P9-CDC-898

Jay Parini MD

A Primer of
Child Psychotherapy

Paul L. Adams, M.D.

Professor of Psychiatry
University of Louisville School of Medicine
Louisville, Kentucky

A Primer of Child Psychotherapy

Little, Brown and Company, Boston

Copyright © 1974 by Little, Brown and Company (Inc.)

First Edition

All rights reserved. No part of this book may be reproduced in any form or by any electronic or mechanical means, including information storage and retrieval systems, without permission in writing from the publisher, except by a reviewer who may quote brief passages in a review.

Library of Congress catalog card No. 74-124

ISBN 0-316-00936

Printed in the United States of America

*For Evelia Valdés-Rodriguez Adams
and in memory of our mothers*

Preface

This is a primer, written for beginners in child psychotherapy. The beginners with whom I have had most experience and consequently with whose perspective I most empathize are medical people, namely, medical students, pediatric interns and residents, psychiatric residents, and child psychiatry fellows. However, I have had some experience teaching and guiding students of social work, education, psychology, nursing, and occupational therapy and have written from some awareness of the problems they encounter when beginning to do therapy with children. What I present should help any of these beginners, as well as the new breed of lay therapist who has not had prolonged training in any of the traditional disciplines. To simplify my presentation I sometimes use "child psychiatrist" to mean any therapist, and "he" to mean both genders or either one.

This primer covers, in an informal and personal way, some things a beginner might try in getting under way as a psychotherapist with children. What I have written is what my own students have found helpful, for students know very well how to select what is useful. Any and every expert in child psychotherapy will be convinced that he could do a better primer than this one. Good for him, for I certainly would hope to see in print many more technical manuals by child psychotherapists of varied schools.

A word might be in order here about my own background. I worked in the social sciences, particularly sociology and psychology, before I began medical studies. The Sullivanian approach to psychotherapy is the one that has made the most sense to me throughout both of my careers, in liberal arts and medicine. However, I learned to respect both eclecticism and orthodox Freudianism during my residency training at Duke University. My own personal analysis was done with a Sullivanian. My tastes and biases about the ideology of therapy are probably obvious, but I do want the reader to be forewarned that my orientation is interpersonal, both behavioral and dynamic, eclectic, and a bit radical sociopolitically.

This book has less theory, or ideology of therapy, than technology — know-how applied to procedures and techniques. Occasionally, some theoretical discussion appears, whenever it is needed to make some technique more sensible. I have chosen to adopt a dogmatic style instead of making as many qualifications and reservations as a dispassionate writer would be impelled to do. I do not mind disagreement, so I risk it by sometimes writing provocatively.

If I were to expect agreement, I would not get it from John A. Fowler, M.D., who taught me child therapy at Duke University in a truly inspiring way. I can at least acknowledge that whatever I do and say on the subject, if it is sound, is something he gave me. I therefore want to thank John Fowler, a devoted teacher of child therapy who deserves a much higher tribute than that embodied in this little book.

Others whose assistance I appreciate deeply include my wife, Evy; Atalay Yorukoglu and Robert Ollendorff, who read the first draft; Richard Greenbaum, who read the second; and Arlene Berlly, who typed the manuscript with patience and skill.

P. L. A.

Louisville

Contents

A Primer of
Child Psychotherapy

I
Child's Heart and
Child's World

*Man's home is the whole world and there
should be no place in it where he is not
welcome. Man's home is his own heart also,
and there should be no part of it which he
fears to enter.*
—Lillian E. Smith [1]

Lillian E. Smith was a courageous human being who worked as a teacher of
children. She contended that all adults have the double opportunity (1) to make
a world fit for children so that children can extend themselves in an outward
direction with ease and grace, validating their own worth in a society of equals,
and (2) to make the child's inner heart also a place of joyous habitation, with no
part of his inner life segregated and alienated.

Child therapy is relevant to human freedom. It is liberating and disalienating
work. It is both inner and outer oriented. For that reason I begin this primer
with two chapters that deal with the freeing up of childhood, seeing childhood
not as a zone for adults to colonize but as a way of life in its own right. These
first chapters concern work with children that aims to allow a free and happy
passage through childhood, and deal with what seem to be some of the most
wholesome adult world views to help children. The conclusion of Part I finds us
trying to specify some of the personal traits of the best therapists with children.

REFERENCE

1. Smith, L. E. Today's children and their tomorrow. *South Today* 8:8, 1944.

1

1
Childhood as a World Apart

The word "therapy" has no verb in English,
for which I am grateful; it cannot do
anything to anybody, hence can better
represent a process going on, observed
perhaps, understood perhaps, assisted
perhaps, but not applied. The Greek noun
from which therapy is derived means "a
servant," the verb means "to wait."
—J. Taft [1]

Child psychotherapy endeavors to wait upon children and to serve them by entering into their separate world. The idea that childhood is a separate world has long intrigued reflective persons. Certain poets have expressed most lucidly, without romanticizing, what childhood is, among them William Blake, a poet whose views about childhood I would commend to a beginning therapist. Blake, juxtaposing the *Songs of Innocence* and the *Songs of Experience,* viewed innocence and experience as "contrary states of the human soul." Very likely, Blake himself did not equate innocence with chronological childhood, or experience with chronological adulthood, but many generations of his readers have come to the sure conclusion that innocence is childish and that experience is adult. A primer of child psychotherapy may take a look at the view that childhood is an undecipherable, distinctive existence.

In some of Blake's *Songs,* childhood innocence and adult experience are contrasted in a way that has bearing for a child therapist. We encounter two versions of "A Nurse's Song," the first in *Songs of Innocence:*

> When the voices of children are heard on the green
> And laughing is heard on the hill,
> My heart is at rest within my breast
>   And everything else is still . . .

Contrast this with its counterpart in *Songs of Experience,* also called "A Nurse's Song" but close-mouthed, hard-bitten, and bitter:

> When the voices of children are heard on the green
> And whisp'rings are in the dale,
> The days of youth rise fresh in my mind,
>   My face turns green and pale.
>
> Then come home, my children, the sun is gone down,
> And the dews of night arise;
> Your spring and your day are wasted in play,
>   And your winter and night in disguise.

The second nurse disvalues and discredits childhood that was wasted in play. For Blake, childhood experience and adult experience were different not merely in degree but in kind. It is not simply that children are more naive or less informed; the child's naiveté is instead a realm entirely removed from adult understanding. For children inhabit a qualitatively different world, a world apart from the schemata of adult life, unexplainable by adult standards of logic and inaccessible to adult imagination. As Blake viewed it, the child is not solely a miniature or immature man or woman. Childhood is a fully separate species of existence.

I adopt much of Blake's perplexing hypothesis — that childhood and adulthood are fundamentally a twain that never shall meet — at the beginning of this primer on child psychotherapy. In so doing I am prompted by much more than a love of perversity, and in fact I shall specify some modifications and exceptions to the Blake outlook in due time. However, at the outset let us be modest about what psychotherapy can effect, as it is carried out between a child and an adult, both of whom are lacking in full empathy and skill. In this spirit of acknowledged limitations, we can conditionally accept Blake's provocative and radical viewpoint.

The polarizing hypothesis that childhood and adulthood are separate spheres is a challenge, a fitting beginning for a book geared to adults who want to share the child's existence in a healing relationship. Such a hypothesis might appear more baffling than promising. It looks antiscientific and antirational. It goes with a crazy belief in discontinuity in human affairs. It shows an affinity for revolution. It disclaims that the universe of man and the stages of human life fall into an orderly, equilibrated, and continuous progression. It vaunts diversity, heterogeneity, and quantum jumps. If Blake's notion seems devoid of reason, we should stand reminded that he also wrote, with more than usual discernment, this epigram:

> The Child's Toys and the Old Man's Reasons
> Are the Fruits of the Two Seasons.

Spontaneous living and playing are childhood; ratiocination is adulthood. To be a child's advocate is to promote a separate world of play, of waste, of consuming without being "productive."

At age seven years, Blake went to work in a textile mill to provide a needed pittance for his family. Blake knew that childhood is not all sweetness and bliss, for he did not have an easy one. But he accepted that a child's world view is not an adult's and felt no compulsion to invent linkages between the two. Antedating contemporary ego psychology, Blake's views point up some characteristics of childhood that many of our present views leave out. Beginning therapists show a ready fascination with the common attitude that all behavior is functional, or defensive, involving conflict and ambivalence. Hence, they feel, everything a child does or says is a defensive measure designed to ward off anxiety or pain or loneliness. It is to that commonly held viewpoint that Blake gives a good anti-dote or contrasting outlook. Blake had a vision of childhood exuberant behavior that has no tangible goal, serves no utilitarian purpose, and gets for the child only those gains that are intrinsic to the activity. Blake foresaw an outlook that seems to be gaining more adherents today, namely, that there is a life above and beyond conflicts and coping devices — a life of abundance, in which the main values are growth and liberated human potential.

Blake could envision noninstrumental behavior in an ego's conflict-free sphere. During childhood, life is at first hand, untempered by the adult variety of social feeling, thought, language, and conduct. In contrast, to be adult is to live a shared, transmitted life — a secondhand life, with second thoughts and manifold consider-ations about others. The fantasy life of the child is life itself for the child. Only the old man plays *to escape* the rigors of his reasons. For the child, using a toy or playing an imaginative game is the substance of life itself. The child's toys and fantasies have primacy and are reality. The young psychotherapist had better understand that. A child's every deed does not indicate "defensiveness" or a "security operation."

DENIAL OF DIFFERENCE AND AFFIRMATION OF EQUIVALENCE

There is much in our culture that functions to disclaim both the distinctiveness and the inscrutability of childhood, and to cap the climax, to stress the similarity of adult and child.

Consolation comes, more to adults than to children, in believing that adults are merely grown-up children, and children are but immature adults. Therefore, as a corollary, adults are made anxious and upset when the world of childhood is described as discretely (not continuously) different from that of adulthood. As with all ideologies, the viewpoint of continuity and similarity has specific historical roots; it is an outlook appropriate to certain perspectives but not necessarily made in heaven for all men to hold. Obviously, when children worked in the mines and mills, certain groups looked on them merely as younger workers, on a continuum with adult workers. This perspective – i.e., of continuity and sameness – is made to work out, as a self-fulfilling prophecy, in the modern world. But it is not necessary to have that social perspective if one is to meet a child in psychotherapy. In fact, the perspective hampers psychotherapy with a child.

In the history of western Europe, childhood as a stage of human development has been viewed several different ways. The vagaries are of real interest. Childhood, as it has been looked upon by Europeans, is quite a wandering epoch; there has been great variation in European views of when childhood ends and what childhood comprises. Ariès [2] has written a book that focuses on the history of childhood, and of great interest, too, is the new *History of Childhood Quarterly: The Journal of Psychohistory*. The historical perspective on childhood as well as on therapy should aid the child therapist. As public attention to childhood grows, it may be reasonable to hope that we are entering an era in which women and children, and family groupings – all of which have been viewed as "soft constituencies" – will take priority over the military, economic, and governmental complex – all heretofore seen as "hard institutions."

Numerous other features of our society buttress the ideology that children are not very different from ourselves.

Many parents and educators are self-styled as progressive and reasonable. In line with this self-appraisal they ardently want to "understand" their offspring and to predict and control the child's behavior. They cannot accept bafflement with resignation; instead, the failure of their predictions sends them looking for an answer and a new route to certainty. According to Blake's thesis, this pursuit will never succeed, since there is more in the child's world than they can dream of in their psychology, that is, in their old men's reasons.

Many professional people who work with children take pride in the belief that they, adults, know and understand their "subject children" thoroughly. They have a peg handy onto which they hang every bit of the child's behavior. Sometimes it is only their ideology and interpretation, not the behavior of the child, that they peg. Very young children perceive that these pseudo-omniscient adults do not meet children where children live. Children pick up their bad vibrations. Many times, children sense when empathy is lacking in the adults around them.

Such adults when dealing with children pretend to themselves that "child behaviors" are cut and dried, totally patterned, and formulable. Very thoughtful intruders, they approach children in the way that, for example, some of Melanie Klein's followers have done: with a heavy-footed manner showing excessive earnestness and with preconceived "interpretations" that, because they are both so philistine and so massive, are veritably "mind-blowing" (in a negative sense). A good antidote in the child therapy literature to this Kleinian overconceptualized intrusiveness can be seen in the works of Virginia Axline [3] and Clark Moustakas [4]. Intrusiveness that is equally abundant, but without concepts, is seen in brain-washers and behavior modificationists. The latter are thoughtless intruders, we may say, if the Kleinians are thoughtful.

An intrusive adult may apply his preconceived formula to everything about the child. He filters childhood through a formulation. Such an adult, for example, may work with a Freudian (or Rankian or Kleinian or Skinnerian) formulation that is all-encompassing. This is often quite gratifying to the adult. The child's welfare is another matter. Or, if the adult is an average parent, some cookbook of child-rearing may suffice to give that feeling of mastery which comes to adults who enjoy outsmarting children. But the obsessive search is always for certainty, or for the illusion of certainty. Nothing is allowed if it portrays childhood as mysterious, unfathomable, or beyond our ken as adults. Lost is the motivation for experiencing a child afresh, on his terms. Firm certainty precludes empathy. Jean Piaget [5], looking at the child's egocentrism, made a point that applies equally well to the "egocentrism" of some therapists:

... the very nature of the relation between child and adult places the child apart, so that his [the child's] thought is isolated, and while he believes himself to be sharing the point of view of the world at large he is really still shut up in his own point of view.

The metaphors of a therapeutic ideology, even such metaphors as libido, id, and superego, can become blinders if we take them for real events and things. We grasp a fleeting reality. We name it, and having named it, reify it. We are not even disposed to "wait and see" because important values and basic preju-dices are always at stake in matters concerning children. We adults feel that we cannot afford the leniency and openmindedness to which a confession of igno-rance might lead us. We are with them *to teach!* It is positively "un-adult" to admit ignorance, not to be forearmed with conceptual schemes, not to have our "old man's reasons" about children. The adult way is to ride roughshod

over those very children whom we are reputed to know so thoroughly and love
so tenderly.

THE SHOW OF CERTITUDE

Psychotherapists have more than their adulthood in common with parents. Why
do we all as adults *have* to know, or pretend to know, everything that goes on in
the mind of a child? Why must we intrude? Why are adults (both parents and
therapists) so insistent about knowing? Primary is our belief, especially if we are
parents, that we have a right to see into anything and everything having to do with
our children. We justify our practice of total surveillance over children. Literally
stated, the omnipresent struggle with our offspring's generation is enough of a
bother to us; it would add insult to injury if we admitted that we do not know
what they are doing. The better to conquer our little enemies, we need to feel
as if we know all about them. However, these authoritarian parental attitudes
can make therapy impossible.

Yet adults feel better fortified to combat the upcoming generation when pretending to themselves that childhood is made of perfect geometric figures. If I
may take over the metaphor of T. E. Hulme [6], in reality childhood seems to be
made of unclassifiable cinders and not of smooth-surfaced planes or solids.
Childhood does not have easily measured parameters. Nor can it be fixed easily
by formulations, especially by those related to static and closed systems. Childhood is much more truly "grasped" if we use the thought models of open systems,
immediate experiencing, cataclysm, *satori,* and the unequilibrated fluke. Only if
we can think of childhood in these ways can we grapple with growth, sudden
change, creativity, and becoming — all the basic stuff of childhood.

Childhood is like psychoanalytic time as Norman O. Brown described it [7]:
"not gradual, evolutionary, but discontinuous, catastrophic, revolutionary."
These terms might describe the way the experienced world, and the world of
childhood, really is; but they unnerve adults who feel that to concede such a
view of reality means to lose control over their children.

Again, we adults have to "know" the child's mind because our own unresolved
childhood conflicts persistently intrude into our current lives, reactivating ancient
affects and defenses. We become exercised to reenact these early conflicts *as we
see them in retrospect.*

Parenthood is not the therapist's best model. Our identification with a child
of our own can be intense, and when not nastily intense, it is both human and

healthy [8]. Petit bourgeois intellectuals, when they become parents, notoriously carry these compulsively "protective" sentiments into their parental roles. They become child-worshippers who fool nobody — it is easy to see that their goal is to dominate children. Be that as it may, we adults occasionally do feel impelled to know the child's mind in order to win some of our own old and lingering battles. What is accomplished thereby is a victory once removed via intellectualization and projection. Wholesome adults surely can find happier ways to accomplish adult tasks, if they can but live a little more in the present. Some of the solution is to *live, not prepare to live* — sound counsel for both parents and child psychotherapists.

Adults envy the joyful wildness of many young children. Hence we feel compelled to know the mind of the child not merely out of concern with our own childhood conflicts but also from our yearning to reparticipate vicariously in some phases of childhood behavior. We want to "become as little children" so that we may enter into some kingdom of heaven where impulse, directness, and spontaneity are the rule. Norman O. Brown [7] has made a stirring glorification of childhood, especially of childhood sexuality and the unfettered pleasure-seeking he equates with childhood. His Freudian thesis is radical, making some Freudian child psychiatrists appear pallid and conservative by contrast.

Friedrich Nietzsche [9] pointed up some of the same values in childhood, when he wrote in *Thus Spake Zarathustra:*

... what can the child do that even the lion could not do? Why must the preying lion still become a child? The child is innocence and forgetting, a new beginning, a game, a self-propelled wheel, a first movement, a sacred "Yes." A sacred yes is needed: the spirit now wills his own will, and he who had been lost to the world now conquers his own world.

In *The Cult of Childhood,* George Boas [10] described such high valuations of childhood as cultist, but for many of the wrong reasons. Boas propounded an interesting argument that our culture is beset by primitivism, a trend that makes us become interested, it seems, in such "savage creatures" as children or women. The list could even include blacks, poor people, and the mentally ill and retarded, one imagines. Most of us, however, in contrast to Boas, sense that the creative person is in some respects the person who is in fullest communication with his own childhood experiences. Primitivist or not, as adults we long to immerse ourselves in the feeling that our originality, our free spark, remains intact.

Observe the quest for ecstasy in adults consuming LSD. Often their rapture derives exclusively from their reenactment of infantile innocence and spontaneity. They view childhood as a good "trip" and worth taking again. From one psychiatric standpoint their drugs may seem ridiculous, but their placing a premium upon more spontaneity may not be pathologic after all. Some people need this kind of unleashing – alas, even some children. Herbert Read [11], in *The Innocent Eye,* dealt with the poet's success in recapturing lost joys:

... my childhood, the first phase of my life, was isolated: it grew detached in my memory and floated away like a leaf on a stream. But ... as this body of mine passes through the rays of experience it meets bright points of ecstasy which come from this lost realm.

It is arduous for any of us to grow up from being unrespectable children to being responsible grown-ups. "Such, such were the joys" sums up the glorified recollection of childhood that survived infantile amnesia as we became adults. Sometimes the shift that was required in our perspective was profoundly shocking as *we* moved from innocence to experience, from child's role to grown-up's role. Even with psychoanalysis, few of us made the transition without big gaps, and we long to leap backward over the gaps once more.

In essence, therefore, we want to know the mind of the child because we cannot know it. We are impelled to fathom what we cannot fathom and to search for the devices that we have lost irretrievably. Discrete, critical moments – sudden flashes – comprised our own childhood, our *temps perdu,* and it is just these same imponderable flukes of existence which make up the childhood of our offspring and of our patients. To work with children assuredly is to live with unforeseeable and unequilibrated flukes.

WHERE CHILDHOOD WENT

This brings us to the important question of why it is that young children are not to be understood fully, even in the most productive therapy. Why are our own lives at ages three, four, or five years so largely beyond recollection? The answer might help us.

So far as we can detect, in the utter chaos of years three, four, and five, a child acts all in one piece, with an unadulterated rage, for example, which brings about temporary disintegration of his personality and involves every cell of his kicking and screaming body. This unselfconscious mass action is the kind of thing we seldom encounter in adults, even when they are drunk, high on marijuana, or psychotic. We adults do not lose ourselves very easily. But children do. Witness the child whose true identity is altered in play or who expects a grown-up to step aside so that his imaginary playmates can walk down the hall. An imaginary playmate is not pathologic, of course, but it assuredly and eloquently testifies that the child is emotionally isolated from us. Similarly, we adults are isolated emotionally from the child. In the process of being adults we have developed a clearer picture of who we are and of what the adult world is like for adults. And in doing so we lose forever that knack for dissolving totally into momentary rage, or joy, or fear — the knack of losing our identity and then recovering it.

As adults we are more modulated, inhibited, and reserved. We are more self-conscious and other-conscious than a child. Gone is immoderate ecstasy. We commit ourselves to emotion in a less wholehearted fashion. We play it safe. We practice only limited commitment. And that is what the world of experience is like — so remote from the wholehearted emotion of the world of childhood that an unbridgeable gap is set up between the two worlds.

From a larger standpoint, not all of our sociocultural imperatives move us to sameness, with the corollary that a big discrepancy is promoted culturally between ourselves and children. In our society we do not provide adequately for a smooth transition from irresponsible childhood to responsible adulthood. By our culture we construct gaps (or, in Ruth Benedict's formulation [12], "discontinuities") that set childhood apart from adult life. We consign not only our three- and four-year-olds into a career of sexual ignorance ("innocence"), but also send our thirteen- and fourteen-year-olds abruptly from a world of supposed sexlessness into a world with sexuality at the center of all functioning values. Moreover, the adolescent is shoved from the role of a weakling into the role of an aggressive, assertive competitor without an adequate transition. This developmental trauma blocks out childhood. All of this tends, culturally and thus artificially, to create hiatuses between innocence and experience and to turn adolescence into a stormy period of conflict and confusion. Hence, the very identity forged during adolescence is so dissimilar from our childhood selves that our infantile amnesia thereby becomes more rigid, more total. Culturally, we enhance the separation between childhood and adulthood in the way we handle adolescents.

Furthermore, many events occur in childhood that become outlawed and tabooed later on. The Freudians can teach us on this count. What is interdicted in the child is forgotten by the time the child becomes adult. An experience (of thought or act or feeling) will be suppressed initially, then pushed into unconsciousness, to operate there in all the intricate ways that psychiatrists see in their dealings with adult patients. What is repressed is usually the sexual, or the self-indulgent and pleasurable, according to the Freudian view of psychoanalysis. This psychoanalytic view may be, as some opine, only a partial view that over-emphasizes sex; yet it seems to make a lot of sense in explaining a big part of what we do in our society. Why quibble about a partial view if it looks at a big part of life?

American adults — even aspiring child therapists — steadfastly cling to the viewpoint that children are sexless and devoid of sexual curiosity, interest, capacity, or experience. We see this even among sophisticated parents in our society. We see it even while their sophistication tells them that the human animal really ought not to be exempt from some of the endowment that birds and bees fall heir to. Such parents, sophisticated but really ignorant or unconvinced, sometimes inspire a sense of fear and guilt when the child has sexual experiences that are actually natural and normal for that child.

Then what is the child to conclude about feelings that are so naturally and spontaneously *his*? He often concludes that he is bad, basically and naturally bad, "originally sinful." Without therapy, the child has a formidable cross to bear throughout life, even if he bears it only in his unconscious. Unfortunately, through repression, childhood becomes a world quite apart, and we "put away childish things" at a tremendous psychic price.

Another fact is that in our society childhood is regarded as obscenely unproductive, pointless, and parasitic. It is filled, in essence, with a plethora of things to be outgrown and put away. Childhood is a time when biologic aims are not always obvious, such as in "functionless" play during childhood. Some people balk at the idea that young human animals are not altogether good capitalists, go-getters, or church-goers. They are "polymorphously perverse"; they do non-instrumental things. Noninstrumental behavior exists, and it is not favored by functionalists, utilitarians, or rationalists. Some of the rationalistic or utilitarian attitude I refer to cropped up in this statement of Anna Freud [13]:

Since play is governed by the pleasure principle and work by the reality principle, the disturbance of each of the two functions has a different clinical significance.

Many generations of psychological experts have been unable to demolish the view that what is functionless can still be important. It was William McDougall [14] who, among psychologists, first contended seriously that play properly has no goal. It exists for the feeling of enjoyment alone, and it is pursued for its own sake. Blake knew that and was only pretending to adopt the voice of a "square" when he wrote "your spring and your day are wasted in play." For McDougall, play emanated from that "surplus neural energy" which affluent (my term, not McDougall's) young animals possess — when they are well fed, well watered, well rested, and free enough from constraints and inhibitions so that their play is made feasible in a life of abundance. Such overflowing exuberance does seem wasteful to the penurious, and a psychotherapy that utilizes certain types of childhood play as an adjunct has not been an easy product to sell. Adults do not hesitate to derogate play therapy as well as play.

There is another possible reason why childhood is alien to and impenetrable by an adult. That reason has much to do with language or with skillfulness in symbolic behavior. At ages three and four, the child's language skills are four or five times as developed as they were at age two, since the maturing human organism is a very teachable and malleable creature; but language behavior is not perfected by any means at three or four, when the child can be said to have more speech than true language. A little later the gift of tongues will have flowered, but vocabulary is limited and conceptual power is not extensive even in the superficially verbose three-year-old child. But the talking child at six years of age has become decidedly more reachable; and that age, by no accident, is when he goes to school seriously. At age six he can communicate better with adults, on adult terms. He now uses the coin of the realm. By school age he can be reached through a shared, mutually comprehended language, and the epoch of his utter apartness is ended. Some convergence of the two worlds becomes a possibility forever after that.

To some extent, the enormous gap between childhood and adulthood is bridge-able by language, through dialogue. At age three or four there are still language idiosyncrasies, private words or words with private meaning, or enunciations that only a close parent can understand, that "only a mother can love." Before he speaks our language the child lives in a world decidedly apart, a world where adult labels, categories, and concepts do not apply and do not reach. Until he speaks our language he expresses himself with gestures, bodily movements, and with his viscera. The mother who has sensed great pain in her child and has said, "If he could just *tell* me what bothers him" knows how childhood, without proficiency in adult language, is indeed a world apart. In almost the same spirit, the psycho-therapist who has been trained to overvalue verbalizations will feel helpless (he who is set up to help) if the child is not verbal; for example, because of the child's age, or selective mutism, or the mutism characterizing psychosis.

We might surmise that things happen and are registered and interpreted in the nervous system of the preschool child, but without adult understanding his categories must be cruder, less distinct, and probably idiosyncratic relative to ours and to other children's. The categories cannot be shared, and they pass into oblivion from disuse when the child matures further, as Schachtel [15] first described so aptly. We, of course, *define* the child's further maturity by his becoming a better talker and developing the socially approved apperceptive mass that is believed and reinforced by the powerful and powerful-talking adults.

In summary, then, there is a moderately plausible case for the thesis, *childhood is a world discrete from adulthood*. With all-or-none emotional responses that engross his entire being, and with spontaneity and directness, the child under six years of age seems to inhabit a world apart. When he represses his self-indulgence and takes on the dictates of the reality principle, he puts his own child's world apart from himself in a way that makes childhood almost irretrievable. Again, when he learns the language of adults, the categories and values of adults, he pushes his own childhood into a world apart. He obtains a firmer identity in the adult world as he grows up, to be sure; but it is not implausible to speculate that the rudimentary picture he had of himself and of us beforehand may have been an entirely different thing from the final product that appears after maturity.

To sermonize, I advocate that we as adults let alone the child who is not too unhappy, allowing him the comfort of his world apart. If we undertake to help out, perhaps it should be with his parents when the child is a preschooler. We should mean to practice a peaceful coexistence with every child. We should let him have his full share of inner experiences — unvarnished, undisguised, and un-buffered — and we should be content to watch his own unique humanity develop. In the process, adults are givers and children are takers, but both can be happy and free. The case I am pleading is only for a more casual and empirical approach that is, after all, in a noble liberal tradition. It is, moreover, in a respectable western tradition that is "scientific." The case has been expressed by Bertrand Russell [16], who like Rousseau regarded all child-rearing as a matter of cultivating instincts, not suppressing them. It was enunciated again by Martin Buber [17] when he described that aspect of education consisting of "pumping" — or drawing out or evoking — in contrast to "funneling," or pouring into the child.

However alienated and rationalized our adulthood might become in bureaucratic mass society, let us condone in children the unfolding of that sense of wonder which draws children into experimentation and direct experience if we will but allow it to happen. If we can permit childhood to be sustained as a world apart, we may conserve a small pocket of that freedom, that liberality of spirit, which currently appears to be in scarce supply.

Even when we encounter children who are unhappy or emotionally disturbed, an overall attitude of waiting and trusting is a very good one. Psychotherapy is, after all, not something done *to* anybody. Therapy is a word pointing to serving and to nursing. Often unaccustomed to receiving adult respect, the child benefits, sometimes immediately, from his association with a therapeutic adult. At first that adult might be a professional person, his therapist. Later, it *must* be his parents and his friends — so-called real objects, with whom he has real-object relations — persons who respect him, love him, and make his life livable, even as they undertake to allow him his separate world.

REFERENCES

*1. Taft, J. *The Dynamics of Therapy in a Controlled Relationship.* New York: Dover Publications, 1962. (Original, 1933)
 2. Ariès, P. *Centuries of Childhood.* New York: Alfred A. Knopf, 1962.
 3. Axline, V. *Play Therapy.* Boston: Houghton Mifflin, 1947.
 4. Moustakas, C. *Psychotherapy with Children: The Living Relationship.* New York: Harper & Row, 1959.
 5. Piaget, J. *The Moral Judgement of the Child.* London: Routledge & Kegan Paul, 1932.
 6. Hulme, T. *Speculations: Essays on Humanism and the Philosophy of Art* (2nd ed.). New York: Humanities Press, 1963. (Original, 1924)
*7. Brown, N. *Life Against Death.* Middletown, Conn.: Wesleyan University Press, 1970.
 8. Adams, P., et al. *Children's Rights.* New York: Praeger Publishers, 1971.
 9. Nietzsche, F. *Thus Spake Zarathustra.* In W. Kaufmann (Ed. and Trans.), *The Portable Nietzsche.* New York: Viking Press, 1954. (Original, 1883)
10. Boas, G. *The Cult of Childhood.* London: Warburg Institute, 1966.
11. Read, H. *The Innocent Eye.* New York: Henry Holt, 1947.
12. Benedict, R. Continuities and discontinuities in cultural conditioning. *Psychiatry* 1:161, 1938.
13. Freud, A. Indications for Child Analysis. In *The Psychoanalytical Treatment of Children: Lectures and Essays.* New York: Schocken Books, 1964. (Original, 1926)
14. McDougall, W. *Outline of Psychology.* New York: Charles Scribner's Sons, 1923.
15. Schachtel, E. On Memory and Childhood Amnesia. *In Metamorphosis: On*

*Throughout the book, references marked with an asterisk are highly recommended readings for all beginning therapists who want to go further than the material of the chapter.

the Development of Affect, Perception, Attention and Memory. New York: Basic Books, 1959.

16. Russell, B. *The Education of Character.* New York: Philosophical Library, 1961.

17. Buber, M. *Between Man and Man.* New York: Macmillan, 1965. (Original, 1947)

FURTHER READING

Talbot, T. *The World of Childhood.* Garden City, N.Y.: Doubleday, 1967.

Wickes, F. *The Inner World of Childhood.* New York: Appleton, 1929.

2

Child Psychotherapy and Child Psychiatry

Children in a group are diverse and heterogeneous persons. Just as individual diversity appears to all who will recognize it in adults of the human species, so it appears conspicuously in children. Children are themselves. After all, children have not yet been subjected fully to cultural patterning. Consequently, they will display wide variation and individuality if they are not regimented. Patterns form out of their diversity, however. To watch the interplay of uniformity and uniqueness among children when a child psychotherapist sees them, either as a group or as individual persons in a series, offers intellectual and esthetic gratification to any adult who is seriously committed to studying and helping children.

In this primer I often speak of "children" as generalities. They are not. Even when children come to us as patients, they only partially and reluctantly assume the generality of the role of patient. They show a weak commitment to being patients, and since their personal differences outweigh their similarities, they are right in holding back. Only for convenience do we call them patients, clients, or by some other term. Some workable uniformities have come out of psychotherapy with children, but the unique child is always more fun than the rule. And, to continue the spirit of Chapter 1, we need to recall that the most intensive and thorough work with one child does not touch all the facets and potentialities that are inherent in that child. Imagine, then, the greater problem of dealing with a series of individuals or, above all, a group of children.

GROUPING BY AGE

What are some of the uniformities? A great deal of our most sensible grouping or grading is age-based, age-related. Teachers, pediatricians, and other child experts do age-grading of children, and it makes sense. Rarely are children under four brought into therapy, for example, and the major help is given to such children through the parents. Those above eight years of age are, for the most part, different from those seven years old or below. In general, young scholars (five to nine) are different *as a group* from children who are ten or eleven, nearer the end of elementary school. Children in the four- to seven-year age range go where they are taken. Docility seems to serve them well. They need to consume a lot of security. They are more dependent. They may show this unmistakably if they experience primary separation anxiety in the form of dreading to go to school, that is, school phobia.

The therapist-child relationship when the child is four to seven years old may be primarily associated with the child's separation anxieties. What the child does with the therapist may be to forge a new dependency relationship and then learn greater autonomy on that basis. It is generally gratifying to the therapist to relate to a very young child, such as a preschooler, if the child is not severely damaged — for example, psychotic. Chances are that such a child will be easier to manage than an older one. It is simpler to coexist with the younger child because the therapist can set up a good, friendly relationship that has deep affinity to the parent-child model. Some child psychiatrists would rather work with preschoolers than with any other age group.

A friend of mine who had learned child psychiatry primarily through clinical work with preschool children found only after his residency was completed that, as he stated it, "Ten-year-old children are really not adults." Others "discover" still different age groups to be attractive and challenging when they enter into the broad experience of practice that will compensate for their narrow training. Many child psychiatry residents find that their work *with adults* improves radically after they have learned about children and how to work psychotherapeutically with children. Therefore we could say that even adults are "discovered" by people with child therapy training and experience.

One child psychiatrist might prefer to work with preschoolers, another with preadolescents, another with older youths. None of these psychiatrists is reacting purely to stereotype or illusion, for personal tastes can be real forces in the lives of reasonable people. Preferences are not necessarily analyzed away, even though on the average a personal analysis and a provocative supervision make therapists a great deal better. Each stage of the life cycle has its own delights, so it is not surprising that various people prefer children of different ages.

The child from eight to twelve years of age, for example, is further advanced in elementary school; and although I do not wish to imply that later elementary schooling is utopia, he may have embarked on a serious academic life. The fun and games of early schooling are over, and he is embarked on goal-oriented tasks, even demonstrating a longing for "chumship" and loving attachment to an age-mate. He is obviously in a very different age-based milieu, with a different style of living from that of a four-year-old child; and if a therapist forgets this, he will lose the child, because he will make the older child feel like a baby.

When a child is ten or eleven, an appointment with the child psychiatrist made by his parents is a threat to his emerging independence; yet he may accept the therapy sessions because he still sees his parents as all-wise. But by twelve years of age, stronger stirrings for independence typically occur. The child has become an adolescent. Usually, by twelve years he has discovered that his parents are far from infallible. Indeed, he might have learned that they are corrupted and confused. These "peculiar people," adolescents, pose sufficient problems to warrant giving them a separate brief chapter (Chapter 12).

The issue becomes: When *can* children cut off, with some expected ease, from their parents? The time of easy separation centers around the child's dependency and his consumption of security. It is related to the extent that his life is preoccupied with, and dominated by, the necessity of receiving infusions of security from adults. If he needs constant reassurance to overcome his mistrust of his parents, he will "need" to be with his parents constantly. Contrariwise, if he trusts his parents, he can accept separation. Where does this child stand in relationship to getting security from his parents? Where does he conceive of himself as situated in his dependency-independency relations? These are the primary questions the psychiatrist asks as he orients himself to the parent-child "system" when parents and child arrive to make use of the therapist's helping skill. As a rule, I see mainly the parents of a child under four or five, and after that age I work with the child directly, separately from and together with the parents.

Otto Rank [1] and his followers greatly influenced child psychiatry in this country by their fundamental emphasis on separation and individuation. The Rankians believed that every parting was sweet sorrow, because every parting connoted a birth, or rebirth, as well as a death — a relinquishing of ties. They believed that therapist and child engage in a struggle of wills so that when therapy terminates, it is a bittersweet and ambivalent ending and growing, with joy and grief admixed. In their view, the very operation of a child guidance clinic acts out the child's condition and teaches him a lot; he is separate, going his separate way with a psychologist or psychiatrist, while the parents go apart from their child with the caseworker. The caseworker does not have to be Rankian, or "functionalist," in order to get across the ideal of individuation! The message is inherent in the nature of the clinic's procedures.

MOTIVATION FOR CURE

What of the child's willingness to come regularly to the psychiatrist? Do any generalities cover children's motivation? In general, the willingness of the child to obtain help depends on his degree of hurting. Without having learned techniques of social withdrawal, the more he hurts, the more acute is the brewing of the child's anguish and the more willing is he to see the doctor. He will be attuned to therapy in some direct correlation to the recency and severity of his symptoms.

Often parents hurt more than the child does and are better motivated than the child. That helps in the overall motivational picture for the simple reason that most children have to do what their parents want. However, some children come to a therapist but show no desire to cooperate. A smart psychotherapist clears this up as he acknowledges that the child *can* fight back if he chooses. He tells the child that the child can resist and oppose the parental arrangement with the psychotherapist. Very early, the therapist informs the child that he is "for the child." Occasionally, this will be the very first time a parent has envisioned that he does not have total ownership and control of the child's life, including the child's problems. It is usually not news to a conflicted child, however, that he has his parents over a barrel, for little can be done against the child's determined wishes.

If the child patient does not hurt greatly (for example, he lacks neurotic symptoms but instead has personality or character problems), he certainly will talk to a psychiatrist more freely if he knows that his parents are behind him and that *they* are troubled by his behavior. The child should know it if his parents have a feeling of helplessness and are sold on the need to obtain outside help. If they hurt, and the child knows of it, he is likely to be better motivated for therapy. To summarize, therefore, motivation increases with the recency and severity of the child's hurting and with the depth of the parental hurt.

Child psychiatry is not diluted or shrunken-down adult psychiatry; it is a separate specialty. It is built on general psychiatry, however, and that is sensible. In child psychiatry two generations, child and parents, come to treatment. At times, there is a third generation, the grandparents, not so dimly in the background. Compare this to "adult" psychiatry, in which the illusion exists on a grand scale, in the heads of doctors, that psychotherapy is a one-generation phenomenon.

A process of "justification" for the anticipated treatment has always preceded the initial interview. Everyone in the household has been busy asking "Why turn to a therapist?" Many times this justification procedure in and of itself has already brought about a shift in the sibling relationships of the child patient before he gets to the first encounter with the therapist. The child has undergone a change in self-image while he was becoming identified as a bona fide patient. In the process, the parents may have had second thoughts whether *this* is the child who should be referred, or whether it should be another of their children. The child patient is a part of the reshifting of forces within the family and often assumes a pivotal role. He is not neutral, not passive, and not aloof. He may enjoy being spotlighted or may abhor it. He in turn may talk with his brothers or sisters about what is involved. They may give him direct support or derogation, or they may only serve to feed his fearfulness.

A child does not escape his brothers and sisters merely because he comes to the therapy session without them. Sometimes child patients who are keenly rivalrous will come into the first interview asserting that they want to bring in their most hated sibling. Or they may express the wish that the particular sibling come in who is the family's prize exhibit of their "well child," or their "best foot forward." The child patient may plead to bring him, claiming he would feel better with his brother present, or saying he cannot comprehend the interchanges of the sessions without his sibling at his side. The child therapist, as we shall see, should not be trapped by this maneuver. He should make known to his patient that his interest is in the child patient exclusively and not in his sibling. Thereupon the child often beams, filled with a surprised, but deeply craved gratification.

Child: Can I bring my little brother Tommy with me the next time I come here?

Therapist: When you come to see me, you want to bring along your little brother?

Child: I wondered if I could.

Therapist: I know you a little now that we have worked together today, but I do not know your little brother, and I don't care to know him. You are the one I am interested in.

Child: Okay, I won't let him come.

The therapist needs to convey to the child very early that he is eager for a personal psychotherapeutic encounter with the child. If he can give the message that psychotherapy counts, and if he can ally himself with the child's healthier longings, then the therapist has entered right into the heart of child psychiatry.

Child psychotherapy is the heart of child psychiatry, I am convinced; but we must always bear in mind that the heart of child psychiatry is not its entirety. Child psychiatry is a medical specialty, but with many nonmedical practitioners brought under the umbrella for interactive, mutual dependence [2, 3]. The entirety of child psychiatry enfolds drug treatment, milieu therapy, peer group therapy, community consultation, special education, consultations with pediatric colleagues, political action on behalf of children and families, psychologic testing and scoring, social casework, clinical and pure research, teaching of medical and other professional students, and many activities other than psychotherapy directly with children.

Child psychiatry has always simultaneously looked inward and outward — inward to the psychic depths of one little girl or boy and outward to the social forms that both enhance our humanity and produce ills that require changing on behalf of all children and their family living. Therapy itself is not all aimed at only the "inner" child, as we will see. It is not enough to will to change the child; we must also determine to change the world. Social activism or "child advocacy" *and* intrapsychic concerns have always been welded together in the field of child psychiatry. However, the core psychotherapeutic skills of the child psychiatrist influence (or determine) those many acts and attitudes that bring a broader spectrum of child psychiatry into being. These skills come first in this book, even though they are not believed to constitute the whole picture.

PRIVATE WORLD

What can we teach a young therapist, who has already learned the essentials of psychotherapy with adults, when he comes to learn psychotherapy with children? We can teach him primarily what it is to know the inner world of one child, then another, and then another. We can acknowledge his tendency to subvert or act out by his demanding to see the parents instead of the child, or by insisting that family group therapy is the only good therapy. But we should stick firm, insisting that the real heart of the matter is the child himself and that within the child is where the opportunities for his new, fresh learning abide.

The challenge contained in psychotherapy with children is to understand the individual child's world. Here, *understanding* has not much to do with facility in sterile abstractions but has everything to do with direct, respectful intimate dialogue or nonverbal sharing between the therapist and the child. It has to do with relatedness. The therapist wants a close view of how the child perceives, evaluates, emotes, copes, thinks, and acts. For the therapist to be able to obtain this view, the child himself must see it and relay (largely verbally) what he sees to the therapist. Seeing it, the child can be helped to modify it in the service of his health and happiness. The therapist is of use to the child in many ways, but mainly as an adult who bothers to know it "like it is" with the child.

Experiencing events as they are and then reporting them as they are connote the kind of integrity in both therapist and child that makes reasonable (if imperfect) decisions possible. The focus that is distinctive in child psychiatry is on therapy with children: how to play, talk, and live with children; how to stand in their shoes and view their lives as they view them; how to savor their uniqueness as persons in their world; how to help them solve their problems. This presupposes that children themselves are valued positively.

To say "children are valued positively" is a North American phrase easily uttered but standing for very little in everyday life. We all say children are important but then proceed to abase them and to subject them to adult colonization and exploitation. Women and blacks rightly proclaim that they will not be treated as children. Dishonesty and casuistry suddenly appear in everyday speech whenever the conversation turns to the ways children are treated by adults. The psychotherapist, too often, finds ways to enter into the universal game of demeaning and disrespecting young people. The child does belong to his parents; the child is a chattel. The child legally is less an entity than is a business corporation and has fewer legal safeguards to rely on. The child is held weaker than he needs to be, more dependent than he has to be, and is subjected to a despotism and tyranny within his circle of "loved ones" that is almost unmatched in the modern world. George Bernard Shaw [4] perceived this as early as 1910, for he wrote of the child's lot:

It has no rights and no liberties: in short, its condition is that which adults recognize as the most miserable and dangerous politically possible for themselves: namely, the condition of slavery... it is impossible to ascertain what the real natural relations of the two classes [parents and children] are until this political relation is abolished.

If our fascination is with the powerful and the free, we had better not spend time learning psychotherapy with children. All economic classes of adults in our nation share in the oppression of children, sometimes called "childism." The upper middle class rationalizes it as in the interest of their individualistic values. The lower middle class and working class do it for the sake of the family as a whole (which is another way of saying for the parents). For example, even lower-class black parents who are being offered the token help of parent-child centers often get themselves organized to extract the goods and services that *adults* want, giving the good excuse that "what benefits the parent is for the child." To value the child and to want to stand with him is an unusual position for adults to take.

FAMILY WORLD AND CULTURE

In child psychiatric work the child is both interesting and important. But a child does not present himself voluntarily to any doctor, whether his illness is bacterial or emotional in origin, whether he has a broken leg or a broken mind. He is presented by his parents or some responsible adult. He comes to the doctor as a human being who is related dependently to others. He is, indeed, a member of his family. The parents complain on his behalf, and more than this, the parents put forth the child *as their complaint.* Consequently the child is presented, in a sense, as a symptom of his parents' anxiety. If they were not anxious, they would be managing on their own and probably be functioning as good parents. But they are at the doctor's, and they are there precisely because they can no longer tolerate the burden of anxiety and helplessness they feel and which they believe to be due to some sickness in the child. Not the child alone, abstracted from his interpersonal relations, comes to the psychiatrist; the family comes, with him and in his imagery, and for this reason a family-centered approach is the natural approach for child psychiatry. Later, the learner of child therapy will do a great deal of family group therapy, but at first he will have to acknowledge and overcome his resistance to working with *one child alone.*

An illustrative case of the complex worlds we must know is that of a young boy, Alfred, who, although involved deeply in his mother's problem, was seen separately in therapy.

A 50-year-old divorced woman came to a child psychiatric clinic to ask advice about her son, Alfred, who had shown an acute flurry of obsessive rituals, doubting, thinking, and questioning. He asked permission of his mother to urinate and defecate, seemed worried about sexual topics, and seemed to "be in deep study," which he would end to ask his mother questions about the Bible, about perfection, and about the unpardonable sin. At times he fell into a semistuporous state, appearing frozen as he sat with his fingers pointing towards the floor. The mother had oversold herself as a moral judge — indeed as a god — during the boy's earlier childhood and had made continual attempts to deprive him of his independence and autonomy. She had deserted the boy (and her husband) for several months when he was four years old, and at times she expressed fully her lack of concern for being a mother. At such times she would neglect her son, ignoring his welfare. Afterward, she would go overboard in compensating for the neglect and scorn she had shown him.

This woman had grown up in an impoverished Southern rural family. Knowing deprivation as a member of the lower class, she sometimes felt driven to inflict deprivation upon her son.

The boy was not psychotic but had severe obsessions centering around his masturbation guilt now that he could ejaculate. The mother-son relation was critical, but she blew hot and cold as a mother, an authority figure, and as an instructor or trainer. Having reached an age that elicits mellowness in many, she found that she had no identity, no joy, no sense of worth, and no sources of security available to her. Her preachments, derived from a fundamentalist approach to the Bible, rang hollow to her. She was an embodiment of the alienation that characterizes our era.

The mother was seen in a community mental health facility by a psychiatric social worker and on occasion by a child psychiatrist. Alfred was seen in individual, one-to-one psychotherapy covering seventy-five hours. Although he was seen separately from his mother, on whom he was overly centered anyway, his therapy was undertaken as a kind of highly personalized instruction in learning how he lived as a unique being, enfolded simultaneously in close bondings to his mother, his father, and a large, extended kinship group. His "curriculum" concentrated on his special and complex relations with his mother, and that was what helped him to get the most relief and undertake the most change.

Parents often would wish to be firm with their children and to indoctrinate or teach them. But what indeed do they have to teach their children? That was a predicament shared by Alfred's mother. How can parents come across as authentic when they feel unreal? What do parents value? What do they themselves stand for? Many parents feel alienated from, uncommitted to, and divested of most of the things that carry meaning. They are strangers to the tools and products of their work, deprived of the gratification of vibrant sexual activity, feebly involved in competent parenthood of their children, and hungering for enjoyment of an inner life with depth and richness. They perceive themselves as rigid and empty beings in an empty, rigid, dehumanized world. Life today in our bureaucratized, highly structured mass society is not all joy for most parents.

To be of help to such persons as Alfred and his mother, the child psychotherapist needs to have multiple skills and perspectives. He has to have a grasp of the cultural patterns of our time. They cannot be taken for granted, but must be held up as live issues. He must see each family he helps against a broad sociocultural backdrop. In addition, he must understand the particular economic class and subculture as well as the individual. He must be attuned equally to the mother's sense of alienation and to the highly significant disruption of her marriage, her "family of procreation." He must understand her sense of powerlessness and be cognizant of her poverty-bound helplessness and anxiety. He must be adept in helping *her* to see these things clearly. He must help her to understand the modes of adapting that her son employs, so that she can perceive (and honor) her son as an emerging, independent human being.

In order to accomplish all these tasks, the child psychotherapist must explore and elucidate some of the early roles that the mother (of our case vignette) developed within her family of origin. Herein lie her greatest "transference" problems, her inappropriately carrying forward infantile attitudes from her own infantile experiences *into the sixth decade of her life.* As it is frequently stated: A woman cannot give wholesome mothering to her offspring until she has come to regard, or to relate to, her own mother more realistically.

The typical mother of troubled children is younger than our example, but she, too, carries the burden of her "baby family" over into her family of procreation. She distorts what her husband and children really are; she finds herself unable to relate meaningfully to her "grown-up family," consisting of her husband and her offspring. Fathers, too, assuredly manifest this transference. A father misperceives his wife and children in terms that may or may not have been appropriate for his siblings and parents when he was in his baby family, but which are certainly inappropriate for his wife and offspring.

Therefore, because of the infantile images that both parents carry around in their heads, children psychically still grow up bathed in the attitudes and influences of their grandparents. Family problems do encompass three generations! The extended family is declining in our culture as a palpable, actual unit, and most middle-class families seen by child therapists are small, conjugally focused, nuclear units. Nevertheless, many of today's parents are engrossed in the lives of their parents. This gives to a detached conjugal family many of the same emotional features possessed by the extended family of yesteryear.

The child guidance approach to psychotherapy is often berated. The beraters refer to a wide spectrum of evils when they allude to child guidance. They usually mean that they dislike the collaborative team approach to the child, viewing a child as a separate person from his mother and father. Sometimes they mean that they dislike the emphasis on mother-child relations to the exclusion of father-mother-child relations, that is, to the exclusion of the father. They wax poetic about the patriarchal family and would almost allege that child guidance clinics are destroying the patriarchate, if not the flag.

A child psychotherapist who does *not* give concentrated attention to the mother-child unit is the one who stands in need of some intense learning. Children are molded by mothers, that is, by women, and by the quality of loving that the particular mother has to bring into the relationship. Our families are started in the United States with the conjugal relationship at the forefront, and we call our middle-class type of family a conjugal family because it stresses the husband-wife relationship so strongly. But when it becomes a true family, that is, when there are children added to the household, it is the mother-child relationship that arises to paramountcy during the child's early years. In fatherless homes, found increasingly in the United States, this generalization warrants an even greater stress. The core family relation is between mother and child.

Thus, in an epidemiologic or public health sense, child psychotherapy is the primary way of helping the mother-child relationship. It is hard to evade that emphasis in child psychotherapy, to sweep the mother-child relationship under the rug, even if, by emphasizing it, we may be leaning toward male chauvinism.

DESIRABLE PERSONAL FEATURES OF THE THERAPIST

Certain personal characteristics or social skills of the child psychotherapist are important and desirable for his work. One feels tentative and apologetic about formulating criteria or standards for healers, but several traits consistently appear invaluable.

1. The child psychotherapist needs to possess a great willingness to know himself — to know and not just to act out. The psychotherapist who works well with children benefits from an understanding and recognition of his own mixed feelings, an understanding of his own childhood and of his reactions towards his own parents: his love, hatred, and envy.

Of course, to know oneself is not necessarily to love oneself more! However, self-knowledge brings about a certain good humor with respect to one's own foibles; it advances a tendency to be accepting of nature as it operates in oneself. Self-knowledge accompanies a readiness to expose one's countertransference when conversing with the supervisor ("I don't like this kid; he annoys me") and a rather natural liking for direct and explicit communications. Self-acceptance does not mean neutrality or complacency. It means being balanced, but dynamically and not statically, and with more humility than might come naturally. Otto Rank and his followers (and Carl Jung and his followers, if the piety of the Jungians does not throw one off course) make a very convincing presentation of self-acceptance as a dynamic balance. Ambivalence contained and balanced within oneself is healthier than projection, certainly. Ambivalence is all too human. Jessie Taft [5], a Rankian, wrote: "Life is ambivalent but so are we, 'born and bred in the briar patch.' " Without leading to perfection, therefore, one's personal therapy and supervision assist the kind of self-knowledge that makes for a good psychotherapist [6].

2. An ability to take up, in imagination, the role of the child, regardless of how bizarre the child may appear initially, is an important asset. Recoiling from the weirdness of a patient should clue the therapist that he is recoiling mostly from a feared and dissociated part of himself. The child psychotherapist recognizes that the bizarre behavior of a disturbed child is not meaningless. No behavior is meaningless, and for that reason it is a challenge to the adult's understanding. It is *not a reflection on the child* for him to be mad and misunderstood, since the therapist's job is to undo both child madness and therapist ignorance. The therapist gets into the child's shoes, in empathy, and can understand how the child feels and thinks, how he initiates and reacts, in his own personal, private version of childhood in his subculture.

3. A deep satisfaction in being an adult is a personal asset to the child therapist. The therapist is lucky if he enjoys being grown up even more than he enjoyed his childhood. After all, to be an adult is not to be hopelessly blemished or accursed!

The therapist is lucky, too, if he derives some security and some gratification from behaving "appropriately for his own age and sex." If his sexual objects are grown up, not children, he can be of surer professional help to children and their parents. Without losing a needed childlike quality, he is not *childish*. He can empathize with a child without losing sight of the parent's predicament or of his own involvement in the interaction. A rich imagination and a broad empathy for all in the human condition go a long way in child psychotherapy.

4. He has an awareness of his own social situation and of the ways in which his position influences his perspective. This is another example of self-knowledge that few analysts take into account, but it is important nevertheless. Stated alternatively, the therapist is not embroiled in "false consciousness," as the Marxist

would term this misperception. He does not try to see all mankind as being very like himself. Empathy transcends differences between doctor and patient once they have been made public and clear, but differences must be made explicit and accepted.

The child therapist should have an aversion to stereotypes, especially his own, for they can too easily be his prejudices; and prejudice is a form of countertransference that always impedes therapy. For example, a black child who automatically is viewed by his doctor as a no-good nigger headed for a lifetime of only manual labor and music needs a better therapist with fewer prejudices [7]. Some greater objectivity is achieved when the therapist realizes that his own race or economic class or religion is not the necessary condition for all humanity. This greater objectivity is not a paralyzing nihilism, leading the therapist to believe in nothing and to see all values as relative or as masks for self-seeking. The child deserves a therapist who stands for something but who can accept others even if they stand for nothing, or for other values.

5. A disinclination to take a negative stand toward the patient's parents and siblings is vital. This ability shows itself in the doctor's willingness to hear fully all the child's reports about his family members while remaining clear that these are the child's opinions. Such a therapist will not try to "unravel" the psychopathology of any family members who are not present in the consulting room. The rule is, *only unmask present company,* if you must unmask anybody.

Ultimately, the child will end therapy and return to the "real objects" in his world – his parents, siblings, peers, and teachers and other adults. Ultimately, a child who is lucky will come to love his parents. Parents need not love their children passionately; a benign protectiveness, in a household that resembles a fairly attentive and wholesome dormitory or commune, might suffice to provide children with the major part of what parents can give, or have to give, to children. Children, however, do need to love their parents, as a prerequisite for their own self-esteem and as a preparation for a lifetime of loving relations with others. A competent therapist will not seek to undermine that love.

6. Willingness to work enthusiastically with tentative hypotheses prevents the stultification of treatment. Some medical people are so committed to quantitative biology or to their familiar style of cookbook chemistry – "experiments" in which the outcome is measurable, foreseeable, and preordained – that they cannot tolerate the ambiguity of interpersonal relations in a free range. Some psychologists are so smitten with heavy methodology and technology, often for the investigation of petty and irrelevant questions, that tentativeness in exploration turns them off completely. Moreover, I observe that some teachers, social

workers, and psychiatrists prize mechanistic stuffiness and eschew tentativeness. Ideologic cults (even those claiming scientific justification) may come and go, but the human process of people helping people survives these fads.

Some honesty in inquiring and some desire to control bias are required of a child therapist and should be assumed. He rejects or confirms his earliest formulations as the process of therapy continues, for as unmistakable evidence unfolds, it is grasped by both therapist and patient. Both a healthy skepticism and a refusal to fit the child into the therapist's own mold are the assets required. Therapists who belong to a cult or feel omniscient are not suitable; nor are those who demand the obsessive's certainty found only in "purely scientific" work.

The beginner in child psychiatry realizes the strenuous effort required to achieve these personal traits if he does not possess them already. These traits add up to social skills or competencies that enhance one's therapeutic effectiveness and one's own enjoyment. Most physicians who elect the child psychiatry specialty fortunately have at least the rudiments of these personal traits before they begin their training.

Changing ourselves is difficult, slow, and tedious. A personal psychoanalysis is useful in freeing up the personal gifts of the aspiring child psychiatrist and can hardly be urged too strongly. Even when he has been analyzed, however, it is imperative that he continue to seek validation by consulting and collaborating with his colleagues. Otherwise, his blind spots will impede his fuller development as a therapist. Psychotherapists help one another. Psychotherapists need each other, at least for the down-to-earth assistance that guild members can give to each other. They learn this lesson best by utilizing supervision during their training and then by continuing it, on a formal or informal basis with colleagues, the rest of their lives.

REFERENCES

1. Rank, O. Will Therapy. In *Will Therapy and Truth and Reality*. New York: Alfred A. Knopf, 1945. (Original, 1929)
2. Adams, P. Some lessons from child psychiatry. *Ala. J. Med. Sci.* 6:384, 1969.
*3. Krug, O. (Ed.). *Career Training in Child Psychiatry*. Washington, D.C.: American Psychiatric Association, 1964.
4. Shaw, G. B. Preface to *Misalliance*. In *Prefaces by Bernard Shaw*. New York: Scholarly Reprints, 1971. (Original, 1910)

5. Taft, J. *Dynamics of Therapy in a Controlled Relationship.* New York: Dover Publications, 1962. (Original, 1933)
6. Adams, P. Child psychiatry as social psychiatry. *Int. J. Soc. Psychiatry* 14:311, 1968.
7. Adams, P. Dealing with racism in biracial psychiatry. *J. Am. Acad. Child Psychiatry* 9:33, 1970.

FURTHER READING

Adams, P. Work with Paramedical Professionals in Academic Child Psychiatry. In Adams, et al. (Eds.), *Academic Child Psychiatry.* Gainesville, Fla.: Society of Professors of Child Psychiatry, 1970.
Adams, P., et al. *Children's Rights: Toward the Liberation of the Child.* New York: Praeger Publishers, 1971.
*Allen, F. *Psychotherapy with Children.* New York: W. W. Norton, 1942.

II
Forces Favoring a Good
Outcome of Treatment

Psychotherapy, even with the very young, is suspect in many quarters. Many like to point out that nature itself is the great healer. In some circles it is fashionable to lump the untutored good will of a nonprofessional volunteer together with the expert and wise technology of a flexible child psychotherapist, to call both of their workings *psychotherapy,* and then to show that their combined outcomes are little better than chance alone, or not more than could be expected from natural history if the child is untreated. This extreme pessimism, although chic, is not warranted. In general, however, the support of life circumstances (without any treatment) produces these results in disturbed patients: improvement in one-third, no important change in one-third, and worsening in one-third. Thus we can see that the natural history of many milder childhood disturbances is a happy story.

Unfortunately, with some delinquent and psychotic children, the prognostic odds are much less favorable. Therefore, a beginner in child therapy whose therapeutic endeavors with a diversity of disturbed children yield considerably better results than one-third "improved" and fewer than two-thirds "unimproved" is doing something more than nature. He has followed the good Oslerian rule, "First of all, do no harm," and another rule, which we might add: *Second of all, increase the improvement statistics!* That is, both refrain from doing added damage *and* make a positive contribution, if possible.

In this section (Chapters 3–6) of the primer we look from an optimistic perspective at all the agents or actors in the treatment scene – parents, siblings, children identified as patients, referral source, the child psychiatry facility, the treatment staff, and the enveloping community. This optimism is not the result of any special pleading for simpleminded pollyannaism. Rather, it is an approach that underscores all prospects and possibilities for some positive change within disturbed children and their interpersonal world. We ask concerning everything in the child's life: How can we increase the odds so that more than one-third of our child patients will improve? What circumstances can we find, create, and capitalize on to facilitate an improved treatment outcome?

3

Parents and Siblings

*I had analyzed a fictional small girl and a
witch instead of the patient and her mother.*
—S. Fraiberg [1]

Predominant among the forces favoring a good treatment outcome are the
child's parents and siblings. Although we might tend to shy away from the child's
relatives and mistrust them, seeing them as malignant forces, still, within the
child's family circle there are constructive possibilities, and we will look at them,
trying to find ways to shore them up. In this fashion, we can try to enhance the
outcome of child psychotherapy. Although they are internalized as fantasy
objects, the child's family members are also real.

CONSIDER THE PARENTS

Down with Parentectomy

The concept of parentectomy is derived from the belief that parents are foes
who can only do harm to their child. It is a concept that places the helping adult,
whether a Bettelheim or a juvenile court judge or a pediatrician, in direct confrontation with the parents. Note, however, that the confrontation usually occurs
when the parents feel weakest and most helpless to cope with their asthmatic or
psychotic or delinquent child, and hence it is not a fair fight. Consequently, if
the parents do yield, giving up the child and allowing their own "excision" to
occur, it is not a great triumph for the helping professional. He won because he
fought against weakened opponents.

Those who advocate parentectomy, even when they mouth only a little moral
pride, are sure that they have something the child's parents lack and something
they can supply without parental endorsement or involvement. These people
actualize the kidnapping fantasies of most child psychiatrists and "snatch" children
away from parents but without feeling the burden of self-examination most child
psychiatrists feel obliged to carry. If I love a child more than the child's parent
does, I have to call it *countertransference* and do something to bring myself in

line with decent ethical and technical practice. But the advocates of parentectomy do not question it; for them, parentectomy is axiomatic, assumed, given, like an article of faith or something perfectly obvious to any sensible person.

Boarding schools and college preparatory schools condone parentectomy for unwanted children of the affluent, particularly in the North. Military schools legitimize parentectomy for unruly children of the affluent in the South. Summer camps thrive on time-limited parentectomy among the middle class in all regions. Juvenile court judges invoke the doctrine of *parens patriae* and sever the family ties of lower-class children, predominantly, in all areas of the United States. The parents, labeled neglectful and abusive by the courts, are cut off from their customary (so-called sacred) ownership rights on their offspring. The state takes over in lieu of the parents, but not so much to give new rights to the children, or primarily to enhance their welfare, as to change ownership to a more powerful group of adults. General pediatricians rush to get mentally retarded, asthmatic, blind, and other unusual children out of the home and into an institution. And they have an elaborate rationale built up to support this parentectomy. Mental health professionals, blameful of parents, urge residential placement and enforced separation of severely disturbed children from their parents on the supposition that the children need to be set free from a pathogenic family by being placed in a children's madhouse. What the doctor can order!

Certainly, you as a beginner should aim to keep parents and their children together and to consider the physical preservation of a family as a top priority. Indeed, your job is to help children and their families *to experience change.* Ultimately, you will help them to separate physically when the children grow up into healthy sexual and vocational maturity. But if the family's liberation from neurotic patterns can possibly be accomplished while everyone is living under one roof, the change will be much deeper and more organic. To go to a slogan: Regard parents as friends, not foes, of your child therapy efforts. Work with the hypothesis that for the child's inner and interpersonal life, familial assets will outweigh all the combined good parent substitution that can be offered by the school, court, physician, and hospital. Strengthen family welfare and you truly strengthen children. Children belong at home. Life, like charity, should begin at home.

Once I met a female therapist who worked intensively with a psychotic child by taking the child into her own home and providing the child with around-the-clock care. She made it her practice to telephone the mother occasionally, stating, "I want you to remember that I love *you* too." Hers was a very direct way of keeping parents involved.

Even in residential treatment the preferred places are the places that require parental visitation, not those that require parental absence. The beginner should keep alert to these matters whenever he is considering residential treatment or hospitalization for a child.

Some psychotherapists, usually ones who have been taught and given practical experience in settings that are confined to one discipline — that is, are unidisciplinary — view parents only as necessary evils in the lives of their children. Psychologists trained in psychology clinics are often in this group. Teachers of elementary school children often have that attitude. The early child analysts around Anna Freud in Vienna toyed with the idea that child therapy could be done irrespective of the parent's involvement in treatment. Later, however, the requirement shifted so that only children of analyzed parents were accepted into child analysis! This was the viewpoint adumbrated when Anna Freud [2] wrote:

Today, I would not undertake the analysis of a child where the personalities of the parents, or their analytical understanding, did not provide a guarantee against such an outcome [prematurely breaking off the analysis of the child].

Finally, today, at the Hampstead Child Therapy Clinic in London, the Anna Freud group definitely acknowledges the importance of concurrent casework, treatment, or analysis for the parents, with special emphasis on the work with the mother [3]. The added richness of information about both the reality and the fantasy life of the child is as highly desirable today as it has always been for Hermine Hug-Hellmuth and the Freudians. The work with the parents, we all know, aids the therapy, understanding, and real-world interpersonal adjustments of the child in therapy, including the child in the end phase of therapy.

A taste for the heroic inspires the therapist who tries to work solely with a child in an ahistoric, unreal vacuum. Anna Freud spared herself these heroics by having the good sense throughout many of her decades to insist that the child is immersed in the current reality of home and family, or of those grown-ups other than parents who function as the child's guardians. It was in that same spirit that the distinguished North American child psychiatrist J. Franklin Robinson frequently affirmed that an identified child patient must have an identified parental force operating in the real world every day of the child's life. Robinson went further and insisted that a dependent — say, orphaned — child from a welfare department must be properly placed, in a home with committed parents, prior to the onset of psychotherapy. He was convinced that this was a precondition of treatment. Robinson's demand held good especially in the residential treatment of childhood disorders, paying off many times by expediting the therapy. If valuable for no other reason, a firm decision on where the child will live spares the therapist from the recurrent frustrations of realizing that therapy alone will not render a child placeable. Until a child has residential and custodial stability, he often cannot become an appropriate candidate for psychotherapy.

Virginia Axline [4] qualified her early contention that good child therapy can go on heedless of the child's parents, finally conceding that, "One can see how much simpler and complete [sic] the recovery would be if both parent and child received help." But at the end of the same brief chapter the heroic won out [4].

There has been some play therapy done in schools where only the child was given therapy and the results in the attitudes and behavior of the child were very gratifying, not only in improved school relationships, but also in his home relationships. This adds a rather pertinent factor to the treatment of the problem child and indicates very strongly that curative forces within the child are potent.

Look closely at Axline and the Rogersian therapists as a group and you will usually discern, in some form or other, the Rankian view that it is only the clearly enunciated, differentiated, and self-conscious will of the individual that counts on the side of health. The human proclivity for self-healing through self-assertion and self-acceptance is pushed very far by these therapists. Indeed, it is not unexpected that individuation should be rated higher than peace within the family circle in any evaluations made by these therapists. The family ideology and the individuation ideology are not necessarily mutually exclusive; but the emphasis on the one often has to be made by the minimization or dismissal of the other. The Rankians and the Rogersians opt strongly for individualistic ideology.

As much as the child's inner world and will are to be cherished by a therapist, this does not diminish the necessity that the therapist have a firm access to the parental acts and values that constitute the child's real outer world. Thus I attempt to show in this chapter and in Chapter 6 the urgent necessity of intimate dealings with the child's family, either by the therapist or by a collaborating caseworker or other parental therapist. Although I advocate the liberation and emancipation of the child, in the individual case it is always my hope that the child's rights and interests will be consonant with the best interests of the child's parents. My hope is that, better still, the child's liberation will be acceptable and appropriate in the parent's eyes and will be embraced by the parents as part and parcel of their own liberation. For to cite again the assertions of Anna Freud [2], therapy does pertain to the liberation of the child.

The fear of his real father in the outer world originally drove him into carrying out the repression, but the success of this achievement depends for its maintenance upon inner forces. The Father has been "introjected," the super-ego has become the representative of his power ... only the laborious historico-analytical dissolution of this super-ego will permit an advance in my work of liberation.

Seeing Parents First

If one truly wants to help parents, the tone can be set from the earliest contact, when parents come in without the child for the initial meeting with the therapist. This gives one a valuable opportunity to test them out as individuals, spouses, and parents and to begin the process of getting to know them in order to help them. Parents suffer for their child. Their child is not only relevant to their own respective narcissisms, and to their identifications, but also to their object relations. That is, they see the child in two ways: as somehow a reflection of themselves and as a real object of their emotional world. Talk about these things on your first contact with the parents. I never aim for a sterile first session. See parents to assess them *and* to plan with them for an evaluation of their child. Exploring their assets for psychotherapy, in case that eventuates, can also be made a part of your agenda. Later on you'll be glad you did.

Parents can be told to come without the child for an initial interview and appear to do it readily, but once they are there, it is good practice to ask them straight off how they feel about it. Their answers are enlightening. Parents who are aloof (rejecting) often say they were surprised you wanted to see them before seeing the child, that you were "supposed to be an expert with children," and they had expected "at most" that you might want to see them in their child's company only after a few weeks had passed. Parents who are wallowing in guilt and helplessness will say they know it is their "fault" so they "weren't surprised" to have you see them before seeing the child, and that they have expected you "may not even need to see the child" after talking with them. Some parents will tell you how fearful they are to have their child see a psychiatrist, how therefore they felt relieved to function as forerunners and how they crave some advice on what to tell the child. Some will say they have secrets they'd prefer telling you in the child's absence. Some parents will state, very clinically, that they speculated that you wanted to elicit some of the background information from them, the parents, the powerhouse. What I have found is that you miss a lot if you *don't* start with a statement such as, "I do want to see your daughter (or son) but I asked you to come in beforehand. Did you have any feelings about that? What did it mean to you?"

Next, ask the parents about the child. What are the problems? Why do you come just now? Why not earlier; why not wait and see? Precisely when did you first notice the trouble? What was going on then? Is it a recurrent difficulty? Who in the family other than the child is all involved in the problem, all in a stew about it? What makes it worse? What, if anything, seems to help it? Do the symptoms hamper the child, or is he progressing anyway? What does it mean to you as parents, individually? What impact does it have on the entire family's life? On sibs? On grandparents? What do you imagine the final outcome may be? In short, what does it all mean? What could your child be telling you in the language of his symptoms?

Next, ask the parents about how they got together to form a family. Some variant of Satir's [5] question is always fruitful: "Out of all the people on earth how come the two of you got together?" It is astonishing how many parents are embarrassed and stymied when faced with this question; but usually they recover and can say something about what they saw in each other, what kind of relationship they had at first, and what kind of major changes in relationship they have undergone subsequently. This is "where parents live," and child psychiatrists need to tune in on these concerns. Occasionally it is said that the only reason for the marriage was convenience, or perhaps "cultural incest" — "I married him because we had so much in common. He reminded me of my brothers." What fatherhood meant, what motherhood meant; money problems during the marriage; current relations with their respective parents; how they live as a small group of human beings — these are the things that parents ought to be more aware of and that you ought to know about, too. The child therapist's interest in family life can be heralded in this initial interview, and later, when a home visit is carried out, observations will be facilitated greatly because of this focus on parents and family during the initial contact.

Parental Personal Traits Aiding Therapy

Lest we forget that parents themselves can be deaf, blind, mentally retarded, psychotic, and so on, we ought to look briefly at some of the clinical features of parents that will enhance their child's course in therapy.

Any and all parental ego strengths help mightily, whether in the realm of perceptual, emotional, or cognitive functioning. Parents who are themselves soundly coping will be able to assist more fully the psychotherapy of their child.

Their child can love and respect them and identify with their wh<
the parents are not profoundly absorbed by their parental roles.
many successful women and men contain stories of parents who v
negligent of their children. Nevertheless, the child's love of paren
parent's love of the child) seems to be the necessary ingredient foi
growing up. Still this has been a consoling and useful fact for man
ful fathers than mothers, I suspect. An intact parent is more lovable, and if only
for that reason is a boon to therapy and personal growth.

Consequently, it is a good omen when the parental intelligence is not severely
impaired by brain damage (from drugs as well as tumor, infection, and so on). It
is all to the good if the parents are not severely conflicted, or extremely deviant
as, for example, a psychopath might be. And it helps if the parents do not hang
onto physical symptoms (hoping that the child is brain damaged rather than
neurotic) but show some so-called psychology-mindedness. And if the parents
have an inkling of what psychotherapy is all about, that is, they know enough to
want it, this positive motivation will be all to the good. Finally, still another
parent attribute is of critical weight for the child's psychotherapy, namely, what
I would call "some flexibility in their value systems," so that the parents themselves can accept some changing within their family and will not forever resent,
compete with, and sabotage the child's therapist and the therapy team. Parents
need values. We all do, for otherwise we have no identity, no conscience. But
a certain openness, a flexibility that will allow constructive change to occur,
makes the parents' life richer and makes the child's life in therapy easier.

Child and Parental Expectancy

The parents' aspirations and hopes concerning their child should be investi-
gated early in the contact with the family. In some respects the presented child
can be viewed as only the symptom of the parents, an unconscious expression
of their neurotic tendencies. .That is a viewpoint of considerable legitimacy, for
the parents do use the child as their admission ticket to a psychiatric facility,
employing the child as a kind of narcissistic probe, like a pseudopod. Our culture
structures parenthood to give narcissistic gratification in many ways that tend to
make for a fusion of parent and child, but the parents are also related to the child,
however imperfectly. The relationship can occur within a wide range, though.
The relatedness may be similar to a symbiosis, in which the parent has no existence
apart from the child and the child appears in many ways to be primarily a con-
tinuant or a sign of parental narcissism. Or, as analysts say, the relation may be

that of anaclitic dependency, or of part objects, or perhaps of real and whole objects. The child's role in the life of the parents is often diverse and multifaceted.

In any event, it is worthwhile for us to know how the parents form images of and speak of their offspring. Do they see the child as a "bad egg"? Do they foresee a good future for the child, or do they see nothing better than a criminal or psychotic career ahead? Ask them to recount a time when they felt a surging of great warmth for the child, when their hearts melted and they felt that the child was very beloved, very close to them. Ask this of each parent separately. Many parents become tongue-tied and simply cannot think of a time that exemplifies this kind of warmth. Or, alternatively, ask the parents what is the best thing they can say about the child. Or ask them to tell you something the child does very well that gives them pleasure in his accomplishment. Again, this is a challenge that leaves some parents dumbfounded. Also ask what is the worst quality of the child, for example, the most horrible thing the child does, in order to find out how well the parents express their conscious criticism and hatred. Here, too, if the parents are forced and artificial in their dealings with their child, they might find it hard to say anything highly critical of the child, even when they are asked by the child psychiatrist. The family style for living with anger is a most crucial psychiatric datum, so look for this and note it well.

In a like fashion, when obtaining the developmental history from the parents, I like to ask them not only about the motor milestones and history of weaning and toilet training, allergies, and so on, but also about the child's sexual behavior. Many sound (and unsound) children have had a rather vigorous genital life, but they usually have taken some care to conceal it from their parents. Therefore a negative report from parents may not mean much from a factual standpoint. Thus I like to ask the question, not because of the intrinsic relevance of the child's genitality, but because sexuality in childhood is a relatively taboo topic. What parents do with taboo topics serves as a useful index of how well they are likely to take to any sort of new ways, make changes, and at least cooperate with the child's treatment. Do they expect the child to be a lustful, genital being? What games of deception, subterfuge, and denial might these parents play? Is this a family in which "id strengths" — lust, zest, vitality, bodily pleasures, and sexual actions — are condoned and enhanced?

Involving the Father

Advocates of family group therapy are usually the most conscientious of all therapists about involving fathers in the treatment process. They insist upon having the father present. Once the father is there, the family group therapist, even if he does little else, often helps to restore the family to a more patriarchal style, allying himself with the father. This is not to say that all family group therapy enthusiasts are male chauvinists, however. We can all learn a lot from family therapists about effective ways to convince fathers to come in, or to reach out to the father's home for contacts.

In my own clinical practice, when the mother says the father will not come, I become suspicious that the mother does not want him there. So I call the father and tell him that I think it is necessary for him to come in. The fathers' favorable response rate has been almost 100 percent. Fathers are not so eager to be shadowy and forgotten figures as some child psychiatrists pretend they are. I would urge any beginning therapist to *insist* that fathers come to see the assigned therapist, whether it be the child's or another therapist. Some fathers embrace psychotherapy with zeal. Child psychiatrists learned long before the advent of the current women's liberation movement that fathers can be involved in child-caring and in family life generally. I guess it boils down to the rule that whenever there are two parents in the household, they should be taken advantage of by insisting that they both be involved. It enhances therapy to have the father take part.

Some fathers like to be involved regularly. Middle-class fathers in particular are willing to talk an egalitarian and "concerned" line, and that has served to give them the good reputation of being highly workable. Too, working-class fathers, less egalitarian and avowedly more patriarchal, can be safely regarded as potent figures within their households and in the life of the child being treated. Lower-class fathers also, whenever they can be located, provide many positive resources for a happier family life and should be relentlessly sought after when a child needs therapy [6]. Involve the father.

Preparing for Psychotherapy

Both child and parents will need some preparation for psychotherapy. If you had the child present at the initial interview, this could have been done by you directly; but if you see the parents alone for the initial evaluation session, you will have to discuss some things that the parents might do to prepare themselves and their child for continued evaluation and therapy.

The parents should be informed and consulted about the terms of the contract with the child's therapist: the cost and payment plan; the timing of evaluation, feedback, and therapy sessions if required; and the precise way in which parents must be involved in the child's evaluation and treatment processes. The parents need to know that, welcome or not, the therapist will become a kind of house guest in spirit, and perhaps in fact, since the therapist undertakes home visitation sessions. It also helps if you alert the child's parents to some of the resentment they may feel toward the therapeutic intruder and encourage them to grumble to you, the therapist, not to suppress their anger or discontent until there is a blowup that involves withdrawing the child precipitously from therapy. Indeed, I tentatively negotiate at the outset for some weeks of warning prior to any termination. All these deeds and discussions help parents to see the seriousness of the work to be done and the indispensability of their aid and support to the project's success. The chances that everything may get worse before improving should be spelled out — a warning of the possibility that it is darkest before the dawn.

Confidentiality in the child-therapist relationship must be conceded early by the parents. They must be assured that you cannot be corrupted on this point. They must expect not to be in control of the relationship, but let it take place between the child and therapist without their nosiness. This means that they are discouraged from "pumping" the child about what he does and says when with the doctor. Similarly, they are dissuaded from prompting the child as to what he should report when he sees the therapist.

In my experience, the best way to accede to the parents' legitimate desires to be in on the continuing therapy is to have them see a caseworker concurrently with the child's seeing a separate therapist. In that way, a more organic evolution of the child's therapy and their therapy can take place day by day, so that both are getting help and both are making changes from inside a structure of relationships. There is, as a result, less need for long-winded preparation of the parents, trying to alert them before the fact to resistances, affects, and the like. These are highly complex things to try to polish off in a single session, after all, and it is both more sensible and helpful to use some of the child guidance format of separate, concurrent parent and child therapy.

The parents can help the child before his first session to understand that he will be seeing a psychiatrist for help with some problems, which the parents will spell out for the child. This help prepares the child, for in that way they will have divulged that you are a psychiatrist, a doctor who works with children and their families when problems such as his occur. There will be no deception or pussyfooting about the kind of doctor being consulted or the pertinent problems, and for some parents this is something big. Won't the child be afraid of the very idea? What if he tells everybody about it? What about the Senator Eagleton phenomenon? Aren't people suspicious of anyone who has seen a psychiatrist?

Isn't there a stigma on psychiatric treatment among children? Shouldn't the child hide the fact of his psychotherapy? Won't this upset his teachers? Won't it go on his cumulative school record? Won't his brothers and sisters ridicule him? Isn't seeing a psychiatrist and being labeled as a deviant, or sick, or crazy, a bad thing?

All these dire outcomes are possibilities, with our cultural ethos being what it is, and with gossipiness and fear of psychiatry being what they are. However, parents can be told that far more children speak to close chums about their "analyst," or "shrink," or "doctor" with more pride, even boastfulness, than with shame. And as for the school, who can say? You may want to talk with the child's teacher, certainly, and will have to take your chances on the misuses to which the school might put their knowledge of a child's treatment. At the beginning there may be no need to let the school know of it. Besides, many teachers are more knowledgeable about child therapy than the customary stereotype indicates. Not all teachers have medieval attitudes on psychiatry. And in any event, the prospects exist (if faintly) for a school destructuring that will permit greater respect for children's overall rights. As things now stand, teachers cannot be blamed for the system; in fact, teachers may be instrumental in changing it on behalf of children.

The parents must be involved, not merely to "bring the child, arrange the appointments, pay the bills, support the analysis, and allow the child to get well," as Samuel Weiss and his colleagues [7] said, but also as an integral and continuous part of the treatment process. Preferably, the parents will be in therapy (casework) separately, and the therapist's relation with the child can be more dyadic and private than when all three members of the parent-child trio are seen regularly by the same therapist.

Parents are needed to give information, to get help in making changes themselves, to prepare the child for psychiatric intervention, and to cooperate with the therapy. We will come back to the special excitements of working directly with parents in Chapter 6. If parents are aided in doing their part, the child's prognosis is brightened greatly.

CONSIDER THE WHOLE FAMILY

Actually, everyone within that basic small group, the household, must be of concern to the child therapist. Think of your own infantile domestic life and of the primary self-concept you developed in your own first two years. Who was important to you? Perhaps mother above all, then father, sibs, and all the others who were in your daily intimate world. Chances are that, even today, regardless of whether you have had psychoanalysis, you carry over into current life some of your very early attitudes toward self and others. If, in the retrospection of the grown-up, infantile objects were so very important, then for the child patient his intimate household world assuredly assumes paramount significance for therapy. Regardless of race or party or gender, you will have to know the "significant others" in the home of the identified child patient.

Family group therapy has become quite the "in" thing in recent years, and it makes good sense to see the entire family group. This is required especially for therapists who cannot trust others to work with the parents (and sibs) while they do their work with the identified child patient. As a group, family group therapists still have a long way to go before they are as skillful as psychiatric caseworkers. I prefer to work collaboratively with my colleagues, even though I have learned a lot myself about the life of real families as small groups since my residency in child psychiatry — more than I would ever have surmised from my analytically oriented training experiences.

As a general observation, I can say to therapists in training that both analysts and social scientists approach real-life families with a heavy load of theory that needs freshening up and adjusting to the actual situation. In some ways, the same can be said of family group therapists, who are frequently inclined to dogmatize and overgeneralize. Moreover, whether general psychiatrists or others, they are most often wrapped up in families in which the identified patient is a young adult who is schizophrenic. Their skill with children may be meager at best. Although they sometimes work with families that contain prepubertal children, these children are usually given short shrift because the family group therapist is primarily working with the parents, some to strengthen fathers, others to strengthen mothers, others to help get the parents off the child's back, and so on. Children who have sat in sessions of family group therapy often attest to the fact that the sessions consisted mostly of therapist grown-ups "rapping" and discussing with other grown-ups. I do not deny, of course, that adults deserve the chance to talk to one another and that sometimes children should be quiet while grown-ups talk.

The big question about studying family groups is whether we can apply the same concepts that refer to individuals to small and large groups. It seems doubtful that Murray Bowen's early views of the family's having an "undifferentiated ego mass" can hold water and be fruitful as a concept to aid our work with families. It is of interest to note that Bowen now sees mainly the man and wife pair, omitting their offspring. That may be a trend for family therapists as a group. Small groups do tempt us to trot out our psychodynamic explanations, explanations whose value, if any, is for the single individual as a person or in his interpersonal relations. The beginning therapist had better stick to individuals until he has had social science training and training in group dynamics and small group theory. Psychiatrists know little of group processes until they have had special training.

If social science and psychiatry are ever to be fused, it will not be a triumph for psychiatry's individualistic concepts, I suspect, because social science will contribute the greater and richer share to the amalgam. Sociocultural interpretations of families make most sense when they are seen against a background of the extended family, the neighborhood, the subculture, and the culture. Family behavior, on the other hand, makes less sense against a background of libido and mortido; cultural values account for more family behavior than do even ego states. One of the soundest steps toward systematic and comprehensive family study has demonstrated the centrality of values, and values are totally socio-cultural. However, the Committee on the Family of the Group for the Advancement of Psychiatry said judiciously [8]:

In any case, the description of cultural and family strains is only the beginning of the diagnostic process. It approaches the background of the problems in the family, delineating normative expectations and departures from them on the basis of which health or pathology in interpersonal relations is perceived. Interpersonal, intrapsychic, and biological levels of integration must all be explored for a full elucidation of any state of illness.

What I would suggest is that the average beginner in psychotherapy can learn best to work with interpersonal and intrapsychic (and perhaps biologic) matters, leaving family group work to those with more appropriate education for the job required. Obviously, many fine people disagree with me here; but I'll say it my way, and the reader can know my position and stay as open-minded as he chooses.

Home Visiting

It is possible to know the family aside from meeting with them in regular family group therapy sessions. One good way is the home visit by the two therapists, one for the child and one for the rest of the family. Most of the things that family group sessions can tell us will come to light on such home visitations, and often more can be learned on home ground than elsewhere.

The beginner, probably the only one foolhardy enough to consult a primer, should do home visits as a part of his therapeutic work with every child. Where the family lives does matter, and much in the way of respect and sincere interest is communicated to child and parents when they are visited on their home ground. Many child psychiatry residents have told me convincingly that they saw more about family life in an hour's home visit than in dozens of hours of conjoint family group or collaborative psychotherapy. Hence, home visits can almost be considered a necessary step in appraisal of any child's world.

My preferred style of home visit is to accompany the parents' therapist and for me to spend some of the time with the entire family group and some with my child patient alone. From the family group I want to learn how they interact with each other, how as a group they receive the professional people whom they've known theretofore solely in a businesslike and clinical setting, and what they seem to have going for them as a family. I also stay on the lookout for any tendencies to scapegoat the child who has become my patient, and I continually try to ascertain what the child means to the family as a group and as individuals. From the child I ask for a look at where he plays, sleeps, seeks solitude, and so on, in the house and neighborhood. If during the time I am with the child patient one of his sibs becomes a tagalong, I might say to the alien member of our trio, "Could you allow your brother Hank and me to have some time alone? Will you go somewhere else?" This doesn't always get rid of the sib, but it scores with my patient that I am for *him.*

Both at the office and on the home visit I do not clamor to see my patient's brothers and sisters. However, in my office, my own territory, I discourage it more actively than I can on the family's home soil. It is only as a reaction against his sibling hatred, I know, that the patient ever says he wants to include his sib in his psychotherapy sessions. Or he wants to bring his brother or sister to resist working in psychotherapy. Anyway, I adopt a fairly strict dyadic therapy approach when I take sides on this argument. I don't want to do sib group therapy.

Child as Family Expert

Children serve as able informants about the values and patterns operating within their families, if children are taken seriously and if family data are considered desirable by the therapist. The child can be asked to draw a sketch of his entire household — all the members of his family and everyone else in the house. Young children may think of cats and dogs as equal members among the family group. Surprisingly, pets assume a big place in the drawings executed by many rather guarded children. Few children have difficulties in getting along with household animals, while their relations with people may be a completely different story. The pets that are included in the drawing often tell us a lot about what the child projects from his own inner self-picture onto the household animal.

Though I have not had especially good luck in this, several of my students have been able to elicit from many children some very imaginative and revealing "kinetic" drawings of the family, that is, drawings of the family as a group doing something. Theoretically, kinetic drawings will elicit not only *structural informa-tion* about the family as seen by the child but also some *process information* about the caliber and flavor of the operative family culture [9].

Even a clumsy sketch of stick figures, perhaps reminiscent of a puerile depic-tion of a police lineup, can be a useful springboard for eliciting a "story" about the family as depicted in the drawing. The narrative, if not the crude drawing, turns out to be pure gold, more than compensating for the drawing's esthetic lack. One can listen with sensitivity, noting how far the child can go with the tale-spinning, and one must always gauge the amount of inquiry that will enhance the alliance and, by contrast, the amount that will arouse the hackles of childish resistance. Don't push your luck.

The basic lesson to be learned is how to convey to the child your concern to know about his family because its members are the figures who inhabit his intimate daily world, real and fantasied. And do this without giving him the notion that you are building up a "case" and playing detective. To share his perceptions of his family with you, he has, as a prerequisite, to trust you. Remember that it might be the first time an adult has ever taken his viewpoint seriously, and that aspect all by itself can make it take on an awesome quality. The burden is lightened greatly when the parents can tell the child unequivocally that they allow and expect him to "spill the beans" to his therapist.

When you are eliciting the family story from the child, it is imperative that you listen and probe for meanings and nuances of family styles. But do not assume that the child's family structure in some way is closely akin to the family of orienta-tion that *you* remember. Stereotypes come easily and naturally when we are talk-ing down to little children, about mama and papa and sibs, but stereotyped assumptions are hellish interferences with therapeutic accomplishment. Stereo-types should be guarded against with diligence. What you and your family for generations past might have thought about the role of the father, the value of the penis, the fear of castration by penile amputation, the mother's role as masochist and maker of chicken soup, and so on, may have nothing at all to do with how your young client exists in his own familial world. So do beware of facile generalization about what family life has to be like. Every child's private familial world is fresh and new, unlike any other child's. And that is why it is best to listen and not to intrude with views of marriage and family forms that supposedly are made in heaven.

Most of us who have studied pediatrics grow accustomed to getting all our facts from the child's parents. And if a pediatrician were honest about it he would say *mother* instead of *parents,* for pediatricians seldom know fathers, either as involved fathers of their patients or as repositories of valuable historical information. Pediatrics in this regard is rather more congenial to the lower-class family in which the father may be nonexistent. In my limited experience, public health physicians, too, share in the pediatrician's reliance on mothers as the only responsible informants about a child's life. With the fatherless poor, of course, talking with fathers often is impossible, for mothers and maternal grandmothers *are* the only adults in charge. The early child guidance clinics knew this, too, and worked with a mother-child focus as long as they dealt mainly with the poor. When they began to serve largely the middle class, they *needed* to learn something out of the family group therapist's book, namely, that fathers are worth seeing also. Be that as it may, children themselves of every economic class — and not only their parents — are excellent informants about family style and family history. I would suggest your finding out about the family from the child. Only the child can tell you how it seems from his standpoint.

PARENTS WHO FACILITATE THERAPY

What kind or kinds of families enhance psychotherapy with a child? Isidor Bernstein [10] pondered the matter for a panel of the American Psychoanalytic Association in 1956 and stated the ideal qualifications of parents whose child is being psychoanalyzed. These parental characteristics constitute a list that would be hard to improve upon.

1. Willingness and capability to supply historical materials the therapist (analyst) calls for
2. Willingness and capability to give the analyst reports on the child's (and family's) daily activities
3. Some encouragement of the child's forming an alliance with the therapist

4. Some discouragement of the child's deriving gratification from his neurotic operations
5. Some recognition that the child is troubled by inner conflict, suffering, and inhibition
6. Willingness to stick out the analysis even though the analyst refrains from advising and prescribing for the parents
7. Strength to handle the "stigma" of serious mental illness implicit in frequent and long-lasting treatment sessions for their child
8. Toleration of a close, prolonged, and secret relationship of child to therapist
9. Willingness to have the child become healthy and to be more independent of them
10. Some faith or expectancy that the treatment will have a helpful outcome, in spite of its costliness in time, tension, and money — what Bernstein meant by "value placed upon the analysis"

The beginner in psychotherapy will surely require as many of these facilitating parent-traits as will the experienced child analyst. However, help to a child can sometimes be rather astonishing without meeting all of Bernstein's criteria for the parents. Bernstein and other analysts recognized that "mere psychotherapy" sometimes can do with fewer optima than analysis, particularly if the psychotherapist makes arrangements for involving, and perhaps even treating, the parents.

REFERENCES

1. Fraiberg, S. A comparison of the analytic method in two stages of a child analysis. *J. Am. Acad. Child Psychiatry* 4:387, 1965.
2. Freud, A. Introduction to the Technique of the Analysis of Children (trans. by Nancy Proctor-Gregg). In *The Psychoanalytical Treatment of Children.* New York: Schocken Books, 1964. (Original, 1926)
3. Freud, A. *Normality and Pathology in Childhood: Assessments of Development.* New York: International Universities Press, 1965.
4. Axline, V. *Play Therapy* (rev. ed.). New York: Ballantine Books, 1969. (Orig. ed., Boston: Houghton Mifflin, 1947.)
5. Satir, V. *Conjoint Family Therapy.* Palo Alto: Science and Behavior Books, 1967.
6. Adams, P. Functions of the lower-class partial family. *Am. J. Psychiatry* 130:200, 1973.
7. Weiss, S., et al. Technique of child analysis: problems of the opening phase. *J. Am. Acad. Child Psychiatry* 7:639, 1968.

8. Group for the Advancement of Psychiatry, Committee on the Family. *The Case History Method in the Study of Family Process.* Report Number 76. New York: GAP Publications Office, 1970.
9. Burns, R., and Kaufman, S. *Actions, Styles and Symbols in Kinetic Family Drawings (K-F-D).* New York: Brunner/Mazel, 1970.
10. Bernstein, I. The importance of characteristics of the parents in deciding on child analysis. *J. Am. Psychoanal. Assoc.* 6:71, 1958.

FURTHER READINGS

*Hobbs, N. Helping disturbed children: Psychological and ecological strategies. *Am. Psychol.* 21:1105, 1966.

Malmquist, C. Problems of confidentiality in child psychiatry. *Am. J. Orthopsychiatry* 35:787, 1965.

4

The Child as a Favorable Treatment Prospect

Help must be directed to the more positive aspect of the self, with the interest focusing on what can be done rather than on weakness and what cannot be done.
—F. H. Allen [1]

We need to know the child as a person and to discover some things about the child himself that make treatment go more smoothly. It is necessary for us to do some concurrent diagnostic work if we aim to do therapeutic work. Diagnosis, understood simply as the clear identification of problems, is ideally done *preparatory* to treatment. Only by diagnosis do we know what problems we're trying to solve. It is rather ridiculous to discard diagnosis simply because it is a feature of the "medical model" of problem-solving that some may decry. Diagnosis is a process of assessing which continues, an ongoing elucidation, and so it overlaps treatment; treating and clarifying interact. In fact, the problems are sometimes identified best only as termination is occurring. The desire to help is inseparable from the desire to understand, and children can spot the same kind of quality in a therapist when the therapist wants to discover and to unearth, as well as when he wants to heal. If we do not get to know and understand the child, how can we give him any kind of reliable help?

No matter how hard we may try to separate diagnosis from therapy, the gray zone of overlapping between the two is always immense. Diagnosis in the abstract is not something done to the child. Theoretically, it is a mental operation that goes on strictly within the helping adult. Yet if a school-phobic, panicky child sees the doctor discovering that the child's fear is not of school but of separating from his mother, the child takes heart that he is being understood and that his problems are being fathomed. So willy nilly, diagnosis becomes something *done to* or with the child, although its major significance may remain within the therapist's head. Therefore, let your diagnostic work be as helpful as possible under these circumstances. I will attend to diagnosis and how it is done in Part III, particularly in Chapters 8 and 10, and will not dwell on diagnostic techniques here. I will instead describe some of the child's assets that we hope to be able to count on as enhancers of psychotherapy. In talking about these assets,

I will be sounding as if they are all internal or intrapsychic, but the reader should remember that in the final analysis they do not appear to be deeply inward. It is only customary to describe them as inner.

SEPARATION TOLERANCE AND PROGNOSIS

Until the child is age five or so, we can permit him to want to do a certain amount of clinging to the mother when the child appears at our workshop in the company of the two parents. Anyone who has watched waiting room behavior in young children would have no doubt that it is usually the mother to whom the child clings, not the father. And I must say, I seriously doubt that it is the parents' problem. That is, the parents have not conspired to make the child prefer to be attached to the mother; the child himself has made that mother-oriented bonding long before he entered our therapy environs. However, if only the father is present, the child under five may cling to him and weep in protest against separation. I say we can "permit" this clinging in the preschool child (meaning that we do not hold it to be highly pathologic) although many urban preschool children have had nursery school, day care, and kindergarten experiences that have made them either feel safe away from the mother or else able to hide their fears on separation. Still, some protest and wailing when we first undertake to separate the young child and the parent is normal and frequent. Any child is entitled to have suffi-cient ambivalence to make him rather fearful of being out of his parents' sight. Still, clinging beyond the age of five years is not healthy. Parents sense that it is not love alone that motivates the clinging older child. Consequently, we will only be agreeing with the laymen, the parents, when we aver that the child's clinging is not a favorable prognostic sign and that his willingness to be apart is a good sign.

Especially, clinging that persists in a child of five or more years beyond the first few sessions is a bad prognostic sign. To a limited extent, it is true that the disturbed child's family is a blob of protesting symbiosis, a mass of union-fusion-blurring of individuality-narcissism-identifications-loss of ego boundaries, and so on. Yet it is not a contented blob. Each member of the family longs somehow in his heart of hearts to be set free from this tyranny of role diffusion and blood bondage; each person longs to be individuated, intact, and whole. As Rank might have put it, each person longs to break out of the collective ideology and to become individualized, even individualistic. Hence the child above five years of age who separates readily and who seems already to have considered and accepted the eventuality of his separateness is a child for whom the prospects of therapeutic success are greatly increased.

EGO STRENGTHS TO LOOK FOR

The child whose ego is sturdy is a better treatment prospect than one whose ego is weak or frail. The precise defining of ego strengths (even if I could do it) would not be appropriately done here, for that is a problem in metapsychology or philosophical anthropology that would carry us either too far afield or into too murky zones of pure speculation. Yet some children do seem, when we compare them with their age-mates, to be basically better protoplasm, basically better put together, basically better able to cope and make out and make do. By convention, we pretend the strong ego is in the child, but we only see it in his relationships. It is a mistake, though, to take the psychiatric mechanistic conventions so seriously that we actually believe that ego strengths are real things apart from a child's interactions with other persons.

In the terminology of Freudian ego psychology it would be said that we are favored as psychotherapists if we have a chance to work with children who show relatively greater, and not lesser, *memory, speech development, reality testing,* and *control over motor functions.* Anna Freud [2] considered these functions, plus such functions as *intelligence, logical cognition,* and general *"secondary process functioning,"* all together, as indicative of growing ego strengths. As the preschool child develops along the ego axis — or, as Anna Freud preferred to describe it, "on the side of the ego" — he becomes a more definite, stronger person who is simultaneously a better analytic prospect. Not trying to push our skepticism or love of paradox too far, we could state it in this way: The child who has greater ego strengths will do better either with or without therapy!

Or, in a slightly different terminology, but with a theory drawing upon a wider range of behavioral science tools and information, the anthropologist Clyde Kluckhohn and the Jungian psychologist Henry A. Murray defined ego strengths as a close correspondent of id strengths [3].

Since the ego system is the differentiated governing establishment of the personality, it is not possible to estimate its power (relative to other ego systems) without some knowledge of the strength of the id forces with which it has to cope. Some "egos" are sitting in the saddle of a docile Shetland pony, others are astride a wild bronco of the plains.

Murray and Kluckhohn [3] wrote further that the criteria of ego strength are (and I paraphrase and concretize them rather liberally):

Conation
1. Ability to stick by a promise
2. Ability and willingness to take responsibility
3. Initiative and self-sufficiency
4. Ability to express some impulses directly and spontaneously
5. Ability to make some decisions
6. Ability to live, within limits, an ordered life
7. Ability to persist when frustrated moderately

Intellection
8. Ability to think about real issues
9. Ability to say what one is thinking
10. Ability to concentrate on problems till solved

Perception
11. Ability to see reality without distortion
12. Ability to see oneself realistically
13. Ability to foresee consequences of one's actions

These are undoubtedly not present to their fullest extent in any child. Indeed, at the other end of the life cycle, they would characterize only an adult who is super-adequate or "hypernormal." Nevertheless, they do stand as criteria of what makes for integrity and strength of ego, and as good developmentalists, we child therapists must make allowances for the child's age as we look at each of these criteria. When they are found, these criteria of ego strength also serve us as the indices of a child's therapeutic workability.

ID STRENGTHS TO LOOK FOR

Most dynamic psychologists today follow the Jungian more than the early Freudian conception of what id is and "where id was." Freudians, before they became ego-oriented, tended to equate id with everything wild and unacceptable in the personality of child and adult. Somehow the child had a preponderance of id, a paucity of ego, they contended. They also insisted that females, "primitives," and people with "ego defects" had rather unbridled ids. In opposition to this, Carl Jung broke away, insisting that love, creativity, religious sentiments, and other such human (and for the Jungians, noble and desirable) things emanated from the id. Once more, we can appeal to the authority of Murray and Kluckhohn [3] for a succinct statement of what criteria of id strength we need to be alert to:

1. Intense energy, zest, spontaneity, enthusiasm
2. Intense needs and appetites
3. Intense emotions
4. Abundant, vivid imaginations

That is a conception of the id as a powerhouse of rather healthy childlike exuberance. Stated in that way, there is nothing particularly repugnant about a strong id, nor would "impulse control" be the only goal of our psychotherapy. As a consequence, we would not have to equate id with original sin. Id is not unfavorable, therefore, and conceivably it could be of great aid to us as we undertake to mobilize the healthier assets of children with whom we are engaged in a process of psychotherapy. Id strength is salutary, then, if it only existed; but it doesn't, except as we infer it from the child's behavior in relations with us, with his family members, and with his compeers.

PHYSICAL ATTRIBUTES AND PHYSICAL EXAMINATIONS

Even though it is not easy to build a convincing case for the intrapsychic location of id and ego, we come now to some aspects of the child which do seem definitely located in the individual child. I refer to the fact that the child does have certain physical traits that help to influence psychotherapy positively. I refer to such circumstances as good health, adequate nutrition, intact sensory and motor apparatus, a brain that is functioning within a range conducive to coping. In a more negative way we could state it that the physically ill child, the hungry or malnourished child, or the child with sensory or neurologic deficits or brain damage is a poor candidate for psychotherapy.

The beginning student should recall that all these physical attributes in the demographic mass are indices of poverty, of lowered economic life chances. For large populations they simply demonstrate the ways in which our class system becomes imprinted into the individual physique. The presidential address of Benjamin Pasamanick [4] to the American Orthopsychiatric Association, entitled "A Child Is Being Beaten," gives a speedy summary and convenient reminder of the many research studies that show how poverty undermines both the physical and mental health of young children. Hard-core-poor children thus present a more challenging therapy undertaking than do the affluent and strong, and they require the best therapists (but usually get the least accomplished ones).

Should every child have a physical examination as part of an overall health survey before psychotherapy is embarked upon? I think so, and I think it can be very instructively carried out by the child's own therapist. However, each young therapist will have to be bound by what his supervisor at a particular time and place may pontificate on this subject. If a young physician refrains compulsively from doing any physical examinations, he seems a little silly to me. Contrariwise, if he compulsively does all physical examinations, even on children who have just been attended by an excellent pediatrician, he seems both silly and untrusting. I guess the best rule is to ask oneself what will be of the greatest help to the child, not what will make the doctor feel best. Obviously, if the child's therapist is not a physician, he must universally rely on others to do the health survey for him. If he is a physician, though, I see no reason for him to tie a hand behind his back, particularly since some very worthwhile skills might atrophy from disuse.

David Levy [5] and William Schonfeld [6] are two writers who have published worthwhile papers on this issue, and both of them take the view that there is much to be gained from doing a physical examination that has psychiatric relevance. Discussing physical findings, images, fantasies, and self-pictures while examining the child can yield some worthwhile psychiatric data, they contend. Physical things such as age, skin color, body size, gender, habitus or physique, and even the child's intelligence, can all be discussed and evaluated with the child during the physical examination.

I do not want to leave this subject with the impression that a child who is retarded, or deaf, or brain-damaged, or epileptic, or economically poor is beyond hope. Something can be done by an astute psychotherapist for all these children. The decisive condition is not what the child has, but what the therapist has in the way of motivation. Still, the fact stands that the child's body and the child's images of his body are important for the course of his psychotherapy.

THE CHILD IN RELATION TO HIS FAMILY

A child who was wanted from a time antedating his conception is a better treatment prospect than the child who was unplanned, undesired, and hated or resented. The child who has not been a big realistic disappointment (mental retardation, costly sicknesses and injuries, and so on) to his parents has a more satisfactory course of therapy than the unwanted child, and so does a child who is not discriminated against because he is too dark for his black mother's tastes. A child whose temperament from birth has been congenial to the mother's tastes is also a more hopeful prospect in therapy. A child who is not an outcast, or scapegoat, or emblem of a family's conflict is a better treatment prospect. In other words, we always have to come full circle back to family relations whenever we are appraising the therapeutic workability of a child. Although it may border on overstatement, another way to put this is: The child's treatability is a function of the parent workability.

TREATING THE CHILDREN OF FRIENDS AND COLLEAGUES

When I was a resident and worked in a community guidance clinic, it fell my lot to evaluate a young black boy whom I'll call Jerry, whose parents I had known well in a social setting. I brought forth the usual arguments against any mixing of social and professional contacts. I wanted someone else to see the boy, someone who had not, as I had, shared certain recreational beverages with the boy's parents. It would have made me feel very good to shy away from that challenge and to have someone else take up the task. I felt well covered and rationalized as I tried to back off from therapeutic work with Jerry.

An experienced colleague said to me, without making me wince and squirm, "I'm just not in the habit of thinking of emotional conflicts as disgraceful." I retorted that I had been misunderstood, that I had not meant that there was any stigma associated with being seen by a psychiatrist. But the colleague's point had been made eloquently and I had to yield when the colleague asked me, "If there isn't any stigma, why can't we help our friends too, as well as strangers?" I did it, and it went rather well, neither strengthening nor eroding the preexistent friendship I had had with Jerry and his parents.

I could say there were some outright advantages in working with Jerry because I knew him and his family. The advantages are that you are doing something that brings pleasure to Hygeia and Hippocrates and all the other figures in our medical and psychiatric hagiology. It is pleasant to help out people whom we know. It is even pleasant to get the goods on them without ever taking advantage of what we know of their private madnesses and foibles! But Jerry was only one case. In most cases, after many years of being flexible and extending courtesy to my friends and associates, I see some persistent disadvantages in working with the children of one's friends and colleagues. For no matter how we slice it, it adds complexity to one's life — perhaps to one's social life more than to one's professional life. But for a psychiatrist, accustomed to great loneliness at best, and with membership in a specialty known to have the highest suicide rate of all, his social life is a highly important aspect of daily reality. At best, the psychiatrist's interpersonal life shows restlessness; witness the number of divorces among us. At worst, it is altogether lacking in verve; witness the puppetlike style of members of the psychiatric establishment at official psychiatric social functions: dull, stilted, bourgeois, lacking warmth — the words that come are not very complimentary. Psychiatrists need every bit of meaningful social life that they can grab, for so much of their time is spent questioning and analyzing relationships. Hence there are weighty arguments against seeing friends as patients.

To analyze is to stand outside of relationships to some extent. The good researcher is a marginal man, not the eager member of the in-group. A certain marginality is required of any behavioral scientist, whether he be anthropologist, psychiatrist, sociologist, or psychologist. Who could study human behavior if he accepted it and endorsed it? I believe, or maybe just want to believe, that child psychiatrists are a much more "swinging" crew than psychiatrists in general. Still, child psychiatrists always run the risk of contracting some occupational ills that general psychiatrists suffer from: loneliness, work alienation, boredom, unhappy love life, feeling powerless but longing to shake the earth, fear of nonconformity, and an eagerness to don what Benjamin Spock called "the professional man's muzzle." The pose of analytic neutrality does nothing to alleviate these occupational ills, and many psychiatrists I know would probably benefit from risking the treatment of a friend's child occasionally. Beginners should do it reluctantly.

REFERENCES

1. Allen, F. *Psychotherapy with Children.* New York: W. W. Norton, 1942.
*2. Freud, A. *Normality and Pathology in Childhood: Assessments of Development.* New York: International Universities Press, 1965.
3. Murray, H., and Kluckhohn, C. A Conception of Personality. In C. Kluckhohn et al., *Personality in Nature, Society, and Culture.* New York: Alfred A. Knopf, 1954.
*4. Pasamanick, B. A child is being beaten. *Am. J. Orthopsychiatry* 41:540, 1971.
5. Levy, D. Method of integrating physical and psychiatric examination with special studies of body interest, overt protection, response to growth and sex differences. *Am. J. Psychiatry* 9:121, 1929.
*6. Schonfeld, W. Body-image in adolescents: A psychiatric concept for the pediatrician. *Pediatrics* 31:845, 1963.

FURTHER READING

Berg, L. *Look at Kids.* Baltimore: Penguin Books, 1972.

Cohen, D. *The Learning Child.* New York: Pantheon Books, 1972.

*Levy, D. Capacity and motivation. *Am. J. Orthopsychiatry* 27:1, 1957.

Sobel, R. The child's role in therapy: A comparison of the child's sick role in treatment as seen by four disciplines. *J. Am. Acad. Child Psychiatry* 6:655, 1967.

5

Referral, Professionals, and Community

Child psychotherapy tends to be vacuum packed while cultures and subcultures rage around it. There has to be an insistence that therapists tune in more to the signals of the culture and the dynamics of the subculture so that a dialogue can occur.
—W. Herron [1]

In this section we will shift our gaze from the child and his family of orientation to you, your colleagues, and your community. The therapist's setup in the community, the organizations of the community, and the referral process by which you are brought to encounter a child in need of treatment are matters for our present attention. Naturally, the child himself and his parents and siblings are very important, but the nature of your own operation and the character of human services in your local area, as well as the referral, are also of great concern. There are optima in each of these that can assist the child's psychotherapy, and we will consider how each of these can be made to do their best on behalf of disturbed children.

THE REFERRAL

If the referral of a child — that is, of a child's parents — is done correctly, it will expedite and enhance the child's psychotherapy. Referrals are not ordinarily within the therapist's control (a fine reminder once again that we have a wholesome lack of omnipotence), but there are some educative influences that a therapist can exert on his referral sources, especially if he is a rather stable, staying-put member of a given community. Hence, after years of working with people who send us patients, the referral process does improve. In all events, the referral can either advance or hinder subsequent therapy, so it is important that it be done just right. And if it is not done correctly, the therapist has to be aware of that and contend with trying to clean up a needlessly messy beginning. A young beginning therapist is often more transient than a well-established one. Hence, beginners need to study referrals more closely and more systematically than do therapists with deeper roots in a community.

The referral has predefined the situation and has established a preset, a prejudice if you will. The referring agent has done two things, and occasionally he has done both badly:

First, he has told the parents (at least) of his reasons why you are needed for their child. The message the child finally received can chill your blood occasionally, and the child's blood also! In any event, you need to know the terms and the context of the preset.

Second, he has told you, or some intake agent of yours, about the child and about what he has done with child and family. This can be off-base, relatively, or rather accurate and informative. The referral agent has done more, and less, than make a social introduction. He has filled you in on clinical details about bedwetting, incest, foibles, family style, and the like that are assuredly *not* shared background data in a cocktail party introduction. But, on the other hand, he has usually done *less* in the way of giving you his personal endorsement, through a warm recommendation, than if he were playing matchmaker as friends sometimes do at cocktail parties. To begin with, nobody loves a child psychotherapist that much; in addition, even if you are well liked by the fellow professional who refers a conflicted child to you, your colleague tends to refrain from going overboard in your behalf; he might be less restrained about endorsing a used car dealer. Social workers, lawyers, clergymen, educators, psychologists, pediatricians, and other physicians are clever enough to know that the child and his parents may dislike you under the best of circumstances because of personal tastes, complex transference blocks, and mythic dissonances [2]. They know that not every family hits it off with every psychotherapist. Your style may put you at odds with this entire family.

In addition, the referrer might have acquired some deep reservations (resistances, fears) about referring any child for mental health care, even to an Anna Freud! The ambivalent referrer is about all we get in this field, so only the extremes become conspicuously noticeable to us. The rule is: Expect an ambivalent referral, with abundant misgivings mixed into it. Don't be astonished if an almost paralyzing doubt was injected at the referral source.

We all know pediatricians whose young patients have died; judges who misjudged; psychologists, general psychiatrists, and social workers who goofed; clergymen and teachers who went berserk; and so on. We who work in child psychiatry need to avoid the kind of compulsive honesty that leads us to utter the grave warnings about our professional colleagues that they do about us.

Many of our referrers talk as though what we do is so inexact, or so hit-and-miss or totally unpredictable, that there is no way to forecast what may happen. Granting the safety of such extremely cautious views, we can quarrel some with their ambivalence and with the poor reputation they may give to child therapy and child therapists. In my experience, it is rarer to get a referral that oversells than one that undersells me. This happens despite the fact that I am rather reliably competent to do some useful things in psychotherapy with young people. It is generally much better that the therapist himself, rather than the person making the referral, supply the needed modesty.

Some Reasonable Expectations

When a child therapist receives a referred child and family, he has a right to hope that the referrer has not depicted the child therapist as someone whom the referrer is testing — "Let's see what Dr. Adams comes up with, if he can do anything." The child therapist also has a right to expect that he has not been represented as a magician, but recognizes that some referrers either demand everything or expect nothing. The child therapist further expects that the referral has not been made as into a wastebasket or dung heap with the implication that nothing *real* is wrong. We are entitled to expect some reasonableness and decency. Finally, the child therapist should expect that referral to a child therapist was neither the first thought nor the absolute last resort for the referrer. Only when some of these reasonable expectations are met will the referral contribute best to a happier therapeutic outcome.

Referrals by General Psychiatrists

The general psychiatrist may refer a child, for the parents, to the child psychiatrist. In the typical instance, one of the child's parents has been the referring psychiatrist's patient. These parents quite often are like members of what Charles Kadushin [3] so wittily named "Friends and Supporters of Psychotherapy." Kadushin concentrated on a species in New York City, but related variants exist in Miami, Philadelphia, Atlanta, and San Francisco — in fact, all over North America.

Referrals by general psychiatrists can be ineptly done and thereby impose problems. First of all, general psychiatrists cannot always be counted on to have seen the child and to have done an evaluation. They may not even have asked the first psychiatric question: *"What is the meaning of this child's troubles?"*

"General" psychiatrists all too often are merely psychiatrists for adults who will not deign to work with young people. So they aren't very general, only adult-oriented, and they often appear to do whatever the child's parents ask of them. At least, the children often perceive that the general psychiatrist values only the adults within a child's family. General psychiatrists in the future will be able to function, I hope, as bonafide generalists, including all age groups in their clientele and, when appropriate, making informed referrals of some children. A general psychiatrist should be able to do some generally therapeutic and helpful things with all age groups.

Odd as it may seem, when the circumstances are just right, general psychiatrists who are seeing one or both parents are among the finest collaborators with the child's therapist. I used to think I had to have exclusive input to a family in order to do my therapy with a child, and I approached "sharing a family" with trepidation. But with experience I have been able to make out very satisfactorily in conjunction with a parent's psychiatrist.

The child has me for his primary therapist. The parent has his or her general psychiatrist as primary therapist, and I function as a secondary therapist with the parent, concentrating on the parenting sector much as a caseworker might do. This goes smoothly if the other psychiatrist and I trust each other, have a basically respectful attitude, and are willing to share but not intrude. Under these conditions I tell the parent(s), "If I get into anything that you think you'd better work on with your personal therapist, tell me to lay off and I will respect that. I want to help, not hinder, and so does your psychiatrist, and that is why we are dividing the labor but still trying to work toward the same goals." And it works. I recall one lesbian mother who invoked the rule and refused to discuss (with me) certain sexual indiscretions, although these had become very well known to her child, insisting she would work it out in *her* individual psychotherapy. That was a productive way to deal with it.

Referrals by Pediatricians

Referrals by pediatricians can be the best or the worst imaginable. Anybody in a civilized society who works with children had better be able to relate to pediatricians. I described some of the joys and sorrows of dealing with pediatricians in the chapter "Techniques for Pediatric Consultation" in Schwab [4], giving therein a fuller view of my ideas on this subject. To make a short list of some of the most disadvantageous features in the pediatrician's referral, we would need to include:

Referral as rejection forever
Referral as insult
Referral as "omniscient completeness"
Referral as abject surrender

If the pediatrician tells the parents that they are up against problems that seem not medical but psychiatric and that he is referring them to a psychotherapist, the parents may conclude that their child is undeserving of further pediatric care and that the pediatrician is finished forever with their child — rejection, into the trash can. To make matters worse for the family, imagine next that the child psychiatrist puts them on a waiting list or tells them he is of the opinion that what they need is "not psychotherapy but good-quality pediatric care," or in view of their financial status he sends them on to a public facility! We, as well as our pediatric colleagues, can reject children and families in artful ways. The best referral is one made *without the pediatrician's dismissal of the case.*

If the pediatrician is obviously angry and fed up when he makes a referral, he often tells the mother that he thinks she is misbehaving and causing her child to be emotionally disturbed. "You won't do a thing I suggest, so I have no recourse but to recommend that either you or your child see a psychiatrist." A bad referral is one that cashes in on the stigma of mental illness in order to make the referral source feel better and to put down the child and his parents.

When the pediatrician has run up a big hospital laboratory bill for the family and has called in neurology, psychology, speech pathology, and metabolism consultants, he may tell the parents that "nothing has been found wrong, so I recommend that we call in a psychiatrist," which is obviously a worse referral than one giving positive reasons for requesting psychiatric help. Pediatricians usually know enough about child behavior to do better than diagnose emotional upset by exclusion. Also, they have enough self-knowledge not to be so obsessively thorough that they recommend a psychiatrist just to "leave no stone unturned." This pediatric search for omniscience makes for a clumsy, even a silly, referral.

Real and Apparent Referrers

Child psychotherapists become known in a community and come to be acknowledged as helping resources. Schoolteachers in particular have told parents about me; whereupon, the parents checked me out with their pediatrician, and the latter made a referral of the family to me. The pediatrician appears to be the referrer in such cases, but in reality it is the schoolteacher. General practitioners and internists, too, will often front for the hospital nurses who spot child and adolescent problems and suggest contacting a child psychiatrist. If the parents permit it, I like to have sessions jointly with the parents and the *real referrer* — teacher or nurse — or in some sensible way to relate to the person who really instigated the consultation. The real referrer is the one to talk with whenever feasible.

Medical and Nonmedical Referrers

As awkward as their worst referrals can be, medical people as a group make the referrals that most enhance a helpful psychotherapy course. The reasons, actually not fully known and studied, are surely diverse and complex. Psychiatric expertise has permeated postbaccalaureate medical training. Postgraduate physicians-in-practice keep current with the emotional factor in their patients' illnesses. *Any* doctor can do some psychiatric screening as a result. In the average town, the one person most active on the front line against mental illness is a physician.

This is not to diminish nonmedical referrals — for example, from social work agencies, school psychologists, and counselors — but to acknowledge that, despite their potential for blundering, our medical colleagues can be counted on to perform that effective peer review that keeps us growing as well as keeping us honest! Each time we get a referral from a physician, we know we have passed muster or have undergone an informal peer review. We are held accountable by our fellow physicians; and the more psychiatry they know, the better for us and for our patients.

The Mandatory Referral; the Unwilling Patient

In a town where I once lived, a judge required an adolescent woman addicted to heroin to enter a specific private psychiatric hospital at the family's expense for a two-year term as a condition of her probation. It was a complex judgment that had many praiseworthy features, including some political aspects, but only the problem of the obligatory psychotherapy will be of concern to us here. A psychotherapist hopes for motivation from within his patient, not from within a judge; but judges often impose psychotherapy as a condition of probation or even as a part of a young person's overall punishment regimen. That seldom makes the psychotherapist happy if he has not been fully co-opted by the forces of law and order.

School principals, too, are great ones for requiring psychotherapy as punishment, as an alternative to immediate expulsion or suspension from their Edenic establishments. A headmaster who is used to coercion and compulsion in his school expects a psychotherapist to "buy into" coercion without any misgivings. A good psychotherapist, however, seldom relishes having to say, "Come to me or you get chucked out of school"; or "Come to me lest you get sent to reform school." Whenever a child and his parents want my arts and crafts, therapy is enhanced. By that same token, therapy is hindered when the child and his parents are made to come not from love but from fear.

The patient's unwillingness impedes therapy, we say. But does it? To be realistic, and attend honestly to what actually goes on in our psychotherapy, all children are rather unwilling patients. Coercion by parents is the child's way of life, so the best we can hope for is that parents will want the therapist to work with their child, even if the child does not.

Undoing an Inept Referral

Your good will and intelligence will ultimately shine through, but there are some things you can do to clear the decks more quickly when a poor referral has been made. For example, you can ascertain at the very first session what the parents were told by the referrer and make some needed counterassertions then and there. As I have come to ask parents and children routinely about what the referrer told them, I have been able to get the red herrings out of the way and get right on with the needed work. When I did not inquire of everyone what their expectations were and what they had been told by the referrer, I often found myself embroiled in a burdensome hassle. Look at it this way: Even an evaluation needs to be carried out free from excessive transference. Attitudes that the parents have picked up from the referrer may or may not be accurate. If they are inaccurate, they can distort and subvert a realistic and professional relationship with the young child and his parents.

Beginning a relationship by talking about the actual expectations of both parties to the transaction makes good sense. Only by talking about them can preconceptions get out into the open, where they can be dealt with as a part of the therapeutic process. This would not be a good rule for a love affair, but it certainly is for psychotherapy. Some things are supposed to be "talked into the ground" when psychotherapy is being done in a verbal interaction.

Also, for the delicate reader or the more orthodox one, let me say that what I am advocating is simply a part of the preparatory "rap" that psychoanalytically oriented psychotherapists advocate. Call it "preparation for psychotherapy" if it makes you feel more comfortable with it. But do it. If the referrer has misrepresented you by maligning or belittling or overvaluating, this needs to be considered, discussed, weighed, and evaluated. Otherwise, it is an omnipresent cloud darkening the therapy process; like a gentleman's agreement, it is not brought out into the open realm of dialogue. Being enshrouded in silence will enhance its influence.

I introduce parents to my way of operating when I underscore or fasten on the hostility in what the referrer told them about me. This gives them an example of how I look for motives that are not made explicit. They note that I am not going to pussyfoot in my work with them; that I see hostility as a natural part of life in our society; and that hostility does less harm when acknowledged than when denied. Similarly, if the referrer has stressed my kudos and overcomplimented me, I like to undo that kind of distortion also. I do this by emphasizing that I would like always to be of help but that unfortunately I do not always have smoothly consistent results from my good intentions. I will tell such parents that the results depend as much on them and their capability to make changes as it does on me, so "Who is there who will give me a glowing recommendation on *you?*"

While engaging in this form of talk and looking at the here and now, one gets some insight into how referrers were real objects as well as professionals in the lives of the referred family members. That pediatrician was a beloved or hated object, not simply a caretaker of the good health of their children. That attorney is not just a professional acquaintance but a person whom the parents revere because of his high social status in the community. That caseworker in the family service agency who recommended individual therapy for their child was not only a social worker who was involved in couples treatment or marriage therapy, but was also like the mother's kindly aunt and like the father's secret girl friend in Chicago! So talk to child and parents about the referrer. Transference distortions of this variety pour forth rather readily if they are facilitated by what you say and do in the very first hour. The added bonus is that you are looking at the referral, too.

How to Communicate with the Referral Agent

In general, it is only the health professionals acting as referrers who expect or deserve a note of acknowledgment that they have sent someone to see you professionally. Grateful former patients do not warrant this courtesy, nor friends of the family, nor the person who was answering calls for the Teen Hot-Line. But professionals do. Also, I believe in giving information that is nonincriminating to social workers, counselors, therapists, physicians (including osteopaths), and special educators. At times, the information that can safely be given is almost noninforming too. A child and his parents must be the final arbiters as to what the referrer is to be told about the actual psychiatric findings.

Then there are others who deserve to be told everything, and these are people who come under the rule of medical ethics and medical confidentiality. Again, it is not just the official role or position that is determinative; what governs is the concrete situation between the therapist, the family, and the referring physician. Physicians who ask for psychiatric evaluation and patient-oriented consultation are accustomed to being told what you unearth about the patient and will often demand to know it. Nevertheless, they can be deprived of much useful information if it happens that the parents do not want this information released. On the other hand, in consultations that are limited to brief evaluative interventions, the therapist is expected to communicate thoroughly and in full detail to the referring physician. In this setting, if the referring physician is a psychiatrist, he and I can quickly come to an easy but fully ethical interaction which abides by every nuance of the etiquette of our guild, the psychiatric confraternity.

Whether or not the patient or family have asked for confidentiality, I find that I can often trust my own cautiousness. Hence, I will sometimes resort to quasi-mystifying euphemisms. For example, the father's Swiss bank account and income tax evasion may become "certain paternal business transactions that are kept covert." I laugh at myself occasionally for such talking around the point, but I must recall that by so talking I honor some of my teachers whose artfulness in these practices I can never hope to match. For one of my early psychiatric supervisors, homosexuality was never called homosexuality but "erotic preferences that are sometimes adjudged unconventional."

Also, I find that I can get by supplying abbreviated information such as, "Much of the first two sessions was spent detailing the kinds of inner and interpersonal conflicts that cripple both these parents and their child." This is a commentary on the themes we explored, but does not give the actual substance. This sparseness is well justified if you know that the referring physician misuses your consultation reports, passes them on to unauthorized persons, for example, or hands them to the parents to read and make copies for their household. You must be able to take it for granted that anyone who sees one of your evaluation reports can be trusted to use it properly. This means that the clerk who reads the hospital chart and breaks security must be fired at once from the medical records library for unethical conduct. And it also means that the physician who violates confidentiality must be confronted, admonished. and perhaps ultimately boycotted.

I used to keep two sets of records, one for the chart and one for my own professional improvement. The set for the chart was almost ridiculously "blah"; my own "impounded" set had all the data I had accumulated. I decided, however, that I'd simplify record-keeping and concentrate more on trying to do good work with patients. Therefore I now keep virtually all case records in the hospital chart. In this one short life I have found better things to do than to play games with supersecrecy and hyperconfidentiality. Many others have contradictory views; see Thomas Szasz [5] for opposing opinion.

THE CHILD PSYCHIATRY FACILITY

The physical setting in which child psychotherapy is carried out is important. Looking at the physical facilities around you, you'd probably never guess it. Urban decay is reflected graphically in most of the child psychiatry clinics that I know. The child psychiatry facility is often an old mansion that was overtaken by the city slum, stood empty for many years, and may have had rather prolonged intermediate use as a funeral parlor. Its final fate was to become a child mental health structure! Or another history that is commonly built into the bricks-and-mortar setting of the child mental health program is: A tuberculosis sanitarium or polio hospital gets a slight altering and refurbishing and is now the child psychiatry clinic. Who says child psychiatry is not moved forward by general improvements in public health? Find an illness that disappears and you find a prospective setting for a child therapy facility! Still one more historical pattern I have observed is that abandoned school buildings are made available for child psychiatry clinics. Condemn an old school building, declare it unfit for human occupancy, and you have excellent material for housing a city's child psychiatry facility.

Nancy McDonald and I [6] wrote facetiously about the way that the physical setup of a clinic can turn off poor people. Perhaps what I am saying now is that the clinic is often in such a slummy building that it should make a slum child feel right at home. Were the poor not turned off by such things as our vocabulary, life-styles, manners, procedures, and furnishings, they might find our physical setting sufficiently impoverished for congeniality.

Somebody once told me that the heart of a child therapy operation is the receptionist or secretary who meets the new referrals, or the clerk who answers the telephone. These are often the underpaid proletarians of a child mental health facility, but they are crucial and deserve better rewards than they receive. When they care about people, they can help your atmosphere a lot. As a corollary, the physical environment of the entrance room, lobby, or waiting room is a crucial matter, too. If the room is bleak and unfriendly, it gives out a message to all who enter. If it sacrifices being homelike in order to achieve orderliness and tidiness, that sets the tone of what your whole establishment is out to represent. I remember the days when black patients were summoned by their first names in Southern university clinics, and so I didn't marvel that so few blacks bothered to come for the white folks' mental health. I went further and struggled to end the discrimination against blacks, which is one more way to facilitate their psychotherapy.

The best waiting room is one that answers the requests of the children, not one that imposes an adult's view of what children need in a waiting room. As experience shows us that children ask for paper and pencil, a deck of cards, a few toys and games, a good waiting room comes into being by accretion. The wall of the small sitting room at one child psychiatry outpatient clinic I have known was covered with children's scribblings and paintings, which was fine. But when we hung up sheets of newsprint, the children became even more productive from a graphic arts (and a graffito) standpoint. The wall had been great, but being able to fill up a huge sheet of paper and then replace it with a fresh one seemed to be still more appealing to the children. Had we not taken a cue from the wall-defacing children (the consumers, after all), we would not have thought of such fine waiting room furnishings. It is important to let children know that their enjoyments are honored in this little enclave, and the physical environment in which children are treated is important in enhancing their psychotherapy.

CHILD PSYCHIATRY STAFF

What I discuss in this section presupposes that you are operating in a clinic setting, one in which you are not a solo practitioner but have the good fortune to be engaged in teamwork with professionals from other disciplines. *Teamwork* means many things to physicians, so let me explain a bit of what I mean by the word.

Teamwork is what horses do, we should remember, so teamwork connotes labor first of all. People are combining forces to work for a common goal. But they are not only working together, as preschool children may do; they are also working *in common.* The common goal has to do with providing human services to children and their families. The social worker, psychologist, paraprofessional, nurse, teacher, psychiatrist, and pediatrician pool their resources for an effective course toward that goal.

For many years obituaries, not eulogies, have been written for the child psychiatric team, usually by nonmedical people who may have a bone to pick with the division of labor under psychiatric leadership that is inherent in child guidance teamwork. Since they are opposed to psychiatric leadership or direction, they emphasize such things as the unserviceability of "the holy trinity" of psychiatry, social work, and psychology. They wax satirical in denunciation of dividing up a family unit, and they decry any operation that does not allow the nonmedical professional to do all he can. They emphasize, for example, that many things done by a psychiatrist could just as effectively be done by a social worker or psychologist. These arguments do have considerable validity respecting delivery of service. I believe anyone would concede that people who have worked as a team for several years can reach the point at which they learn, practice, and teach one another's erstwhile special skills. When it comes to my delivering services, I have learned to function as a fairly good social worker, a fairly good psychologist, a fairly good pediatrician, and a fairly good special educator. I could effectively pinch-hit for any team member, I believe. That ease of role diffusion is useful and relevant to my service role.

However, the great virtue of the child guidance team, with its subdivision along collaborating disciplinary lines, is its strong relevance as a *vehicle for teaching* about child mental health. It is made for teaching child psychiatrists, social workers, psychologists, and special educators. The trainee in child psychiatry, particularly, is fortunate if he can work in this so-called old-fashioned way during his apprenticeship. Consequently, I would argue that teamwork has greater relevance for training than for direct services. We must be aware that training is the way we provide for even greater direct services in the future. Adams, Work, and Cramer [7] have compiled and edited a book entitled *Academic Child Psychiatry* in which some of these issues are given a complete airing.

Teamwork is also what is done by active participants in games and sports. It is not exclusively an instrument for serious technical work. For people who value children, not surprisingly, there is a strong positive valuation placed on play. The child's play is the fruit of childhood. The spirit of play permeates much child psychiatric teamwork. Our colleagues in general psychiatry and in pediatrics raise their eyebrows at times when they perceive that ours is not a life-style of pure work, alienation, and long-suffering. Child psychiatry teams have fun. They are, as I wrote earlier [8]:

... professional people who do not live in an isolated practice system, but who are interacting — including reinforcing, correcting and validating each other. This

gives to their very workshop a structuring that negates loneliness and work alienation. In an age such as ours it is small wonder that delight in our work and play
should arouse some suspicion and resentment within uninformed onlookers.

Since the publication of the Stanton and Schwartz study [9] it has become an
axiom in psychiatry that conflict among mental health professionals shows up by
a worsening of the patients' condition. There is a straight line from intrastaff
conflict to patient regression and unhappiness. When we are at odds with our
colleagues, our patients are the ones who suffer. Interprofessional rivalry and
conflict can create havoc, especially in work with more severely disturbed children
(those with psychoses, antisocial behavior, or brain damage). When professional
rivalry happened in the child guidance clinics, more and more clinics found themselves selecting only neurotic or other mildly disturbed children. When patient
welfare is given secondary importance, we move with ease to screen out the poor
and the very sick.

I am trying to stress that wholesome teamwork can enhance psychotherapeutic
work and intrateam struggle can impede and subvert psychotherapy.

Giving Psychiatric Leadership

Child psychiatry is not only a medical subspecialty, it is also an interdisciplinary
or multidisciplinary team, with the medical membership in the minority. Democracy should dictate that the majority rules or that team leadership should rotate
among the team members in an egalitarian way. The prospects for more work
democracy in the factories, fields, and clinics of this world are alluring to me. In
some special circumstances, such as in a radical therapy collective, which concentrates on giving services that will undermine the political status quo, I could envision opting for this sort of team democracy. But my actual workaday world has
been an academic medical setting, which is not anything like utopia. In my actual
world I want to stress the practical need for medical leadership of the child psychiatry team. I regret it when child psychiatrists are not given training for team
leadership.

Medical leadership is necessary because medical ethics permeate the team's
workings. The leader takes the medicolegal responsibility and is accountable for
whatever the team does. Accountability without authority is treacherous, I contend, and like taxation without representation it may be positively un-American!
A leader works for the group and is under pressure from within the group as well
as from the outside to behave as an effective leader. The child psychiatrist has

usually been trained to lead teamwork and to lead it effectively and reasonably.

Being a leader or coordinator, or group consultant or facilitator, does not require Caesarism. A leader does not have to be a dictator, imposing irrational authority on a group of sheepish followers. And, please remember, the team is for the consumers, not for us. A leader of a child psychiatric team is not a czar who cherishes his ability to dispense with all his team members and do the team's work singlehandedly. Far from that, the child psychiatry team is a team of equals who are interacting collaboratively, not in parallel and not on the model of an assembly line where each does his own unrelated thing. While an orthopedist might call it teamwork when he writes a prescription for a physiotherapist to carry out, or a pediatric hematologist might call it teamwork whenever he refers the family of a leukemic child to social service, the interaction of the child psychiatry team operation is much more sustained than that. Child psychiatric teamwork is not a hit-and-run operation by any means.

The work of the respective team workers is distinctive. It is not a virtue, but only a pragmatic necessity, that team members sometimes achieve role diffusion. Even when they underline their similarities, there are still some basic features that differentiate one professional from another. To oversimplify crudely, let's spell out what, quintessentially, each team member can do to help children and their parents.

The child psychiatrist brings his physician's arts and skills: the cognitive style of identifying problems, called diagnosis, and coping with problems, called therapy and rehabilitation. His style is hardly that of the classical medical model, which psychologists frequently debunk but seldom encounter among their psychiatrist colleagues. The child psychiatrist brings some structure and some anxiety-allaying security to the entire team by virtue of his medical background and expertise. Besides that, he brings medical ethics to pervade the operating tactics of the entire team; to control and to provide security to all members and to protect the people being served by the team. It is no accident that child psychiatrists in the United States, especially those trained after 1959, are trained according to rather uniform standards all over the country and are dependable role models of team-leading for child psychiatry residents in training.

The social worker brings to the child psychiatry team a foremost expertness in working with parents of disturbed or conflicted children. He has generic training in the most practical and relevant aspects of the social sciences, namely, community structure, casework, and group work; and although the Council on Social Work Education is altering curricular options, one can still rely on social workers to be rather evenly and uniformly skillful in those three areas. The social worker's ethical code also brings enlivenment to the entire team, with its stress on social action, social change, and the values of human differences and diversities. I suspect that the observation is still sound that, in view of what they can do, after having obtained the required two years of postgraduate training, certified social workers are society's best bargain in the mental health field.

The clinical child psychologist brings several seasoned intellectual benefits to the entire team. He has a broad knowledge of child development and child behavior and a background in scholarly enquiry that is shown in his respect for intellectual competence and his positive valuation of scholarly work. He also has, when he is not off on this or that faddism, a profound knowledge of psychometry, intelligence, and personality testing. The training programs for clinical psychologists in the United States are highly variable, and as a consequence it is anybody's guess what a particular Ph.D. can or cannot do. It is the individual who has to be scrutinized when you want a psychologist you can depend on.

The special education teacher can bring some of the more practical skills of the psychologist of yesteryear, such as psychologic testing, cognitive/academic assessment of children, and testing of psycholinguistic abilities. Although most special education teachers lack psychologists' theoretical grounding, they are expert in therapeutic tutoring and specialized academic remediation. Add also that the special educator can provide the whole team with a better entrée to and liaison with the regular school and is a valuable expert on children as learners and children in groups. Since special educators are an emerging profession, there is a perplexing and disconcerting variability among them. You will have to appraise each one on his own merits if you are not to buy an unknown product.

All these team members make a very exciting and helpful mix, but if they are not careful, they can make a lot of trouble for one another and for the families they are presumed to want to serve. It is an easy fadeout from tension to uncharitableness. You as a beginner can see whether there is backbiting and subversion among the members of the teams with which you are affiliated. I have mentioned previously that sometimes social workers can become proprietary in their work with parents, and that it is not entirely smooth sailing for the child psychiatry team. It should be added that any team member can make trouble by grinding the axe of his particular profession in rivalry with others. Psychologists go off on tangential hobbies rather easily, and among the mental health people, psychologists are rather like Unitarians among the religious, often troubled to define their role or to seek a reclarification of their image. It means at least that they are not stagnant figures but are searching and questing, which is all to the good. But when a psychologist goes from making a fad of a standardized psychologic test to family group therapy to operant conditioning, as I have seen happen with one clinical psychologist within the short span of three years, there is perhaps some reason to wish that the profession was a little *more* staid, not less.

For educating child psychiatrists, a team is needed that can function rather happily together. But above all — and I will try to state this without being too provocative or arrogant — the team members need to train the child psychiatry student for leadership. This can become very sticky, for the child psychiatry resident comes along as a novice, is put to work with highly competent and experienced teachers who obviously know a great deal that he does not. Once they have taught him, however, he will go off to other settings where he will practice what his social work/special education/psychology professors taught him, but where he will be held in greater esteem than his colleagues in social work/ special education/psychology. It has, in all truth, an element of unfairness about it, but it is a reality that can be justified and rationalized. I have made a limp gesture in that direction, at least.

I am sick and tired of nonmedical people who work in, but always knock, a medical setting and who debunk young physicians in specialty training. These critics howl about the indignity of their having to teach the people they also must defer to. For one thing, it is the task of every humanely or democratically inclined teacher to teach his students all he knows, as best he can, and then to send them off into a marketplace where they earn a great deal more money than their teacher earns. I, for one, have accepted that as my fate, as I guess most academic child psychiatrists have also done. A teacher has some of the idealism of a selfless helper. There are other gratifications for me than requiring that I earn more than any of my students, or derive more esteem than they do from the general public. The same concept has to be accepted by nonmedical professionals in any child psychiatry training program: Serving well and teaching are their own rewards.

COMMUNITY RESOURCES

Not all communities in North America make it easy for a child therapist to function well. The spread of human services in the United States is uneven nationally. Sparsely settled suburbs may have more services than densely populous center city areas. Some small communities have many services to aid people in trouble. Some large cities have relatively few helping resources. Sometimes a community makes very specialized services available before the fundamental generalized services are being provided; for example, when a city has a residential treatment unit for psychotic children but no outpatient mental health program.

In certain countries outside the United States, human welfare is of great concern, and as a result it is taken for granted that the public at large has an opportunity or an obligation — not through private almsgiving but through welfare and health structures — to help all those who need it. Norway looks almost utopian in this regard; a small, largely agrarian, peasant culture, with some traditions of seagoing too, it has a keen determination to serve the health, education, and welfare of all. The Norwegians have no atomic or lunar visitation programs, to my knowledge, but they are trying hard to create a social democracy in which human wastage is prevented. In the United States, whenever confronted with human problems, we ask, *"What can they do to shape up?"* The Norwegians ask, *"What social arrangements can we devise truly to aid people with problems?"* The United States has more privatism and more ethical talk and the Norwegians, more "publicism" and more sociocentric utopian talking and thinking. We react as if we were ethical yogis and they as if utopian commissars. We attend to the heart of man and they, to his social institutions. Psychotherapy, without a doubt, is primarily ethical and person-centered, but it requires that an already existent utopian set of thoughts and deeds have been structured in the community. If people are hungry, feeding must come before the repair of fantasies!

The variable relations of psychotherapy to politics are interesting. Seymour Halleck has written a fine book on the subject [10]. Some intellectuals in Czechoslovakia were convinced that a new economy would eliminate the need for psychotherapy, having noted that psychotherapists were typically bourgeois people doing most of their work among the middle and upper classes. These intellectuals had their way for a time, and on the Communist side of the cold war's zealotry, they eliminated schools of social work, institutes of psychoanalysis, and training programs in psychotherapy — for a time. The rationale was that socialism would prevent all the customary forms of human anguish. The experiment failed, and psychotherapy and other direct human services have been allowed again. In Cuba, so very near to us, Fidel Castro asserts that the yogi approach, the emphasis on man's inner heart *(el hombre nuevo),* takes priority. Those who stress the economy have been imprisoned in Castro's Cuba as a dangerous *microfracción.* Many people argue whether social change is more important than personal change. In the United States, as Frank Riessman [11] reviewed the conflicting camps, some intellectuals question whether human services can be humane in this society and whether it is proper to push for more health, education, and day care.

For every benefit to the people there are also some benefits to the system . . . The crucial questions against which service expansion and activity must be tested are: who pays for the benefits? How good are the benefits? Do they lead to redistribution of income, services, and power and to the projection of a new kind of society? How much control do the service recipients and the service workers have over these services?

What kinds of services are required before child therapy can be facilitated? For expository reasons, I like to divide the community's services or helping resources into those that are mandatory and those that are important but less than mandatory. Obviously, the division is not based on a sharp differentiation, just one to work with. Mandatory services that must be assumed in a community where child mental health work is to go well include:

1. Physicians, hospitals, and clinics for child health
2. Welfare and health departments
3. Public education with child-oriented professionals
4. Protective services for children in legal trouble
5. Family service agencies

1. Physicians, working in public hospitals and clinics as well as in private practice, must be present in enough abundance to look after the health of children. Maternal and child health programs are undoubtedly prerequisite to a psychotherapy program. Physicians are not loners, of course, for they are only parts of health maintenance teams. Along with them are nurses, health paraprofessionals, medical technologists, other specialized technicians, health administrators, occupational and physical therapists, social workers, and others. Physicians, both in private offices and in clinics and hospitals, are to a surprising extent out of reach of the poor in the United States. Under our current arrangements, medical care is thus more private and unsocialized than it might be, and a child therapist should see to it that there are public programs to support health and deal with sickness among poor children. If children are sick, poor, and neglected, they cannot avail themselves fully of any form of psychotherapy. First things first.

2. For the middle class, until they are hit hard and quickly made medically indigent, we have regular care, and for the poor we have public health! Both are needed, as things stand, if the child therapist is not always to be diverted away from psychotherapy and into general health and political endeavors. Perhaps I ought to say a word about why I think welfare departments are needed as a community prerequisite to child psychotherapy. It is the same story. I am not

advocating a perpetuation of the status quo, but only trying to be realistic and pragmatic. Even in a class society there are some things to be done to enable a child psychotherapist to proceed in his performance of humane work with fewer obstacles. Only a small proportion of the estimated 20 million poor in our nation receive aid to families with dependent children and other welfare assistance. Yet there has been a strong backlash against all drives to inscribe more of the eligible poor people onto welfare rolls. And backlash triumphs at the moment. Nevertheless, child psychiatrists and other child psychotherapists all across the United States were there, before many with a more strident rhetoric entered on the scene, trying to direct poor children and families to the available resources which might help them with basic life maintenance. After the basics are provided, psychotherapy may have a place of great import.

Moreover, in this ad hoc, unplanned, and largely apathetic-to-human-want nation of ours, a funny fluke has appeared in the mental health programs of welfare departments in the various states. Especially under President Nixon, who sneers at welfare, the anachronism has come about — there is more mental health money in welfare departments than in mental health programs!

3. Public schools are not in the vanguard of humane services either, but they are community preconditions for child therapy. However much you may feel tempted to get rid of the bad compulsory schooling to which young people are subjected, you will find that preschool and elementary school teachers are a child therapist's best co-workers and favorite community resources (the former more than the latter, and the latter more than high school teachers). In addition to a racially integrated school system with teachers who at least do not harm children – and we hope may even enlighten and enrich them — schools bring into the community a band of helping persons: counselors, psychologists, social workers, remediation experts, and others. These are often people with whom a child psychotherapist feels warmly and amiably interactive. They do the basic daily work and once in a great while need a mental health consultation.

4. Children also get into trouble with the law, and child psychotherapy is relevant to a good many delinquent young people. Yet child therapy cannot do everything for everyone. Hence a community needs to have some provisions for children's shelters and refuges as well as probation workers and other court-centered people and services. If they are doing the basic, general work, the child psychotherapist can do his more specialized work with an appropriate few of their clients in an air of sharing and re-referring that aims to enhance the child's well-being.

5. The family agency is the fifth prerequisite for a community in which a child psychotherapist can function optimally. In many ways, the family service agency is the jewel among community agencies. Manned by trained social workers, the topmost family service units are accredited by membership in the Family Service Association of America. Able to provide direct services in the form of casework and therapy to individuals and family groups, they make noteworthy use of mental health consultants, too. Further, in clinical work, the child psychiatrist finds no better resource imaginable than a competent family agency, particularly when what is involved is a "multiproblem family" with, for example, alcoholism, neurosis, delinquency, poverty, tuberculosis, and congenital defects. I prefer a family agency any day to the average sort of family group therapist, especially when the reality problems of a family are admixed with neurotic conflicts.

Now, there are other facilities that can make a child psychotherapist a happier worker in his community. Let me merely list them, emphasizing that they are highly relevant and not necessarily at all secondary for certain individual children, although more specialized than the other services that have been discussed. Their existence in any community gives eloquent testimony to the state of caring about human beings within that community.

Special education facilities for retarded, dyslexic, deaf, and blind children
Child guidance clinics
Orthopedic and physiotherapy clinics
Speech and hearing clinics
Residential treatment centers
Foster homes
Other specialized child-caring institutions

We do not have to engage ourselves in a mire of psychologism, concentrating only on the mental or intrapsychic. In aid of psychotherapy, there are optimal conditions in many segments of external reality: community resources, the child mental health team, the facility in which therapy is undertaken, and the referral to psychotherapy. All these reality factors set the tone and give a pattern to the setting for really helpful psychotherapy with children.

REFERENCES

1. Herron, W. The child therapy scene. *Psychology in Schools* 5:351, 1968.
2. Stolorow, R. Mythic consonance and dissonance in the vicissitudes of trans-ference. *Am. J. Psychoanal.* 30:178, 1970.
3. Kadushin, C. *Why People Go to Psychiatrists.* New York: Atherton Press, 1969.
4. Adams, P. Techniques of Pediatric Consultation. In J. Schwab (Ed.), *Handbook of Psychiatric Consultation.* New York: Appleton-Century-Crofts, 1968.
5. Szasz, T. *The Ethics of Psychoanalysis: The Theory and Method of Autonomous Psychotherapy.* New York: Basic Books, 1965.
6. Adams, P., and McDonald, N. Clinical cooling out of poor people. *Am. J. Orthopsychiatry* 38:457, 1968.
7. Adams, P., et al. Authoritarian parents and disturbed children. *Am. J. Psychiatry* 121:1162, 1965.
8. Adams, P. Some lessons from child psychiatry. *Ala. J. Med. Sci.* 6:384, 1969.
9. Stanton, A., and Schwartz, M. *The Mental Hospital: A Study of Institutionalized Participation in Psychiatric Illness and Treatment.* New York: Basic Books, 1954.
10. Halleck, S. *The Politics of Therapy.* New York: Science House, 1971.
11. Riessman, F. Can services be humane in this society? *Social Policy* 3:2 (September–October), 1972.

6
Helping Parents Be Parents

*Parental authority is the last refuge of a
scoundrel.*
—Will Durant [1]

A parent (Latin, *parens*) is a source from which our whole bodies and many biologic partial features derive. We can thank or blame our parents for being the source of the broad fundamentals of our temperament, physique, intelligence, and vitality, although we know all of these can be modified environmentally. Environmental nurture means nurture by our parents again. Hence, for many facets of what we have, do, and are, our mother and father serve as sources. I like to stress the parent as a source, an originator, a "begetter" in the Biblical terms so important in my own childhood learning. Stressing the parent's generative and initiative functions seems worthwhile to me, perhaps only because the parents of emotionally disturbed children so often take too seriously their role as *animal trainers.* I like to emphasize the parents' function in beginning a new life that will unfold according to its own inner mysteries and to minimize their parental need to do behavior modification on their children. My conviction is that parenthood need not be all that joyless and deadly serious. Why not encourage parents to have a little fun in the private sector when they are raising their children? The parenting age is a truly marvelous time for being human, and its access to parents is one thing that helps make child psychotherapy a fulfilling vocation.

Many philosophical anthropologists have recognized that parenthood marks a vital turning point in many ways. Freud called it full genitality and an alloerotic mode, if fully flowered. Erikson associated it with the human longing to generate life and to care for the young of the species. Weston LaBarre and others emphasized that child-rearing (parenting) means giving security, while being a child means to consume security. Harry Stack Sullivan, ever alert to security-seeking operations, stressed the part healthy parents can play in building in their children a confidence that others will help. Parents live brotherliness and uncalculating love *(Agape)* more fully than almost anyone else. Therese Benedek argued that parenthood can be viewed as a highly developed libidinal phase. Whether we accept (or need) libido theory is not an urgent matter, but it is urgent for a child therapist to know how important the transition to parenthood can be for an adult human being. It is so vital that nobody should experience it perforce, as the advocates of free abortion often say.

Parents are not really patients, and although young psychiatrists want to give them their come-uppance, unmask them, and "therapize" them, it is best to view parents as natural allies instead of as sick. It is far better to enhance their growth than to attack their deficits. It is generally better to approach them as mature people in a challenging life situation who have a prime chance for growth than to regard them as conniving lunatics who are shabbily sending their poor little child to "play the sick role" instead of themselves. Such anti-parents reasoning makes a psychotherapist look very savvy and slick and "one-up."

Parents do have problems in growing to their maximum and in developing into whole, sane, fulfilled human persons. We all do, and parenthood, in and of itself, does not augment or detract from the challenges and opportunities of the epoch of sexual and social maturity. We can safely assume that parenting is *not* so much of a drag that it blights that epoch between puberty and senescence. Before we discuss some of the ways that parents can be helped in being parents, we will consider some of the tasks of parenting, even some of its problems or pathology.

PARENTAL SELF-IMAGES AND ROLES

Parents carry a multiplicity of images in their heads, and that must be understood at the outset. In Chapter 3 there was mention of the images parents might hold concerning their children, but here we are interested in the images they hold about themselves and each other. Parents' images of themselves lie along at least these four parameters: (1) as member of family of origin, (2) as member of conjugal pair, (3) as member of family of procreation, (4) as individuals, a little wild and undomesticated.

Member of Family of Origin

The child psychiatrist Hugh Missildine [2] wrote a pleasant and informative book, *Your Inner Child of the Past,* which stresses how our behavior is always effected within the frame of a self-concept laid down in infancy. A beginning psychotherapist could read the Missildine book with profit, especially if he read it as having high relevance to the parents of child therapy patients. Every time a parent makes a decision with respect to his or her family of procreation (that in which he is father/husband or she is mother/wife), it is done on the basis of ancient "instincts," that is, the parent's own early childhood experiences. He can, we say, either reenact what happened to him, guided by repetition compulsion; *or*, by reaction formation, he can try to outdo his own parents with a belated air of infantile defiance. The Freudians are right: We all do live out our lives under the impress of childhood deeds and fantasies. Every time a parent does something in his family of procreation he calls on his repressed and buried childhood experiences. That is, as the Sullivanians correctly say, what transference is all about, the transfer to the procreative family of one's nursery years. Therese Benedek [3] traced step by step the reenactment process by which parents, in imagination, make their children play their own childhood roles. A lot of transference can be resorted to in the wake of healthy coping.

The activities of parenthood can be the precipitants of rapid mental growth toward a life of commitment to caring for others, toward "alloeroticism." Therefore, if you do use the libido theory, it will be incumbent on you to regard parenthood as it is seen in Benedek's views, namely, as a phase in the human libido's development. In short, you will stress its intrapsychic consequences. Finally, I believe that if parents are having overwhelming problems based on transference as the Sullivanians define it, one or both parents may properly become patients in need of individual treatment.

Member of Conjugal Pair

The typical family in the United States is parent-centered in a special way. The marriage pair, the husband and wife, dominate the family scene. By contrast, an extended family does not give so much importance to the sexually active marital couple. Conjugal families both antedate and survive the presence of the offspring in our society. Conjugal pairs even grow old together. They are more typical of the North American middle class than a strictly nuclear family consisting of a detached household containing only the marital pair and their offspring. Much of the identity and self-picture of parents whom you will see will depend on their conjugal role, their husbandness and wifeness, so to speak. If new to their conjugal roles, the man and woman might have come in as representatives of their respective families of origin and might have had their original families in awareness; but later on — and often this emerges thanks to pregnancy and childbirth — they become cognitively centered on one another and on their interpersonal relation. Parents sometimes value their conjugal relations so highly that they take good care of each other but may actually neglect and deprive their children. However, some parents talk to a child's therapist about marriage to resist talking about parenthood. Hence, a therapist must bear in mind *all* the parental roles.

Everyone is lucky, children and parents alike, if the marital pair are happy and not embroiled in problems. So be sure to ask about the marriage, about the husband-wife transactions, when you see parents. If the conjugal pair is at high risk, marital therapy (marriage counseling, conjoint parental therapy) is called for, but that makes patients of the parents. Not all marriage problems need therapy, and some of the best marriages I have seen have gone under the shadow of the divorce court rather often. Parents, of course, are usually not patients and usually are not candidates for either individual or marital therapy.

Member of Family of Procreation

Here the parent sees himself as father or mother, not primarily as husband or wife, and not primarily as in the shadow of what my wife calls "the baby family," i.e., *the family of orientation*. At stake are the roles as mother and father.

> *Vater werden ist nicht schwer*
> *Vater sein, dagegen sehr.*
>
> (It's easy to become a parent
> But very hard to be one.)

I agree with Wilhelm Busch that copulating and impregnating are not difficult but that parenting is a different matter. Many people have been bound up in problems with themselves and others since early life, and even if they marry and become parents, they cannot make the change in perspective and life-style that parenthood may require. Another way to say this is that if a father is too narcissistic, he cannot do adequate fathering; the lower-class, fatherless child may be better off *emotionally,* though not in reality, than a middle-class child with a narcissistic father. Still another way to say this is that if a woman still hates her own mother in a sadomasochistic relation, she is not able to do the mothering that parenthood requires. So their readiness for parenthood needs to be assessed when we see parents, although this does not mean we should behave like "super-spooks," subjecting parents to our "psychiatrizing" as we talk with them. Besides, most parents have already made a step toward healing when they come to see a child therapist. Almena Dawley [4] said this in a Rankian form:

A parent has let into the closeness of his relationship to his child, a little of the outside, in coming to the clinic . . . until the parent is ready to give up the prop which the clinic represents and to become responsible again, but differently, for his relationship to his child.

And Dawley went on to say what I have been discussing:

The case work process with a parent in a Child Guidance Clinic is quite different from adult therapy because it originates and has its center in a reality problem, namely, the relationship to his child.

Surely that was a very early Rankian rendition of the argument that parents are not patients but can use the occasion of their child's therapy to experience personal growth.

Not all growth and personality change occur on the treatment couch, and Rank and his followers knew that very well. Much growth occurs within the family, and direct treatment of one or two or three members of a family can make for growth without bringing in all the family. I think a young therapist should realize, further, that sweetness and light are not necessary for all growth within a family. Family members fight, and rightly so. They have a lot to fight about! Perhaps, as the Rankians contend, there is little growth without "struggle and fight, guilt and fear."

If we become more tolerant of parental frailties and shortcomings and refuse to treat them as patients, what, then, are the traits that distinguish parents who are making it? We are not demanding perfection, but only humanity and the spirit that allows children to grow up in a healthier way. Some of the features of good, not perfect, parents are the following:

1. Some sign of positive allegiance with the child patient, some hope that the child is good protoplasm that will turn out all right. Positive identification, seeing oneself in an enlarged and emergent form in one's child.

2. Some comfort in leading and teaching young people, some gracefulness in asserting who one is and what one values, some capability in exercising rational authority. Having something to teach, something to stand for.

3. Some willingness to watch and wait while in a peaceful coexistence with one's offspring, not expecting everything to be sweet and rosy in this vale of tears, but having some confidence in nature as it will unfold in any and all growing children. I don't want to be too schmaltzy about this matter, so I will sum

it up and end it by citing Gardner Murphy [5], the eminent social psychologist, who wrote:

... the parent will let the child tell him where his tastes, his loves, his demands upon life lie. The parent will supply restraints and disciplines primarily when the child is defeating his own ends, especially when the child is clearly showing, as most children do sooner or later, that he actually wants goals, order, and a sense of direction rather than chaos. But it will be his first concern that the child live in the child's own idiom before he be asked to understand the idiom of others.

Murphy accurately prefaced that remark by saying, "It takes a good deal of faith in the raw human stuff to do this." In somewhat the same manner, if we trust the raw stuff of parents, they are more likely to pass that same trust along to their children.

Parents as Somewhat Undomesticated, Individualistic Beings

We psychiatrists often acknowledge the importance of parents' roles in their families of orientation, in their conjugal mating pair, and in their families of procreation. Yet we often overlook, especially when we are clamoring for more *social* psychiatry, that all is not social for parents. Parents are more than their roles and transactions, although their interpersonal relationships are basic data in our psychotherapy with their children. The self that is above and beyond roles greatly intrigued Otto Rank, for one. I imagine that Rank would have wanted to encourage parents to be a bit selfish. When we are evaluating parents as parents, we need to go beyond an understanding of what they are in their interactions past and present and to try to get some glimpse of them as persons with inner lives that sometimes overflow the more public, conventionalized images that they present to us. There is some uniqueness, some unsocialized will, some unprogrammed ecstasy, that merits our discovering and respecting.

In a study that John Schwab, Joseph Aponte, and I worked on [6], we found that parents who were fully immersed in domestication were more likely to be the parents of disturbed children. In contrast, parents who had a private life that provided them pleasures away from the familial nest were more likely to have normal children. Hence I have come to look askance at parents who proclaim their total absorption in their children and in their mates — not because I think that they are lying, but because at the least they are not realizing their full possibilities. Family life is glorious, but it is not meant to be the only thing that engages us.

AVOIDING THE MAJOR PITFALLS IN WORK WITH PARENTS

In order to enhance the child's progression through psychotherapy, there are certain things to be avoided, some of which have already been alluded to and some that have not. Our greatest blunders in working with parents show up when we lack empathy for them in their varied roles; when our vision of them is blurred by our hatred, disrespect, and competitiveness; when we assume that we know all about them without bothering to hear them out; when we ignore them; when we regard them only as necessary evils; and when we consider them to be "sick-sick" patients.

For a trainee, work with parents flows most smoothly if the parent work is carried out by a team member. The child guidance collaborative mechanism is a jewel for the learning of child psychotherapy. It allows a safe distance between the parents and the child's therapist, sparing the latter blunders social and professional. Countertransference is lessened while the parents are also getting needed help.

However, even for a beginner, I do not advocate total separation of the work with the child and the work with the parents. Some contact is easily managed by holding family group sessions wherein both therapists join the parents and the child (and the siblings, too, perhaps). Also, after a period of variable length during which the main approach has been collaborative, through teamwork, the caseworker can withdraw from the case, and the approach can become that of family group therapy. Such a shift of style works particularly well if it has been explained to the parents that separate work may no longer be needed and that family group therapy will be the sole approach thereafter.

The child therapist has had the prior obligation to work alone with the child, which is the best learning imaginable, and he has grasped some of what it is to be that child, while simultaneously he has had input from his colleague about the parents and what they are up to. Then when he begins working with the parents, he is much less prone to ignore the child and favor the parents, a fault rather commonly found among family group therapists who do not know how to work with children individually. And once the shift away from individual child therapy is made, it is probably better to stick with the group approach right on through till termination of the case.

Something more should be said about the pitfall of negative countertransference toward the parents of the child patient. Jewish therapists have difficulty empathizing with the child's parents if they are Muslim or Christian, and vice versa, which is an easy countertransference for all of us who grew up with some kind of negative reference group drummed into our awareness, that is, a group that we were made ashamed to be like. In our multiethnic but profoundly racist society, we all grew up with some group of despicable "Irish/Italian/black/white trash/Polish/Spanish" people whom we were warned against. "Don't be like a . . ." is an admonition made to children up and down the entirety of North America. Then add on our class prejudices and antipathies that are used to justify economic inequalities. These lessons, too, are carefully taught. Also, add on certain regional antipathies and grudges that are made explicit in the rearing of most children. Then think of the nationalistic sentiments and the many "enemies" of our country to which we have been acculturated within the past few generations. With all of it piled together, we can see that it is difficult to relate to many of the parents of disturbed children simply because of our negative social group sentiments. Also, some therapists derogate women and find mothers to be universally bitchy. Some therapists disvalue males and find fathers to be universally passive or incompetent. Further, racist views and practices permeate public psychiatric work. Thomas and Sillen's extremely valuable book *Racism and Psychiatry* [7] goes into this deeply. All these prejudices impede therapy, and perhaps the best way to make them conscious and destructible still lies in our own psychotherapy.

Good supervision of a beginner's therapy is indispensable if countertransferences are to be unearthed and mastered. Therefore the beginning therapist should try to put his feelings about parents (as well as child patients) on the agenda for supervisory sessions. This is the hardest thing for even good young therapists to do gracefully, but it must be done.

Parents can be considered lucky when they and their child are under the care of a therapist who knows himself and is eager to help all of them, as well as himself, to live fuller lives.

GIVING PARENTS ADVICE

One small token of our esteem for parents is demonstrated by our answering some of their questions. As we come to know them, we try to be of service. Many young therapists, already cagey about parental wickedness, "give the business" to parents who ask them for some advice. The parent poses a question, and the young therapist becomes devoutly "Rogersian" in his refusal to cooperate. He will only reflect back or acknowledge what the parent said — "You are concerned about the child's schoolwork (or bedwetting and so on)." The same therapist would never adopt such a hostile, withholding attitude toward the child, but the parents are only a necessary evil, to be mystified and scared. This non-committal stance, this aloofness that borders on rejection, is ten times worse if someone else is not seeing the parents. I might be sparing of advice if I knew the parents were being seen by a good caseworker, but if I am the only one whom they have to help them — as parents, not patients — I tend to give sensible (I hope) advice to parents when they ask me about their child's

> Sexuality
> Bedwetting
> School phobia
> Custody changes
> Learning problems
> Physical and neurologic problems
> Cruelty to sibs
> Trouble with the law

I do not know of any area of practical child-rearing that is sacred and can never be commented on during a contact with parents.

There are, of course, some child analysts who are so rigidly pious that they oppose giving any advice or suggestion, although I believe this is a dying breed. These are analysts who, for example, are against sibs' viciously fighting but eschew any advising (unless we can catch them zeroing in on the child's hatred, analyzing it in order to oppose it in a roundabout way). The child knows full well what such analysts are up to and stand for, and what behavior they would endorse or proscribe if it were not taboo to give advice. Further, there are writers of great breadth, flexibility (and even a lack of orthodox piety), such as Stanislaus Szurek et al. [8], who would appear to equate any advice-giving with reprimanding the parents for misbehaving. Others might object on the grounds that in giving advice the therapist risks squealing on the child.

It is, of course, imperative that we do not betray any of the confidences that the child has entrusted to us. Also, we want to be fairly certain that the parents do not use against us whatever we say or advise. In cases of school phobia, sibling violence, and bedwetting, as exceptions, I am even willing to risk being quoted as having said I am against the child's symptom. In those instances I do enjoin parents to oppose in word and deed what the children are doing. I do other things besides giving advice, but advice is an important part of my repertoire in helping.

Parents are more forgiving, thank goodness, than our psychiatric colleagues. Parents of our child patients are also more flexible, catching on very quickly to the point that we are not omniscient, but are (to quote Paula Elkisch [9]) rather like midwives: We do not make or remake their babies. We can only deliver.

REFERENCES

1. Durant, W. *The Pleasures of Philosophy.* New York: Simon & Schuster, 1953.
2. Missildine, W. *Your Inner Child of the Past.* New York: Simon & Schuster, 1963.
3. Benedek, T. Parenthood as a developmental phase: A contribution to the libido theory. *J. Am. Psychoanal. Assoc.* 7:389, 1959.
4. Dawley, A. Inter-related movement of parent and child in therapy with children. *Am. J. Orthopsychiatry* 9:748, 1939.
5. Murphy, G. *Human Potentialities.* New York: Basic Books, 1958.
6. Adams, P., et al. Authoritarian parents and disturbed children. *Am. J. Psychiatry* 121:1162, 1965.
7. Thomas, A., and Sillen, S. *Racism and Psychiatry.* New York: Brunner/ Mazel, 1972.
8. Szurek, S., and Berlin, I. (Eds.). *Training in Therapeutic Work with Children.* Palo Alto, Calif.: Science and Behavior Books, 1967.
9. Elkisch, P. Simultaneous treatment of a child and his mother. *Am. J. Psychother.* 7:105, 1953.

III
Direct Work
with the Child

Any primer is a poor substitute for direct involvement in therapy with a real child and good supervision of that therapy. Hence this primer can only provide one therapist's ideas about some methods, processes, procedures, techniques, modalities, maneuvers, and gimmicks. The beginner can pick and choose freely those he might want to try, if any, and use any that his conscience and supervisor will condone.

Chapter 7 presents some practical suggestions about the conduct of the initial interview with a child. Chapter 8 goes into the diagnostic process in some detail. In Chapter 9 some general pointers about the selection of treatment levels and methods are developed. Chapter 10 spells out some ways to work with children's dreams and fantasy productions, a matter dear to my heart, and Chapter 11 deals with terminating the treatment relationship. Chapter 12 presents the modified procedures that the developmental situation of adolescents requires.

7

Conducting the Initial Interview

*Let us grant that the "when" and "how
much" of the art of therapy can only be
learned through personal experience, and
that each individual has to develop his own
skill. The "what" and the "where," however,
are aspects of therapy which fall into the
realm of science, and with regard to these
aspects a cumulative body of scientific
knowledge can be compiled.*
—J. Ruesch and G. Bateson [1]

The first interview with a psychotherapist can be a tense time for almost any
child. The child is encountering a stranger, and no matter how benign we think
ourselves to be, the child sees us as a little on the creepy side initially. Later the
child may be pleasantly surprised, but he moves into a relationship with the therapist from an original position of alienation and mistrust.

The first rule, as far as I have been able to determine it, is *for the therapist
immediately to say something,* and perhaps symbolically to give something, to
the child. As much as I admire the Rogersian therapists such as Axline, Moustakas,
and Carl Rogers, I think they overdo their injunctions against therapist talk, at
least for the initial contact with the child. College students are able to catch onto
Rogersian style, but a child meeting an adult stranger is not ready cognitively for
the Rogers approach. A child should not be expected to know that the strange
therapist belongs to a special cult whose members are forbidden to be directive or
intrusive and hence can only reflect back what the child says; or, as I have heard
a child characterize them, make "dumb remarks" about everything that the child
does. Even a gentle and essentially nondirective therapist has to do a little talking,
if only to explain his nondirectiveness. Ultimately, the child will feel comfortable
and trusting as he proceeds in the work with the therapist. When that happens,
the therapist can be completely nondirective for brief periods of time and for
work in specific sectors, such as sibling hatred. A general or permanent stance of
nondirection, however, will turn off most children. I sometimes think the child
is right in interpreting the therapist's silence or inaction as indicative of his stingi-
ness, meanness, and hostility.

GETTING STARTED

Behavior in the Waiting Room

The therapist has his first chance to be human in the waiting room if the child is coming to the therapist's workshop for the first of the diagnostic sessions. It could conceivably make more sense to use the term *diagnostician* instead of *therapist* at this point, but since our overwhelming interest is in the therapy, I will make the assumption that the reader will follow me, knowing that it is the therapist-to-be to whom I am referring. The young therapist himself is often a little edgy and feels a bit incompetent when he first sees a new child for a diagnostic work-up. A child does puzzle us. The fact that we have all been children does not help too much if we are overly technical in our approach to communication with children. We might never have been psychotic, but oddly enough, we feel more at home with a psychotic adult than we do with a young child who has a psychogenic learning block, such as a gifted underachiever. The young therapist *can* learn, however, and of course learns to help children more effectively from real work with real children than from reading a primer. Still, in the early phases of his work with children, a technical manual can conceivably be of some help.

The therapist should endeavor to be punctual for the first session. If he is late for any session, he should apologize to the child and indicate his intention to make up for the lateness. However, if the child is late, the therapist cannot assume any responsibility to make up for lost time. I tell this to children, and it helps to provide controls and limits or demarcations to our relationship.

The therapist's behavior in the waiting room takes into account the child's age and any other knowledge of the child that has come out of the therapist's prior work with the parents. First, let me consider the case of working with a very young child and his parents. To the very young I show my most concentrated attention for a brief period and then ask the parents to join the child and me in the office or workshop. I try to welcome the child and to show some real interest in him. Thus I may squat down near the child in the waiting room and comment on what he is drawing or saying or otherwise doing. I may comment on a toy he is using or clutching. I try to show interest quietly and to avoid "coming on like Gang Busters," for when I have been too obtrusive the child occasionally has started crying, which is hardly an auspicious beginning!

Next, let me take the example of the preschool child whose parents are to be seen by a caseworker while I work with the child. In this case, I would expect to introduce the professional colleague to the parents. Of course, if they had already met previously, my colleague would introduce *me* to the parents and to the child, with my colleague banking on the idea that for him to have known the parents is to know something about the child. This is no time to intrude into what my colleague is doing with the parents, so I recommend saying a casual "hello" to parents but a much more seriously attentive greeting to the child. I feel some sympathy for the child who is being overwhelmed by four stalking grown-ups, so I suggest crouching down so as to join the child. By the same token that I prefer to occupy in my office a chair no higher than the child's chair, I want to have my center of gravity in the waiting room down to the child's level as soon as possible.

If the child is of school age but not yet adolescent I am unlikely to crouch down, unless the child is confined to a wheelchair or looks fearful, for instance. Most polite school-age children stand up in the presence of adults during an introduction anyway. With the adolescent there is no need to overcome a gap in height; in fact, the gap is often in favor of the adolescent!

Here are some things that are often said to children in the waiting room by therapists, even by followers of Rogers. "I am Doctor Smith. I want to show you where I work (my office, playroom). There are some toys and other things there for us to work with while your mom and dad are working with this lady (gentleman, doctor). Our room is close to theirs. You come along with me." At this time the preschooler will often take the therapist's proffered hand and accompany him to the consulting room.

Sometimes, even with the warmest and gentlest approach, a child will squawk and protest, and the parents become very involved. They may sputter with shame and embarrassment, feel double-crossed, and swear that they had prepared the child totally. Or, in a different mode, they may jump at the chance to come between the therapist and child; mothers especially may tend to put words of separation panic into the mouths of their children. In the ensuing melee, four grown-ups are seen cowering before a little child, grown-ups themselves sometimes giving mute testimony to their own fears of separation and individuation, a fear with a very human face. Never mind. Let the mother come with you and the child to your workroom, but when there, let her stand. If she makes a nest there, sitting and settling down, you will regret it. Let her stand, and try to reassure her that you can manage without her as soon as she is ready to trust you to be alone with her child.

Every mother I have seen in such a situation has been able to separate from her child after standing for three or four full sessions. However, I suppose if a mother had not been ready to leave at that point I would have tried to set up some special sessions for her alone, in addition to the child's sessions she attended. What I acknowledge with clinging parents is simply how hard, how sorrowful, how bitter parting is. The mere recognition of it helps, I suspect; but also, I do not delude myself into thinking that the parent shuts out my cues that I want to see the child alone in the room! The nonverbal cues and the talk go together well to transmit my message to the parents.

There is no branch of medicine, except pediatrics perhaps, which has to contend with such poorly motivated patients as those who come to child psychiatry. Children are roped in by their parents, and we have been enculturated to expect a certain docility from the children. Since the days of ancient Rome, when child-beating began to be practiced, a "good" child has been one who fears and obeys adults. Sometimes, alas, we do not see this expected juvenile yielding. Sometimes the child will refuse to go with the therapist even if the parents agree to accompany him for an impromptu "family group evaluation" session.

Occasionally, a young tyrant refuses to budge from the car out in the parking lot. In that event, here are some suggestions I have found helpful. Go out to the car. Greet the child and tell him you expect to see him *inside,* for that is where you can work to help him out with some of his troubles. Do not even think of undertaking to manhandle the child. That job, if done, is the parental prerogative. Your job is to see whomever you can help, provided they are willing to see you, but not the defiant ones who sit outside in parked cars. Give yourself the luxury of holding the parents responsible for getting their resistive child inside. Do not see the child as an outpatient (it is that open and shut a case) if the parents are unable to get him into your office. In the long run you will be glad that you chose the path of relatively little intervention to produce the child, since both the parents and the child will be likely to look on you more favorably for having declined the bailiff's function. The parents, especially, will be pleased that they have found, out of their own repertoires, a workable way to get their child into your office.

Behavior on an Outreach Visit

Occasionally, the initial interview is held in the child's home and not in the therapist's office. There is no law against that, and indeed it shows a sincere spirit of outreach that helps to cement good relations with families who have real problems such as confining illness, poverty, lack of transportation, and the like. The practical aspects of the technique for home visits were presented in Chapter 3.

Behavior in the Consulting Room

When a preschool child comes to the consulting room, he should be assured that you keep the promises made in the waiting room. "This is where I work, where we will talk and play. Maybe you'd like to look around at some of the toys and other things that are here." You maintain a permissive, friendly stance that informs the child that he can choose what he plays with in here. While he explores the room and its contents, you are vigilant in trying to discover the meaning of everything he does. No behavior is meaningless, you recall, and you quietly observe his reticences, his anxieties (fears), his sudden stops and shifts, his compulsive and perseverative acts, and his sources of sheer delight while he is at play before your eyes. If you can understand him as a playing, coping child you may not need to do much talking and questioning in the first session.

Although you should be willing to roll with the punches and not try to force a routine on the child, the first half or more of each session will ordinarily be given to talking. The latter segment may be given over to "play observation." At the very end, some summing up, however simply stated, is highly valuable, particularly if it is done by the child.

Eliciting the Child's Story of His Troubles

In Chapter 3, I wrote about the "fun and profit" of regarding the child himself as the most valuable informant concerning his family and his closest daily world. Here I will go further with that idea and consider some of the practical techniques for working fruitfully — as a participant observer — with the child informant.

I like to get down to business. At times it is not successful, but it deserves a try. I ask the child, "I wonder, can you tell me what you are coming here for?" If he pleads ignorance, I respond that his parents have let me know of some of his troubles, worries, problems, things that bother him and make him unhappy.

Indeed, this could be elevated to the status of a rule: *Say everything you say four or five different ways:* troubles, worries, conflicts, symptoms, bothers, unhappinesses. In fact, get into the habit of saying things several different ways, the simplest ways possible and the more highfaluting ways. Do it so much that your spouse will notice and perhaps complain that you never used to be so explicit and maybe you no longer expect her to understand plain English! If she complains, or even comments on it, you have made an important stylistic step toward becoming a very accomplished child therapist.

Using a number of words for one thing is recommended because the child and his family may have different speech patterns from yours and your supervisor's. Hence, it is a good general semantic principle to present a message in various phrasings so that it will get through to the child without surprising or baffling him with any one word you use. Also, I find it is honest and helpful to say things such as, "The words I am about to say may seem dumb or hard to understand, for they don't really get across my idea. But . . ."

Also, I like to remind the child and myself that what I have said does not catch it, and I hope the child will help me to find better words. I often add, "or some such thing" or "and so on." This kind of tentativeness is not an obsessive defense designed to guard me against all risky eventualities, but is done simply to denote the imprecision of my speech and indicate to the child that I am out for dialogue, for give and take, and that what I say is not holy writ but only a starter to get something going between us. All that matters is that we can come to some meeting of the minds.

Now, if the child flatly disclaims (or denies, since I know he has troubles) that he has any problems, I usually say, "I know you aren't completely happy, but I can imagine that it is hard to talk with a strange doctor about it. It will be easier when we know one another a little better. But I would like for you to *try* to trust me and try to talk about some of your problems." If he says no and bids to defer talk about his problems, I say, "I know your parents are in a stew of worry about your schoolwork (or tying knots in your mother's underpants, or taking money from the collection basket at church, or wetting the bed). But sometimes the grown-ups and the child see it differently." This is absolutely true, so sometimes the child looks relieved that you have seen that much. If you are lucky, he will go on to telling what it is that he is concerned about, in contrast to what his parents are concerned about. The parents are hung up about her thievery, but she is hung up about her lack of friends. He sees the curse of incompetence, but the parents see only the encopresis. He frets about his obesity while they fret about his poor schoolwork. The child seems to conclude, "Here is an adult who wants to know how *I* feel."

It is important to inform the child, in Aichhorn style, that you were not born yesterday and that it is not easy to pull the wool over your eyes. So tell him that you know what the discrepant parental complaints are. In addition, ask him to talk this over with his parents, to straighten out the disagreeing stories. Tell him that your goal is to help him and his parents to talk over real issues in a more constructive way and to iron out the different ways that each person in his family sees things. In this way you are throwing onto the child some burden of improving the family communication skills. The marvelous prospect is that by doing this in the initial interview, both you and the child can help to reorient his family.

It is for such reasons that it is difficult to separate diagnosis from therapy. The diagnosis may stop whenever you have identified the problem, and then forever after that, any remedial steps, suggestions, clarifications, or prescriptions are all in the realm of therapeutic work. The difficulty is not a conceptual one, since the concepts of diagnosis and treatment are distinctive and clear enough, but it is a practical one of temporal overlapping and merging.

In connection with eliciting the child's chief complaint, I like to inquire about the preparation the parents gave him, asking him what his parents told him about coming to see me, a psychiatrist. I have spent some time, after all, in working on this with the parents, and now I can determine more or less what was communicated from parents to child. Thus I get a better idea of how competent a reporter the child is or perhaps of how the parents had put it to him. What I am trying to diagnose here is the nature of the interactions between parents and child.

Notice that I have identified myself very definitely as a psychiatrist. The nonpsychiatrist would say "psychologist" or "social worker" or simply "therapist" instead. I abhor therapists who try to conceal their professional identities and intents when talking with children. If we act like secret agents, whose agents are we? I strongly profess what my role is, name what I do, and tell who I am. I have few reluctances to tell children about my private life. I do tend to be a good American who will not divulge things relating to my sexuality and my money, but with respect to almost everything else I am quite willing to supply a straight answer when the child asks. I do not answer my child patients as I would an inquiring reporter, of course; for if the child has a right to know about me, I have a right to ask him how come he wants to know this, what it means if I say yea or nay to his question, why it is important to know whether or not I am a socialist/atheist/Quaker/father of three. The reporter has no right to know any of these things, for I have made no commitment to help the reporter.

Double Standard, Yes; Double Agent, No

At the same time that the therapist is self-revealing, he has to realize that everything he says and does, along with some things he does not do or say, will be used in evidence against him whenever the occasion warrants. Being in jeopardy is a necessary part of doing therapeutic work with children. The child is free to tell his parents or others whatever he chooses about what goes on in his sessions

with the therapist, but the therapist will not divulge anything to the parents without first discussing it with the child, giving him an opportunity to talk the therapist
out of it. Likewise, the therapist can reveal to the child anything the parents tell
him, but pledges not to reveal to the parents (without prior permission) anything
the child reports concerning the parents. This is a double standard but a very
workable one. The philosophic and ethical ramifications are numerous, but from
a practical standpoint the issue is simple. It works well and it facilitates therapy,
both with child and with parents.

If the double standard is not adopted, the child is unduly exposed. He is
already vulnerable, dependent, devoid of rights, conflicted and neurotic, and
incompetent. He can profit from a little stacking of the cards in his favor. If
the dual standard described is not adopted and adhered to strictly, the therapist
will be forced to fall into the role that I have dubbed "double agent," behaving
like a ruthless spy who runs back and forth supplying hot information to both sides.

EQUIPMENT FOR THE CONSULTING ROOM

Some therapists collect items for their playroom as if extravagant and intricate
toys were going out of style, constantly shopping the catalogues and toy stores
for playthings. This devoted attention to details has a laudable aspect, but I like
to remind beginning therapists that it is not necessary to be lavish. One of my
efforts at a witticism, the taste of which I would not vouch for, was to tell child
psychiatry residents that the toilet in the playroom's dollhouse need not actually
flush. I say all this in the spirit of trying to facilitate relatedness between child
and therapist and not because I subscribe to the Protestant virtues of thrift and
modesty. It is not necessary to adopt a no-nonsense frontier spirit in order to opt
for small and simple toys and supplies. They also make it easier to tidy up once
in a while, I grant you!

The best justification for simpler, smaller toys was discerned and explicated by
Melanie Klein [2], who believed that "*ph*antasy" (deeper than "*f*antasy") was
facilitated by the very smallness of the toy objects and by the very simplicity of
the room's furnishings. ("It does not contain anything except what is needed for
the psychoanalysis.") It is much less distracting if the workshop is simply designed
and simply supplied than if it is filled with the Rube Goldberg contraptions some
young therapists seem driven to set up. Less distracting, it also prevents the child's
becoming mutely preoccupied with a multitude of toys, thus resisting verbal interchanges that are the heart and soul of the talking cure.

What play equipment is indispensable? *A gun, a doll family, pencil or crayons, and paper.* The gun is indispensable because it is an instrument for playing out violence and hostility; the doll family, because onto it tenderness as well as hostility can be projected; and pencil or crayons and paper, for drawings. These are often quite enough in the way of basic supplies. One other item that is frequently needed is a soft rubber ball that will bounce, not be too threatening, and may be the *only* vehicle for give-and-take between the child and therapist during many of the early sessions.

A dollhouse, a sandbox, a source of water, finger painting supplies, and clay, among many other supplies, may be useful in certain cases, but success in treatment is not dependent on them. Success depends much more on the therapeutic use of the self of the therapist, which cannot be obtained from a mail-order house.

And what about food? I like to feed hungry children, and although it introduces reality factors, parameters that deviate from a classical model, I think it is a good idea to have some time for eating and drinking with some young patients. This does not have to be done in the office or playroom, however, and I know some child analysts may feel more kosher when they take the child away to a nearby soda shop, not contaminating the treatment setting with feeding! Certainly, a clinic that is set up for training child therapists should have a budget available to provide cookies or crackers, milk, orange juice, or carbonated beverages. I do not advocate a full meal or a banquet — just something for the "munchies" which often overtake children. I do not feed adolescents at all.

Psychotherapy with children is loaded with gimmickry. None of the gimmicks is sacred, and few are evil, profane, or taboo. I knew a disciple of Marguerite Séchehaye who spent untold hours seeking "the symbol" which was to serve as the reliable vehicle for rapport, bonding, relatedness. That therapist made a big point of feeding children and observing closely for regressive, maternally orienting acts, and speech in the child. The symbol was food, sometimes milk or M&M candies (favorite symbols in another cult, that of behavior therapy) or popcorn. If the child gave a purr and nestled against the therapist's body when presented with a specific food, that food became the symbol, the optimal reinforcer.

Another gimmick, equally deserving of the young therapist's clinical trial, is the use of pets in psychotherapy. This has been favorably surveyed and explained by Boris Levinson [3]. I have known psychotherapists who had family groups bring their dogs into the therapy sessions with them. At one place where I worked, a mynah bird was imported in the hope that its speech would interest some of the mute psychotic children who were hospitalized there. The bird was a "bust." He pecked at the children, frightening most of them, and his utterances were confined to blood-curdling shrieks, imitations of a large Xerox machine, calling out the names of a couple of secretaries, and saying, "What's the trouble?" It was an attempt at pet therapy that did not help the children and produced a seriously disturbed mynah bird!

Similarly, the matter of gifts is much condoned, touted, decried, and analyzed [4]. I know of no rigid stance to take in this debate. I see nothing against giving or receiving, as long as it is not done out of a neurotic compulsion within either party to the transaction. The pertinent question is: Does it advance the therapy at this time? Especially when puberty is reached, or at the time of a holiday, or at the time of termination, it seems appropriate for a therapist to give a present to the child if he feels congratulatory and does not need to pinch pennies, and provided it will not harm the therapy's progression.

WRITING NOTES DURING THE SESSIONS

When I began my basic psychiatric residency I believed it was horrible to write notes during an interview. I refused to do it, harking back to my sociology graduate student days and ways. Note-taking, I believed, fractured rapport, built mistrust, and encouraged false reports. I think that entire ideological perspective has some merits in a sociologist's training, but it is a little rigid for a therapist. Our advantage is that, as therapists, we theoretically have something to give in exchange for the information we are collecting. Typically, the social scientist is utilizing unpaid volunteers who are not so demoralized and yearning so much for help.

I was fortunate enough to be challenged in my dogmatism about note-taking and changed as a result. My challenger, a supervisor, cited to me a study of interviewing that showed that a movie (videotape) with sound recording furnished the most information; a sound tape was second best; and notes were third best. However, notes written at the end of the session missed a lot; and when notes were written later, only a tiny amount of the data of the interview could be retrieved. Thus I can advise that unless the session is taped for sight or sound, the therapist should take notes during the session. Only in that way can he augment his fund of retrievable data.

Occasionally, a child will ask me if I write things down in order to report them to his parents or teachers or others. I simply try to explain to the child that I am incorruptible on that score; that I need some memory aids if I am to be of greatest help to him and his family. My notes are for me only. I also tell him that what I am writing down may not necessarily be what he and I say, for sometimes I have a bright idea of something I may do to help him and I don't want to forget it, inasmuch as bright ideas are not given to me in a steady stream.

Now, if a child does *not* ask about my note-taking, I say to him, "I am writing down some reminders to myself. How do you feel about it? I'd like to encourage you to say or ask me anything that occurs to you about my taking notes when we are working together here." Sometimes this unleashes a good flow of reluctances and misgivings. Sometimes children notice, too, that I have developed the knack of taking down everything virtually verbatim, so at selected times and topics they will say, "Don't write that down. It is super secret." I say in response that I won't write a thing about it, and that I'll try especially hard *to remember* what I need to know about what they are saying. After the heat of the occasion has dissipated I try to clear up with the child what my note-taking is all about. I guess the main thing is not to make too much of it, one way or the other, as long as the principle is clear that note-taking is both permissible and facilitative to good therapy.

INTERRUPTIONS ARE STRICTLY FORBIDDEN

Nothing is more unfair to a child patient or more distasteful to me than to see a child therapist who talks on the phone, runs in and out of his office, and seems to be thinking of one hundred other things than the intimate world of this one child who has applied to him for help. A therapy session is sacrosanct, private, and must be guarded securely against extraneous interferences. Therefore I explain to my students that when they are engaged in a therapy (or diagnosis) hour with a child there must be no interruptions.

I also urge them to tell their spouses and children that the *only* exception to the rule is the therapist's own family. The young psychiatrist particularly, in trying to be Doctor Cool, does not take care to give his family members his phone number at work. This says two things to a young male psychiatrist's spouse, for example: that she is not to be trusted to spot a real emergency that might warrant interrupting him, and that she should be ashamed if she does not pose as being just as omnipotent as her spouse. The family life of the beginning therapist has enough strains upon it, I surmise, so I urge the beginner to tell his spouse where to reach him and to call him freely whenever an emergency is felt. Secretaries and others should know this, too. Only a real love partner, or one's flesh and blood, has claims that preempt a patient's claims on us.

AIM TO DIAGNOSE

The initial session is meant to further our diagnostic function. In child psychiatry, as in general medicine or pediatrics, we size up the strengths and weaknesses of the patient and identify what needs our therapeutic endeavors and where we can be of greatest use to the child and his family. Our early session, whether it is held at the bedside in a pediatric consultation, or in our outpatient workshop, or in the child's home, is done in a spirit and image very similar to our therapeutic sessions. We have no special repertoire for diagnostic work. Diagnosis and therapy are us, after all, our presence, our style, and our craftsmanship, as we proceed in getting to know the child better.

What we do during the first, diagnostic session can be either therapeutic, neutral, or decidedly unhelpful. A lot depends on the professional's intent and skill. In general, the most helpful first session will be one with the greatest amount of clear, full, rich, and natural communications between child and adult. If that occurs, then the session is informative or elucidative, hence diagnostic, as well as helpful, hence therapeutic; and it can even empower us to make some rather astute guesses about the outcome of our therapeutic efforts, and so be prognostic. Elements of the three operations (finding, treating, and prognosticating) can occur within the first 50-minute session.

GO AFTER FANTASIES

The Freudians have a convention that makes some sense if we overlook a certain preciosity that is implicit in it. I refer to their spelling of conscious daydreams and reveries as *fantasy*, reserving the spelling *phantasy* for those fantasylike experiences that have deeper unconscious components, lying closer to primary processes. What we all seek in an initial session with a child is some preliminary understanding of *phantasy*, even if we spell it *fantasy*.

There are some people who do what they call "psychotherapy" without invoking anything unconscious in their conceptualization. They do not believe in the unconscious and believe that the kind of educative, behavior-modifying work that, unquestionably, they do does not require any such notions as the unconscious, or the ego, or the other constructs much used by psychodynamic theorists. I do believe in the unconscious and find it sensible to think that some of what I seek to do in working with disturbed children is to help them drag their contemporary conflicts and their early infantile patterns out of the dark of unawareness and into the light of insightful day. I will grant to the behavior modifiers that symptomatic change in and of itself has great humane import and that the heavy theoretical apparatus many dynamic theorists carry around in their heads has precious little bearing on making children's lives more liveable. However, I am not so uncerebral that I dislike all rational conceptualization. Some behavior modifiers come uncomfortably close to being concept-free. They count, and change, behavior, inviting the child to shape up or ship out. They have a great deal to teach about psychotherapy, for their technology is reasonable, effective, and, in many hands, humane. It is far better to count the occurrences of his good behavior than to make unwise interpretations to a young child.

There are others working with children who at first shy away from fantasies and from primary process materials generally. They prefer to wait until later before they permit the child to voice his *severest psychopathology.* They shush up the child in the service of their ideal, which is supportive psychotherapy. But I think they overlook the fact that verbalizing these very things, especially if they are shared with a shrewd and competent professional person, imparts great comfort to a conflict-laden child. The therapist who hears out even the child's bizarre fantasies and who listens to very "psychotic-like" talk actually is more supportive than the back-patter who is afraid to share in where the child is "at."

You cannot do everything in the first session, but in other early sessions you and the child might share in some of the following topics that will help you to help the child:

Play
Dreams: most recent, scariest, recurrent
Heart's three wishes
Earliest memories
Responses to incomplete sentences
Daydreams or conscious fantasies
"Positive identifications," such as favorite color, joke, animal, parents, famous person
Negative identifications, such as most hated person, color

These are so important that they will be considered in detail in Chapter 10.

ENDING THE FIRST SESSION

Some acknowledgment of the limitations imposed by time is worthy of a competent therapist as the first interview draws to a close. Later, the child may be asked to summarize what has transpired in a day's session, but this is not usually requested in the first hour. I do try to give a quick résumé of what I have heard the child say his main problems are. This shows that I do listen and that I am working to hear, to heed, and to be of use to the suffering child. I say that I want to help him feel better and be happier and that I had better see him some more if I am to do that. If the child is under eight years of age I do not try to be too specific about it, unless he inquires for a precise date; I tell him that I will arrange to see him again in a few days and will set it up with his parents as to exactly when. For an older child it is only simple courtesy to say, "I will try to set it up with your parents for you to come back to see me next Wednesday afternoon at three."

TAPING AND LEARNING FROM THE BELLWETHER HOUR

As a vital element in a young therapist's training program he should endeavor to review everything he has said and done in his initial sessions with several children. The technology of the videotape makes this possible. Although for the purist it is odious to think of the "interference" produced by the recording itself, even old-timers can quickly get accustomed to having videotapes made and studied. As I indicated earlier, the tape records things that nothing else can.

Children's responses to videotaping vary considerably from one to another and from time to time. One child likes it, one ignores it, and yet another will make faces, strut, or clown before the camera. Still another will beg you not to let the parents "look." One will dislike it or be ambivalent; another merely wants to know if it will be broadcast commercially. At first it is nearly always an intrusion, like a third person observing the therapeutic encounter; but for both child and therapist this quickly gives way to a phase of inattention to the video equipment that coincides with increased attention to the child's problems and the therapeutic relationship, whether taped or untaped. The stationary monitor with a wide-angle viewing lens is less intrusive than a cinematographically more perfect camera operated by a skilled technician. The voice-record is still important in our age of visual emphasis, so that when the child has his back turned to the camera you will still have available the mnemonic assistance of the sound track. What you are after is any form of technology that will help you to learn to be a more effective therapist.

A supervisory session that concentrates on all that occurred during the initial interview is worth a great deal. In some ways the transactions of that first hour can truly serve as a bellwether. They show us what our patterns and the child's are. The tape projects all the data before us and, along with the sage commentary of a supervisor, can be one of the most enlightening maneuvers made during a course of training in therapy. Bringing the tape into supervisory sessions makes us alert, early on, to things that escaped the eye and ear when the session was in progress. I strongly recommend taping and scrutinizing the first session. In some manner, as the first hour goes, so goes the therapy.

IDEAL GAINS FROM THE INITIAL SESSION

I am afraid that the many activities proposed for the initial hour with a child will already have struck the reader as too much to hope for. That would be a good conclusion to reach, for what I am proposing is a generic and inclusive group of things that might be done all to good ends, in the first hour spent with a child. But it is intended to be like a smorgasbord because it is a fare of many things, and the best plan would be to choose a few items from the totality but not to aim to partake of each and every thing in a single session with a child. After all, we too, as well as children, must work within the real limits imposed by time, and we cannot expect time to stand still while we do everything we know how to do. We have to pick and choose a few things to do, mainly selecting the things that come naturally and easily; "For when the time comes," as an early existentialist stated so reassuringly, "The holy spirit will instruct you what to say" [Luke 12:12].

Nonetheless, if ideals can ever be approximated, some of the ideal achievements from the initial session with a child might be reached by working within the framework described in the following paragraphs. This framework is based on suggestions for work with adults made by the Committee on Therapy of the Group for the Advancement of Psychiatry in their 1961 pamphlet [5], which in its entirety is highly recommended for a beginning therapist with children.

First, we hope in some way to make a faint beginning toward the establishment of rapport between the child and the therapist and perhaps fully achieve it. The ice is broken. The child and therapist who have been thrown together somehow have a feeling of confidence that they can coexist and that the other might indeed prove to be fully *simpatico.* All this means that somehow a relationship with positive components seems to be possible, that is, a possibility emerges of give and take, of cooperation, of mutual respect, of toleration of differences, of willingness to work together. All these things are the simple, practical ingredients of rapport. If something salutary has not cropped up to foretell some positive relatedness in the first hour, the first hour has been a failure. There is no getting around that. However, failure is what life is about to a very important degree. For a learner, failure is only a part of the overall optimistic process. The learner who does not err and fail is not a very exciting student. My love is greatest for those who risk a good bit, make rather egregious boo-boos, and truly profit from the experience forever after. The student who makes no mistakes should be a teacher, not a student. It is the duty of a supervisor to help the student become increasingly competent and to help him make fewer mistakes. Remember that no one is perfect, so mistakes and failures are to be expected.

The second of the ideal gains to be made in the first hour is the establishment, at least in an incipient and adumbrated form, of some coherent and rational *diagnostic formulation.* At the end of the first hour the therapist has the feeling that he somehow knows the child, has met the child, and that what he has seen and heard and divined somehow hangs together with his impressions and formulations of what the child is up to, what pressures are bearing down upon the child (predisposing conditions, precipitating stresses), what the major reaction styling is (diagnosis), and what the degree of the child's disability probably is. In addition, I like winding up an initial hour with some tentative and feeble intimations of other courses of action the child might find to be happier alternative modes for living. But that means that I am already thinking of what the treatment plan will be like.

Third, the *treatment prospects* should be considered in some elementary way as a result of the transactions of the first hour with the child. All of the dimensions that favor a good treatment outcome, discussed in Chapters 3 through 6, are pertinent in this context. Some appraisal of the child's strengths and weaknesses, of the entire family, of the parents in particular, of the referral, of the therapy facility and staff, and of the community's resources for a child like this should be at the forefront of the diagnostician's awareness as he assesses the therapy possibilities for the given child. Often, distance, money, and severity of pathology are the only items considered relevant to prospective therapy; but when those are the principal considerations, it is the therapist who is of questionable worth, not the patient.

A fourth ideal achievement in the initial hour(s) is the early dynamic assessment of the *treatment objectives* that would be most suited to this particular child. These range from supportively putting out the symptomatic fire to total character rebuilding. For any patient, one or the other extreme on the spectrum or one of the many intervening and intermediate goals of treatment would be ideal. Deciding what to do in the way of treatment goals and range of treatment modalities is the subject of Chapter 9 and is taken up again in Chapter 11, which discusses termination.

Fifth, implicit in the sizing up of treatment objectives is the goal of *choosing the type of treatment.* A final closure might not be made after the first hour, but again some general inclinations might be brewing in the minds of therapist, child, and parents, ranging again from brief supportive therapy to a long-term, patient, and slow psychoanalysis.

A therapist is getting quite accomplished at his work if, more than once in a blue moon, he finds that after the initial hour he is able to do several of these things: establish rapport, make a diagnostic formulation, consider therapy prospects, size up therapy objectives, and choose the best available type of therapy.

REFERENCES

1. Ruesch, J., and Bateson, G. *Communication: The Social Matrix of Psychiatry.* New York: W. W. Norton, 1951.
*2. Klein, M. The Psychoanalytic Play Technique. In M. Klein et al. (Eds.), *New Directions in Psychoanalysis.* New York: Basic Books, 1955.
3. Levinson, B. Pet psychotherapy: Use of household pets in the treatment of behavior disorder in childhood. *Psychol. Rep.* 17:695, 1965.
4. Levin, S., and Werner, H. The significance of giving gifts to children in therapy. *J. Am. Acad. Child Psychiatry* 5:630, 1966.
*5. Group for the Advancement of Psychiatry, Committee on Therapy. *Reports in Psychotherapy: Initial Interviews.* GAP Report No. 49. New York: GAP Publications Office, 1957.

FURTHER READING

Harrison, S. I. Communicating with children in psychotherapy. *Int. Psychiatry Clin.* 1:39, 1964.
McDonald, M. The psychiatric evaluation of children. *J. Am. Acad. Child Psychiatry* 4:569, 1965.
Prall, R., and Stennis, W. Common pitfalls in psychotherapy with children. *Pa. Psychiatr. Q.* 4:3, 1964.
*Werkman, S. The psychiatric diagnostic interview with children. *Am. J. Orthopsychiatry* 35:764, 1965.
Wimberger, H., and Millar, G. The Psychotherapeutic Effects of Initial Clinical Contact on Child Psychiatry Patients. In S. Lesse (Ed.), *An Evaluation of the Results of the Psychotherapies.* Springfield, Ill.: Charles C Thomas, 1968.

8

Pointers on the Diagnostic Process

*Since we have found that the forces with
which we have to contend in the cure of an
infantile neurosis are not only internal, but
partly external as well, we have a right to
require that the children's analyst should
correctly assess the external situation in
which the child stands; just as we ask that
he should measure and comprehend its
inner situation.*
—A. Freud [1]

With diagnosis, as with therapy, it is best to think of a total process and not
of substantive categories. Phenomenologists wage long and vital debates with
essentialists on the philosophical issues embodied in the counterposition of content and process. The existentialists (or phenomenologists), along with "functionalist" caseworkers and others, emphasize the vibrant now, the process of
interacting, risking, communicating, encountering, and helping. They stick
closely to what is immediately evident. On the other side of the fence are the
"diagnostic" caseworkers, many Freudians and Meyerians, and others, who
give emphasis to *what* is said and done in the way of history-taking, mental
status, associations, and so on. The former group stress process; the latter, content. At least at present, our concern is not with these weighty theoretical
matters, but solely with the practical effects resulting from the differing styles
of a processual and a substantive approach to diagnosis. The processual approach
is more dynamic and hence perhaps more befitting childhood itself.

The ideal diagnostic process is not a static enterprise or a hollow search for
the pigeonholes into which child reality can be crammed [2]. Diagnosis is not
the be-all and end-all; it is merely a serviceable cognitive process, an intervention
with eyes and ears wide open to find out what ails a growing child and his family
and then to build on our discoveries by formulating a reasonable program to
alleviate, change, cure, heal, relieve, and repair. And, if the rare occasion should
present itself, we can move to total restructuring and reorientation of a life.

Many helpful details about studying and diagnosing the problems of children are provided by Simmons [3] in his book on psychiatric examination of children.

SOME VARIETIES OF TEAM EFFORT

My own favorite way of proceeding with a diagnostic work-up is to get together a team of at least three persons: one to give psychologic testing to the child, one to inquire of and give aid to the parents, and the third to study the child in a setting of play and talk. In the order presented, these are traditionally the "holy trinity" of psychologist, social worker, and psychiatrist. To gild the lily, in affluent clinics or hospitals we can add a special educator and a pediatrician to the team. To leave no stone unturned, we can bring into the team a medical sociologist, an occupational therapist, a speech and hearing expert, and a few paraprofessionals who are equipped to do some of the chores traditionally done by the professionals named.

I have also worked rather effectively in solo practice, lest anyone doubt that a child psychiatrist can go it alone. And other team structures have been useful, too. I have worked productively with another physician who was seeing the parents, with the other physician or I serving, as needed, as our own psychometrists of sorts. Then again, I have been helpful in league with one social worker or one psychologist as my only collaborator. The main thing is to make a rational division of the investigative labor and to try to collaborate fully and communicate well, thinking of the welfare of the family and not solely of the territorial imperatives of the teamed-up professionals. Furthermore, I have done almost anything and everything that is honorable, I hope, in the way of teamwork collaboration with students in nearly every imaginable discipline, and I enjoy that teamwork with students almost as much as what I have described as an ideal form of teamwork, namely, working together with a social worker and a psychologist. None of these work patterns is always thrilling and gratifying, goodness knows. It is enough to hope that they may often be.

PSYCHOLOGIST'S CONTRIBUTIONS TO DIAGNOSIS

The psychologist is a prizeworthy mental health professional. In Chapter 5, I enumerated some of his main skills that we can safely depend upon. Let me say a little more here about his psychologic testing, which can be a valuable diagnostic operation. The results yielded by testing can give us a good objective, or semi-objective, set of pointers to the child's functioning in several spheres. Hence, testing is data-unearthing. Testing also gives us a very good baseline against which to make comparative readings in the future. For example, suppose a severely ego-impaired child shows scattering on the IQ test at six years but a Total IQ of 98, then at age eight shows an IQ of 80 with the same scatter and at ten an even lower Full-scale IQ. The increased decrement over time can be called intellectual deterioration in all good conscience. According to medical thought patterns, what we did was to obtain a baseline reading in relative health that was to serve us as a reference point when assessing later accruing and developing pathology. The electrocardiogram of a symptom-free young adult has a similar utility for later following of his developing cardiac pathology. For that reason we could view IQ testing as a vital part of the health planning for a vulnerable child.

Nobody likes to be asked to do routine testing, and no self-respecting professional psychologist will want to have a medical or social work colleague send him a child with a note saying merely "for testing and recommendations." It helps nobody to undergo testing that is routine and uninformative or not really considered and valued by the therapist. Hence a sensible phrasing of what is desired from a psychologist colleague must contain some specific questions about the specific child, such as: What is his highest intellectual functioning? Does his performance on tests seem to be all he is capable of doing? Are there any signs of organicity? What does this child see of his place in his family? What are the major defensive maneuvers made by this child? What does he do if his first-line defenses don't work for him? What kinds of preoccupations and persistent themes recur in his imaginative productions? The point is to ask sensible questions and to leave it to the psychologist to decide what kinds of tests and measurements will best answer your questions about the child. A competent clinical psychologist can do more for children than serving as a laboratory technician, so I never ask him to do a WISC and Rorschach. In our haste, and given our proclivity for shortcuts and abbreviations, medical people can be quite rude to each other and to other members of the health team. Occasionally the problem is so simple that the colleague does not understand our telegraphese, and if we mean to be understood we should use less jargon.

The assessment of intelligence (intelligence quotient) is of value for a therapist who is getting his grounding in working with children. A competent psychologist can be among the finest teachers of a young therapist who is being trained in any discipline, and as old-fashioned as it might appear, I find the IQ to be helpful. I know, of course, that it gives false negatives, but not false positives. It can under-estimate but not overestimate. I know, too, that it discriminates against blacks, and that 15 or 20 points must be added to the IQ of a black child if we are to get any kind of estimate of his potential, not just of his achievements alone. How-ever, the IQ does provide us with some feeling about a child's possible limitations for school learning, and although an IQ below normal does not indicate any lessening of the child's humanity, it does give us a general clue as to how to pitch our nonmusical work with the child.

When the IQ is below 80 in a white child who has not been subjected to rural poverty, we are dealing with reality or reality problems, not fantasy. The parents usually know that their child is "not too strong on the smarts," and if they do not, a sage grandmother will often know it and say it. More severe retardation poses yet a greater reality problem. Retarded children are indeed human, are lovable, and do love, have feelings, and suffer from emotional conflicts, ostracism, loneli-ness — from all the human plagues. They can benefit from psychotherapy, more-over. Severely retarded children can also learn in other ways than through psychotherapy. Some of the most enculturated, agreeable, and socially poised children I have seen have been retarded children from attentive and advantaged families, making a mockery of some of our stereotypes about the "retarded."

It should be stated that IQ testing gives us important data about many things other than intellectual level, namely, about a child's social judgment, specific topical areas of conflict that come up in the course of the IQ testing, special information about the child's antisocial leanings, visual-motor perceptual prob-lems, linguistic problems, clues to brain damage, and suggestions of psychosis. It is small wonder that child psychiatry has counted intelligence testing as a vital part of its own history and has inscribed the names of Simon, Binet, Terman, Piaget, Cattell, Bayley, and Wechsler among the honored personages of child psychiatry.

Two other instructive instruments are the Thematic Apperception Test and the Rorschach. Both are projective personality tests. The Thematic Apperception Test (TAT) and Children's Apperception Test present pictures that contain variable degrees of ambiguity and inexplicitness. That is, the stimulus is unstructured enough so that the child projects (according to his own perceptual style) what he "sees" in the stimulus picture. The stories told can be very illuminating of the child's projective patterns. The gem of the projective techniques, however, is the Rorschach psychodiagnostic test. Hermann Rorschach was a Swiss psychiatrist, a student of psychoanalysis when Jung and Freud were less opposed to each other, who worked out a set of ten ink blots, some monochromatic and some multicolored, to show patients, who report what they see in each blot. For that matter, the TAT was the invention of a Jungian medical doctor and psychologist, Henry A. Murray, long at Harvard University. The Rorschach test became Americanized, so to speak, through the importation and widely publicized endorsement of the test by David M. Levy, a prominent child psychiatrist in New York City.

Projective tests probe deeper dimensions of the personality that will fascinate and inform a beginning therapist. These can be administered, as can intelligence tests, by special educators with the requisite theoretical and practical training, or by psychiatrists who have had the required tutelage, as well as by clinical psychologists. The supreme experts, though, are the clinical psychologists, by and large, and that is why training programs in child psychiatry tend to hire these psychologists to teach child psychiatry residents how to do testing. Here is another instance of learning best by doing.

The Bender Gestalt, the Illinois Test of Psycholinguistic Abilities, the Frostig, and many other tests can provide telling clues to the problems we strive to identify and resolve. They are all useful in the diagnostic process, giving us helpful clues to intelligence, ego functions, defenses, self-concept, brain dysfunction, family relations, and so on.

DIAGNOSTIC PLAY SESSIONS

Studying how a child plays can help our diagnostic mission. At the start of my training as a child therapist I felt that I could learn a great deal about the child by observing him right at the beginning in two or three diagnostic play sessions. By the end of my training I had begun to feel that the passivity and relative safety afforded both to me and to the child by rather nondirective play observational sessions was not so indispensable an ingredient as I had earlier thought. Hence, I moved from always using play to using it only when I thought it would be facilitatory.

Play is one way to relate without stirring up too much anxiety in the child; it is also a comfortable and consoling way for the therapist to enter slowly and cautiously into the therapeutic relationship with the child. Today, I utilize play sessions mostly with children below seven years of age. It gets out the child's rough-and-ready fantasies in a fairly efficient manner. Children can sometimes be most outspoken only during role-taking, and they will tell us more about themselves through the mask they are playfully wearing than through direct conversation. Play, therefore, is disarming. It aids the guarded, highly defensive child's self-revelation. However, it does require that verbalization not be omitted. If we rely on the play to carry the full weight of the cure, we may, like Selma Fraiberg [4], realize only later that we have dealt exclusively with a fictional small girl and a witch, not with a real little girl and her real mother. It is the real little girl we mean to help.

Play diagnosis is often done by psychiatrist, psychologist, or social worker. It all depends on their training, their experience, and their preference for the modality of relationship through play. Nurses, occupational therapists, and some persons who are without specialized disciplinary training can also do play therapy. I think the best finger painting therapist I've seen was an occupational therapist. Some of the most energetic and innovative play diagnosticians are paraprofessionals (usually young women), who could really be said to practice the profession of play therapist. If the person has a background in teaching, and especially if the person will always try to observe the child among a group of his peers, the value of his play observation is increased. The schoolteacher is often the most astute observer there is of children in groups at play. That is what they are accustomed to observing, and they are truly expert, as a group. I know a behavioral biologist and an entomologist who are equally adept as sensitive observers of children in groups, but teachers are less rare and also reliably excellent. Activity group therapy, based on Slavson's [5] ideas of child group therapy, has had considerable success in a few spots in the United States but has not become widely adopted.

Most child psychiatry and multidisciplinary clinics do not utilize diagnostic play so much as do clinics that train only psychologists or counselors. One exception, known to me personally, is the University of Oslo Child Psychiatry Clinic, directed by Hjalmar Wergeland, where very thorough grounding in play diagnosis is provided for students of all the disciplines who are working and training in the clinic. The skills needed for play diagnosis and play therapy have become, in Oslo, some of the basic ingredients of the therapist's curriculum.

Worthwhile data to gather in the diagnostic play session include the nature of the child's play; the sequences of play content; what the child says or does that accounts for his backing off from a certain kind of play at a given point in its development; whether or not the child relies on the therapist for stimulus or for support; whether the therapist is brought into the play or excluded; and what properties (toys) the child employs in the play. Children vary stylistically in play just as they differ in cognitive style. Even if playrooms are included in community mental health centers in the United States, they become scheduled as multipurpose rooms sooner or later. In some facilities, a large playroom may be the only place provided for seeing children.

Attending upon a child's play is a way to reach and establish relatedness with a child, I can assert with full confidence. Nonetheless, as I think over the groups of residents in child psychiatry with whom I have worked, it has usually been the ones with the biggest hang-ups and difficulties in relating verbally with children whom I have steered in the direction of playing with the children, encouraging play, setting aside time for play during the sessions, and urging them to back off for a time while setting the stage for the child to play freely.

What, then, is the place of play in diagnostic work? People who can learn what they want without play will do so, and people who find that only play reveals the inner child will value play more highly than verbal therapy. Finally, both play and talk seem to go together smoothly for most therapists who are doing diagnostic reckoning.

THE DIAGNOSTIC CONFERENCE

Once the team has gone to work amassing data about the child's and family's problems, a vital next step is to get everybody on the team together for a diagnostic conference. Team members who have worked together and who know how to do so well can be absolutely informal and unstilted in conferring with one another about what they have seen and heard. The diagnostic conference can also be a rather formal exercise — and this is one situation in which a little planning and systematization can help sharpen the wits of all the helpers. In teaching and training settings, the more formal conferences are much better, because they are planned and more serious than the slipshod prattle that I have heard some teams engage in. A formal conference with seriousness and reasonableness is better than the impromptu guts-spilling that some people prefer. Children are best helped by teams who are pondering, in sober reflection, how to help children. The person who has the job of entering some notes about a conference into the clinical record is the thankful beneficiary of those conferences in which diagnostic discussions are more systematic. The impromptu brainstorms are evanescent and very difficult to summarize.

The diagnostic conference is a time for the best teamwork a team can muster. In the wrap-up, the thinking of all the experts is pooled for the benefit of the one child and the family. An example of the diagnostic conference at its finest was the one I visited for a few months at the Hampstead Child Therapy Clinic in London. Everyone there was serious, everyone prepared, and everyone looking forward to the always wise and sometimes unorthodox commentary provided by

Anna Freud. The Hampstead Clinic is proof that one little child warrants the deepest reflection of a large number of very bright and expert grown-ups, and that when the grown-ups are committed to helping people solve problems, some impressive changes can be accomplished.

Let me add a word about the format of the diagnostic conferences I have conducted for several years. This is not a sacred ritual but only a profane, time-tested agenda.

1. The child's therapist-diagnostician presents a basic statement in two or three minutes that identifies the child by name, age, gender, ordinal position in the family, school grade, and class position; gives the basic problems as the parents and the referring source articulated them; and poses at least one problem which the assembled conferees need to help solve. For example: *Is this a child who would benefit most from residential treatment? Is this a child who is obsessional or borderline psychotic? Is this a child and family who can be helped by once-a-week child guidance, or by family therapy? Is this a child with a psychogenic learning disorder?*

2. The person who worked with the parents outlines the family story, the background data, the quality of relationships within the family nest, and the strengths and weaknesses in family functioning, especially portraying the role of the reference child in the family's imagery and reality. This report well may include the developmental, medical, and school history of the reference child.

3. The child's diagnostician again concentrates on what he has done, seen, heard, and otherwise experienced in his time of contact and interaction with the child whose problems are at the forefront.

4. The psychologist, special education teacher, and others who have participated in the assessment of the child make orderly, succinct comments about the nature of their contacts, observations, and impressions.

5. The child's therapist-diagnostician summarizes the findings, pointing up discrepancies and discordances, stressing areas that need further fact-finding or work, and so on.

6. The chairman of the conference states his opinions about the predicament of the child and family members, after which a general discussion ensues. The upshot is a decision of what to do next; whether, for example, there ought to be a rest, or more diagnostic work, or treatment.

7. A concise summary of the work of the diagnostic conference is recorded on the patient's chart.

SHARING FINDINGS

Following the in-house diagnostic conference comes the interpretive interview with the parents of the child, the time to share diagnostic findings with the parents. The child can be present also. This is theory put to practical use and can mark the beginning of therapy.

At such a conference, we can picture for a moment how overpowered the child might feel. He has been identified as the one having the trouble or even as "being" the trouble. He sits there, or moves about, appearing nervous but trying to look cool — one child with the child's therapist, the parents' therapist, the two parents. Four-to-one odds are bound to make him feel victimized. For that reason, the child's therapist and the parents' therapist had better have their wits about them, know how to collaborate, and understand the vital necessity for giving the child the opportunity "to go first." Also, the child needs to see repeatedly that the two therapists will fight for his right to be heard. In short, the child needs our advocacy in that setting.

The time for sharing findings is an ideal time to let the child say the first word. The child's therapist can encourage him to say what it was like to meet all the new people, take all the new tests, and talk about himself and his problems so much. The child often clams up, being trained by hard knocks to remain discreetly quiet when he is in the presence of grown-ups. Yet the therapist encourages the child to tell it the way it was. An obliging parent might butt in, trying to rehash what the child has said or what the parent thinks would be wise for the child to say. Without being a bully, the child's therapist can insist that the child be allowed to say it in his own words. Often the child spills it all out, and there is not much need for the professionals to say or do too much that can add to, or be at variance with, what the child comments. The child's message-sending is step 1.

Next, in the sharing-of-findings conference with the family, as step 2, I would want to ask the parents what they can say now about the problems they have as a family. This often identifies their major difficulties as being within the child, or between child and father, or child and mother, or child and other family members. The clinical workers must add only a mite of reinforcement or clarification to what the sufferers themselves have said. That is a very appropriate way to bring clinic and family worlds into a close working together. The parental message-sending is step 2.

Step 3 may be a recess period. The sharing conference is used to plan for the lull. I am increasingly impressed with what can happen if therapy is *not* undertaken immediately with the child and parents following this session of sharing findings with the parents. A time to wait, for reflection, for internal shifts and coping strategies of their own choosing, can be a sensible course of action at this point. Some therapists do the diagnostic evaluation, share findings, and then let the family go its own way for a period of one to three months, thereupon returning for a follow-up consideration of what is needed most at that point. This waiting is appropriate for many behavior disorders and neuroses, certainly, but does not always seem to be appropriate for delinquent or severely impaired children. The Children's Psychiatric Center in Miami, for example, does a short series of family group evaluation/consultation sessions and then stops its work, to continue only if, after a resting phase, the situation seems to warrant some resumption of therapeutic work. This way of proceeding works well and helps a large number of families each year, and it deploys limited resources efficaciously.

Step 4 comes when the recess is over and the family comes back for a recheck. If one wonders what families do about their relationships following a psychiatric evaluation, one asks the family members. When I have done this, they tell me that the diagnostic process is helpful overall, but that they view it as a change-producing intrusion they have had to learn to live with. They have had to accommodate their older patterns to the new perspective that has been introduced. They have felt bad trying to swallow or assimilate some of the things they learned. They have doubts and misgivings. They develop resistances to certain sore points that have been rubbed during the evaluation or the sharing conference. And they may even brood about and tease over some parts of what they have taken from the clinicians. The family seems to live through a productive time while they are taking a recess, waiting for a second look and a final workable "disposition" when the waiting period has ended.

Human beings do have heads and can work on their problems. Often they are not so neurotic, even in a pathologic social order such as ours, that they cannot think productively and wisely. And they can make plans that will be in the best interest of their marriages and families. Their problem-solving capabilities have a chance to flower during the lull between the diagnostic work-up and the final decision of how to proceed. For these and many other reasons, I would recommend a wait between diagnosis and a final decision of how to work further.

The ordinary thing in my own clinical work, however, is to go right ahead with step 5, which is the course of psychotherapy with child and parents, if it can be worked out. I am a professor and do a limited amount of clinical work, so each hour counts. Sometimes we do not preach what we practice. It is easier to get into the longer-range work while the iron is hot, we say in self-justification, instead of observing a period of judicious waiting. In reality we are trying to do what we can to fill up our own schedule books without too much rocking of the boat. I recognize that this borders on the cynical, but it is true. What I do is similar to the practice of child analysts of trying to experiment and to deviate from purely analytic approaches only when they have an opening in their schedules but have no "good neurotic" available to fit into the available time slot. We are all a little too harried, I suspect, to do everything as we might hope to do it if we had more time.

The diagnostic process includes everything we can discover about the child's complaints and their meaning, the past history of the parents and the child, a developmental history of the child that is as detailed as possible, an assessment of the family as a whole, the exact forms and meanings of the current call for help, and as much as we can discern about the positive assets of the child and of the family. The diagnostic process is a dynamic process of meeting with a child who is not abstracted from his family and peers. It is a process that takes full cognizance of the larger field of community resources, referral, and treatment facility. These were considered in Chapter 5, but it warrants restating now that therapy can be done best when the total field or context is just right.

REFERENCES

1. Freud, A. The Theory of Children's Analysis. In *Psychoanalytical Treatment of Children.* New York: Schocken Books, 1964. (Original 1926)
*2. Group for the Advancement of Psychiatry, Committee on Child Psychiatry. *The Diagnostic Process in Child Psychiatry.* GAP Report Number 38. New York: GAP Publications Office, 1957.
3. Simmons, J. *Psychiatric Examination of Children.* Philadelphia: Lea & Febiger, 1969.
4. Fraiberg, S. A comparison of the analytic method in two stages of a child analysis. *J. Am. Acad. Child Psychiatry* 4:387, 1965.
5. Slavson, S. *Child Psychotherapy.* New York: Columbia University Press, 1952.

FURTHER READING

*Group for the Advancement of Psychiatry, Committee on Child Psychiatry. *Psychopathological Disorders in Childhood: Theoretical Considerations and a Proposed Classification.* New York: GAP Publications Office, 1966.
Gardner, R. *Therapeutic Communication with Children.* New York: Science House, 1971.

9

The Treatment Process: General Considerations

From the point of view of social psychiatry, psychotherapy is seen as using the tutorial method (in individual psychotherapy), the seminar method (in group therapy), and the classroom method (in mental hygiene education).
—R. Rabkin [1]

We can assume that, by a concatenation of parental communications, self-examination, and therapist communications, the child has been prepared to come on a regular basis to see the therapist. We are assuming the child has been prepared for the obvious facets of therapy and that he understands, at least in general, that he will go to a specified place at regular times and work with a particular person whom he now knows by face and name. The ways in which preparation for psychotherapy can be done were detailed in Chapter 3. It is a chore dumped principally into the parents' lap.

The child has some vague notion, at least, that he has problems that need some outside assistance to be resolved, and that as he understands more fully what his feelings and reactions are, he will be freed of his troubling symptoms. He knows that his symptoms stand as tokens of inner conflicts over which he has insufficient control and awareness and that therapy will aim to make him more aware and freer. Therapy will help him to continue growing, aware of his milieu, so that one day he might change his world. If any of this is perceived, even dimly, by the child, we can safely conclude that he has been prepared for psychotherapy.

CHOOSING THE LEVEL OF THERAPY

Once we have become involved in the diagnostic process with a child and find that the child has been prepared for therapy (which blends in with the diagnostic work), we already have some idea of what to do to help. Also, we have some idea of the soundest way to work simultaneously with the child's parents and siblings.

It is clear to any reasonable person that not every child needs all the "big guns" from our therapeutic repertoire. We have to examine our own consciences and countertransferences to see to it that we are not always and automatically recommending our shoddiest or most superficial treatment for children who are poor, or female, or black — just to mention three of our pervasive prejudices in North America. Those three prejudices show up repeatedly in clinical judgments made by trainees in child psychotherapy. Unfortunate are those trainees whose supervisors have similar prejudices, for the trainee's blind spots become compounded by a training that does not question the irrational, greedy, inhumane, snobbish, racist, and sexist attitudes of the learner.

Sometimes a child's problems will require a multilateral approach; for example, depth therapy, good pediatric care, homemaker services for the sickly and overburdened mother, casework for the rejecting parents, special tutoring for the academic handicaps stemming from the child's brain damage, ethosuximide for the petit mal attacks, dietary regulation and counseling to parents and child, and direct economic assistance to all from the welfare department. In reality, then, we cannot be purists and attempt to dispense a pure culture of psychotherapy. Often, the poor and the handicapped child need help on many fronts at once.

Many purists who insist on working within a narrow frame seem to me to be more interested in maintaining some particular image of themselves than in doing what the child and family need done. Several child analysts have revived the idea of pure talking analysis in recent years [2, 3]. Although they do not credit her with being their mentor, their views are vividly reminiscent of Melanie Klein's [4] in her famous debates many decades ago with Anna Freud. Melanie Klein advocated a harder line than Anna Freud, insisting that no warmth need be shown to the child in analysis, that no special talking and explaining are required, and that every activity of the child should be confronted and interpreted. Klein's was a no-nonsense approach and laid claim to being more orthodoxly Freudian than Anna Freud's approach. Anna Freud saw the need of offering explanation, support, love, reparative experiences, and the like to a disturbed child. Klein's view was that all those deviations added up to a therapy with so many parameters (or technical deviations) that it was no longer deserving of the label "psycho-analysis."

Still, it is a good idea to come to some kind of plan about what level and mode of therapy is required. I like to begin by stating what would be an ideal treatment program and then to make concessions to reality by noting what in the program is simply impossible to do under the circumstances. A comprehensive treatment plan should finally be set up that lies within the realm of the possible or just a step or two beyond what is probably realizable. A comprehensive plan is one that specifies the level of therapy, or the goals of the therapy. These goals and levels may not be simple and pure, but complex and mixed. Nonetheless, they need to be thought about critically and rationally and given our clearest possible formulation.

A child with ulcerative colitis provides another example of multilevel, complex therapy, according to some of my reflections on such cases [5]. So, in choosing the level of therapy appropriate to such a child, we would certainly think of the possibility of a family group therapy approach, although we might quickly dispense with that idea in deference to a more promising alternative. We may then consider separate and simultaneous personal therapy for both child and mother, even with a single therapist, as Melitta Sperling has described in classic form [6]. Better for beginning therapists would be psychotherapy with mother and child, using separate therapists. This might be handled as follows:

The psychotherapy with the mother, assuming that she is controlling, would, we will imagine, be personal psychoanalysis that includes visits to her therapist five times a week. In addition, the mother would see a caseworker once weekly for more reality-focused or ego-focused issues. (Some analysts, however, would not allow an analysand to work with anyone else, we must recall.) The child, on his part, would be seen in a more didactic, supportive, change-oriented psychotherapeutic situation. The child's therapist would be rather active, directive, self-revealing, unaloof, supportive, and liberal. He would give suggestions about different ways the child could learn to express feelings. In short, he would be a therapist who employs some of the more effective trappings and skills of the behavior modification school. The child would also enter group therapy sessions in addition to the twice-a-week individual therapy, for isolation from peers is part of the vicious cycle of colitis.

Further, there might also be some explicit environmental manipulation, such as getting the father out of bed with the child and providing remedial academic work if the child has lost out on too much schooling. The child certainly will need to have excellent pediatric care at the same time, preferably with a pediatrician who is able to collaborate with a psychotherapist. The pediatric care alone may make the difference between life and death at critical times. Added to all this, the child's therapist might want to see the child and parents (and sometimes siblings, too) all together. This would be family group work, but on an intermittent, not a regular, basis.

The therapist should not tie his hands behind his back, feeling that only one level at a time must be chosen. He should not be so smitten with the ideology of scarcity that he thinks first and foremost of only the most practical or economical or expedient ways to work with a child and family. Especially for a therapist in training, the ideology of abundance is much to be preferred. There is not an abundance of human services in our nation. Some people frown on such abundance. Corners can be cut all too easily later on, but early in his learning the therapist should take the approach that there is an abundance of human services and helping resources to be used by everyone in need. As a matter of fact, one day that might actually be the case. If it is our obligation to help the lonely, anxious, and pained, we may see the day when therapists become outspoken agents of societal change. Currently, therapists act much of the time like yogis instead of commissars. The tragedy inheres in the fact that most yogis refuse to change the world, and most commissars refuse to look inward. To avoid this tragic predicament, we should choose the best therapeutic modalities we know and keep looking outward as well as inward.

In considering levels of therapy goals (see Table 1), we might give some thought first of all to whether we will be primarily focused upon *change in the environment* or on the *inner world of the particular child.* To focus on the inner conflicts, imagery, and other experiences of a child is certainly one level for a valid emphasis in our approach. I call it ethical because it urges the child to look inward and try to do better. Within an overall ethical-intrapsychic approach, we can choose an appropriate focus in the spectrum of therapy methods [7] ; that is, we can choose to do (1) specialized and theory-laden analytic work, (2) psychodynamically oriented psychotherapy, or (3) supportive psychotherapy. Our choice of methods need not be mutually exclusive. The other extreme of emphasis would be on environmental manipulation and change, a level that can also make for valid and effective intervention. There is nothing sacred about either environmental change or inner change, and perhaps the truly committed therapist will be one who uses both simultaneously. It should go without saying that one can be eclectic and at the same time be clear and precise about what one wants to do. For example, the therapist can outline a plan of therapy that consists primarily of a personal change program, but of the supportive type, with some elements of environmental change included. To the child, who may benefit greatly from an eclectic approach, that regimen seems like no kind of profanation at all, no dilution, no deviation, no heterodoxy. Only those who bend over backward (whether for "utopics" or for ethics) will feel impure by doing whatever seems to help the child.

Table 1. Levels of Therapy Goals and Methods and Behavior of the Therapist

Therapy Goal Level	Intrapsychic Change	Environmental Change

Therapy methods	Analytic therapy
	Psychodynamic
	   psychotherapy
		Examples:
		   Politics
		   Work with parents
		   Work with schools
		   Neighborhood
		      development

	Crisis intervention Supportive psychotherapy Behavior therapy	

General sequencing
   tactics
	Feelings before defenses
	Anger before sexual lust
		Not described
		   in text

Behavior of the
   therapist
	General conduct
	Therapeutic style
	Therapy processes
	   Transference
	   Catharsis
	   Insight
	   Ego strengthening
	   Reality testing
	   Sublimation
	Therapy operations
	   Identification
	   Clarification
	   Imparting information
	   Interpretation
	   Advice giving
	   Reassuring
	   Promoting regression
	   Confrontation
	Therapy techniques
	   Examples:
	      Individual play
	      Individual talking
	      Peer group
	      Family group
	      Operant conditioning
	Technical gimmicks
		Not described
		   in text

In all that follows in this chapter, I omit discussion of environmental change to concentrate only on intrapsychic change and the ways it is enhanced by therapy.

MAKING AN ALLIANCE TO WORK TOWARD SHARED GOALS

No matter whether the therapist anticipates utilizing transference analysis, psychoanalytically oriented character analysis, or ego-supportive psychotherapy, the child must participate in the decision to work toward the goals chosen. The therapist lets the child hear the therapist's explanation that he will "want to be working to help you be more comfortable, not so afraid to be away from your mother, to stop wetting the bed," and so on (supportive to ego and has symptom relief as its main goal). Or "I think we will be working to find out why you keep getting yourself into this kind of trouble with the law" and so forth (psycho-analytically oriented therapy of character change as main goal). Or the therapist might say, "By your seeing me four times each week we'll try to learn what lies behind your problems, how you feel about yourself, about me, about others . . ." (personality reconstruction by means of more analytic, long-term therapy). The child then responds in some way to the verbal invitation. Sometimes the child refuses completely, without batting an eye, especially if what bothers him is not a great crippling inconvenience to him, only to his parents. A child who declines the invitation for "a long journey" of personal analysis is usually not unpercep-tive, but knows very well that *what he wants changed* is not what you are most likely to change. Under the circumstances, resistance is very understandable and human. He can "smell" his gratifications, so to speak. He knows that pleasure is not the course to be expected from your promised therapy! If this kind of an outspoken declination can be dealt with quickly and properly, the refusal can be modified, and a spunky child will quickly form a good working relationship with a therapist.

When a child refuses therapy that I think he needs, I say something like this: "You are afraid you'd get hurt more by psychotherapy than by the hurts you now have?" If the child says he is not so sure, I may proceed with, "I don't want you to be any unhappier, but sometimes you have to get a little more afraid than you ever have been. Yet, with me to help you to find your way, you ought to be able to wind up better off in the long run." I might go on to say that it is all right, it does not "throw" me if he and his parents decide he should not come here to work with me. I grant that it is a little sneaky to remind and forewarn the child, in essence, that his parents may require more energetic convincing than

I do if he is to stay away from therapy! I could add that it is a pity he does not feel strong enough or brave enough to get some help with his problems and that growing up by solving problems is the preferred line of approach. Finally, the child will come around to "signing himself up," but this might evolve only after there has been a conference including the parents, therapist, and child. The parents *must* have a preview of our goals and in some way share them with us and the child.

I think the psychoanalytic views of the therapeutic alliance are correct ones [8] and that the alliance is, as Charles Keith [9] described it, an outgrowth of some self-reflection on the child's part. A child who lacks in self-objectification cannot form a therapeutic alliance. The philosopher George Herbert Mead [10] also described this capacity for self-objectification and self-objectivity in non-Freudian terms that make good sense, without completely contradicting the Freudian formulation. Mead conceived the differentiation of *I* and *Me* as cognates of "ego-splitting." A child has to do more than form a transferential distortion of the therapist and more than have a relationship with the therapist. He has to be able to see his own wholesome aspects as opposed to, or critical of, and as being able to transcend many of the problems and shortcomings that reside in *another part of himself.* He sees he can do it if the wholesome aspects are allied to the therapist's know-how. The good part looks at the bad part and says, "I can subjugate you if the doctor helps me." Mead would undoubtedly have called these the good and bad *Me's,* noting that neither was the *I* (the self beyond roles, the self beyond the expectations of others), which characteristically stays out of the limelight. The therapeutic alliance consists of a joining together of forces, that is, of the healing resources of the therapist and of the drive toward wholeness of the child's own personality, ego, or Me. Also cooperating with this project are the parental reinforcements, if all is to go well in therapy.

PHASING OF THE WORK ON FEELINGS AND DEFENSES

In our nihilistic age, unmasking of one another is in vogue. Some child therapists I have seen feel fully justified in wading into a child's defensive maneuvers equipped with napalm and flamethrowers and all the other technology of modern individual combat. It makes them feel intelligent, deep, and impatient with resistances. It prevents anything therapeutic occurring for the child, however. A child hints that he feels skittish, and the young therapist jumps into the "underlying reasons" for this anxiety and the ways in which the child protects himself — as if therapists themselves do not defend and protect against anxiety.

The sounder approach is this: Whenever defenses appear, to accept them without attack, question, or analysis, and to encourage the child to identify, live with, and embrace his feelings. Emotions and affects are the first grist provided the therapist for a helpful work relation with a child. Thereafter, the work on defenses (such as repression, projection, overcompensation, undoing, and isolation) can be done without destructiveness for the child. There is a great deal to be taught and learned about the child's *affects* in psychotherapy before we begin to do any unmasking. Before we try to analyze defensive maneuvers, we should try to help the child see what he feels and in what sequence and contexts his feelings emerge and to praise him for having his feelings and for acknowledging them. From a technical standpoint, this could mean that some catharsis (some primal screams and the like) takes chronological precedence over any work on ego defenses. I often ask a child in the early phase of psychotherapy to "tell me what, of all the things you felt since you were here last, was the most stirring emotional event." I tell him it can be something that made him sad or joyful or angry or scared, that I am concerned with what was *most deeply felt* in the given experience. Similarly, in working with dream reports, I encourage the child to tell me as clearly as he can what the *feelings* were in different sequences of the dream's story line. If I do nothing else with the dreams reported to me, I try then to identify the affects. This "cues in" the child that I value what he feels and even value his feeling. Once he knows his feelings better, he is in shape to examine his defenses against anxiety and insecurity.

SEQUENCING OF THE WORK ON ANGER AND SEXUAL LUST

Anger and lust, or hostility and sexual impulses, remain the affects that preoccupy most neurotic people of all generational or age groups in our society. Feelings of abandonment, castration fears, sibling rivalry, Oedipus complexes, separation anxiety, inhibitions, perversions — in fact, the central ingredients in almost all the neuroses, developmental disorders, and character disorders — involve lust and anger. Our most unacceptable impulses are channeled into lust and anger as some kind of final common pathways for expressing our psychopathology. I have said that some young therapists seem unduly eager to hack at a child's defenses before they have worked on affects. I am now saying that another blunder a therapist may make *when working on the affects* is to "go after sex" (lust) before going after anger. Children are often made worse and pushed into greater confusion by our adult sexual preoccupations. Childhood sexuality is real, and during therapy it might be apposite to consider it in detail, though one would hope the approach would be fired by motives other than those of spying and finding out. Voyeurism in patients is just a desire to see, but in therapists, it is a need to inquire.

Anger is "where the shoe really pinches" in a child's life. A child finds it easier to conceal lust than anger. Many children who do not feel especially wicked for their incestuous strivings toward the parent of the opposite gender do feel extremely wicked for their rages and hatreds toward family members. To explore the child's hate with him helps him, but to explore his lust beforehand may even be detrimental. Sexual confidences, when elicited prematurely, may touch off a whirlwind of transference and countertransference, so called. Sexual confidences (about genital, not oral and anal, matters) make the relationship become unnecessarily supercharged with eroticism and make the child too slavishly dependent on the therapist, even if he perceives the therapist as his seducer.

I know of one young trainee therapist who violated the rule and began a diagnostic evaluation with a child who had a sex problem by talking reassuringly and in excessive detail about the child's sexual knowledge, feelings, experiences, and "hang-ups." No amount of warning from the supervisor deterred the young therapist, and although he fancied himself to be very analytically oriented, he found himself *during the second session* showing his penis to the child, supposedly as reassurance to the child. The therapist said he wanted to detoxify the subject of sexuality and develop a closer, more accepting relationship. The child did appear to like the therapist (all of him), but that therapist could not extricate himself or the child from a hypersexualized relationship.

Hatred is something that needs to be analyzed. Otherwise, the child will not know when his anger is justified and when it is not. Forms of sexuality, on the other hand, or sexual longings, are universally and generically justified in our postmodern, postindustrial and post-Victorian era. Hatred gives all of us ethical and intrapsychic problems that sexual drive could never hold a candle to. Children of today are not totally emancipated sexually, we can be sure, but their problems are surely less frequently with Eros than with hate. My real point is not which is more important, but only that one can try to help a child to know and to improve himself with respect to both hate and lust, but that the work with hate should be done first.

CHOOSING THE MAJOR TECHNIQUES AND OPERATIONS TO BE EMPLOYED BY THE THERAPIST

Not everyone can do everything that might be helpful to an emotionally conflicted child. So we sometimes offer those techniques we do best in lieu of offering what the child needs specifically for his problems. Then we justify our choice of therapeutic style, therapy operations, and therapy technology ex post facto. We hallow our own capabilities, thinking they were made in heaven. Our craft will be more rationally based and less wildly empirical when we can find specific operations and techniques that best serve a given child's personality and inter-personal situation. That day may be far in the future. Probably the best set of guidelines for this "matching" of troubles with techniques has been formulated up to the present time by proponents of crisis intervention [11], of brief psychotherapy [12, 13], and of behavior modification [14]. The last technique merits a special brief discussion here.

I have alluded previously to the kind of operant conditioning that depreciates all theory, all inferences, and apes the approach of a quantitative hard science by counting the "undesirable behaviors" of a disturbed child and proceeding to reward the child's "desirable behaviors." Then a recount is made later on, show-ing some diminution of the undesirable behaviors. To complete the acid test for research purposes, the "undesirable behaviors" are rewarded next, reappear in high frequency, and finally are extinguished again so that the desirable and rewarded activities will reappear to dominate the child's behavior. This makes for an exciting experiment, but it carries some dangers and disadvantages in its wake. My principal objections to this form of operant conditioning research and therapy refer to its occasional indifference to the child's point of view, its ignoring of ethical matters involving the rights of the child, and its almost universal adop-tion of the definitions and value systems of parents and teachers, not of children. Notwithstanding these objections, I find that much of contemporary behavior therapy (a school larger than that of operant conditioning) constitutes a posi-tive innovation and welcome addition to a general theory of child psychotherapy.

Many of the things I practice and advocate in this primer would probably be sounder if I had learned to describe them in the vocabulary of behavior therapy. The ingredients of behavior therapy that are easily integrated into a dynamic psychotherapy certainly include its emphasis upon the relief of suffering through concentrating on "good times" — always emphasizing what is adjudged to be effective, desirable, or acceptable. I find that to be a useful doctrine soundly based on the greater facility with which we can increase desirable behavior as compared with obtaining a decrease in undesirable behavior. It *is* infinitely easier to increase desirable behavior (that which *the child* deems desirable) by accentuating the positive. Another helpful item from behavior therapy is its consideration of what is going on locally and presently — the here and now — for behaviorists strictly adhere to basing therapy on actual behavior. One additional example of a useful behavioral therapy precept is this: Tie all behavior to its situational context. This has been an old maxim for certain neo-Freudian analysts, and possibly for many Freudians too; but it is all too easy for beginners in child therapy to receive gratefully any verbal statements a child may make without exploring when the reported event (or behavior or response) occurred, what preceded it, and what other conditions formed a part of the overall field or situational context in which the behavior took place.

Certain behavior therapists have begun to include fantasies under the rubric of behavior, and they have found some very helpful ways to decrease the suffering of children attendant upon entrenched phobias, obsessions, panics, tantrums, compulsions, "faulty habits," tics, and other symptoms. Analytically oriented therapy is not at all incompatible with behavior therapy techniques. Sometimes an interlude of several sessions devoted to behavior therapy is interspersed with some of the steps or phases of analytic therapy; sometimes the searchlight is moved from the past or from the unconscious (analysis) to the present and to some starkly troublesome symptoms that can be best alleviated by a behavioral strategy.

Crisis intervention approaches are similar to those of behavior therapy (and of many dynamic and supportive therapies) in their primary reliance not on defects and sickness but on strengths to be shored up, underlined, and depended on. Crisis interventionists are more optimistic, more growth-oriented, and more now-centered than are many of the therapists who denounce them as being too "superficial."

Brief and focused therapy likewise stresses a strong behavioral base and seeks to map out an intervention program that is specifically and explicitly aimed at a particular sector in the totality of the child's life. It is certainly no mere happenstance that crisis intervention, brief therapy, and, to a formerly small but now growing extent, behavior therapy is coming to take the child's family into very serious consideration. The family is the context for much of a child's behavior, both that which is conducive to positive growth and competence and that which we can call defective and decremental, pathologic. I would enjoin every young therapist to watch the literature closely for reports about work in crisis intervention, brief therapy, and behavior therapy. These, as well as the old and wise psychodynamic literature, will be a source of help in one's continuing education.

Sensible, but not so much to the practical point, are the writings of psychoanalysts such as Aaron Stein [7] who want to make treatment fit problems but in a very general, global way. For example, Stein seems to think that he has said something practical and concrete when he makes a distinction between the psychoanalysis indicated for "transference neuroses," the psychoanalytically oriented psychotherapy for character neuroses, and the supportive psychotherapy for patients who have been deprived and mistreated. Such distinctions evoke mental images in many therapists of people they can recognize and approaches they are familiar with, but they certainly fall short of the concrete and commonsense approach taken by the operant conditioners, for example.

The behavior of the therapist is certainly crucial during therapy with a child, although our aim is to have our techniques worked out so expertly that we do not remain centered on them. Instead, our goal is to be exquisitely aware of and sensitive to the behavior and longings of the child with whom we are sharing the brief period (in the light of the child's lifetime) of our therapeutic relationship.

Simply to make the discussion go along, and not because there is any intrinsic merit to the scheme, I will subdivide the behavior of the therapist into what I will call general conduct, therapeutic style, therapy processes, therapy operations, and therapy techniques. From one class to another there are overlaps and redundancies, as will be all too clear to the reader.

General Conduct

The general conduct of the therapist has to do with his objective behavior when he is in a psychotherapy session. It includes his use of silence and watchful waiting, which some therapists do with an uncanny sense of timing and relatedness to the child; his use of questioning and commenting, which some can do in such a way that the manipulative aspects are reduced to zero and the child repays the respect shown him; and his use of the art of listening, with "three ears" and giving feedback to the child about what has been heard and registered. These elements characterize a therapist's activities and behavior in a very broad way. General conduct items are those that psychiatrists would apply to adult patients in the old-fashioned type of mental status examination under the heading of "Attitude and General Behavior."

Therapeutic Style

Therapeutic style is almost as sweeping a category as "general conduct" for describing what the therapist does when he is with a child in trouble. The term alludes to such parameters of working as intrusiveness, directiveness, structuring. Some therapists, try as they may, can never bring themselves to urge the return of a child to school posthaste; they fail with school phobics as a result. Although they work well, with a permissiveness and gentleness that has certain admirable qualities, it must be granted, and is helpful when children are mildly inhibited and in need of "de-repression," they are timid and incompetent when the case demands hard bargaining, as with a school phobic or bedwetter or violent child given to tantrums. Some people are made to sit passively, it seems, while others are made to get rolling and to display a good bit of their own souls as they relate and interact within the therapeutic process. Some people could not do behavior modification if their lives depended on it, and others could not do work in the classic psychoanalytic style if their reputations were at stake. All of us like to justify the stylistic features that fit our personalities best.

Therapy Processes

Therapy processes cut across a variety of therapist conduct and styles. By therapy processes I refer to the kinds of treatment methods that are denoted by six different processes [15], namely, transference and substitution, catharsis, insight, ego-strengthening, reality-testing, and sublimation. These processes are attributed to the patient as they are stated, but in reality they are also a part of therapist behavior, part of what the therapist promotes and condones.

It is a truism that psychotherapy is a transaction in which the therapist is *the sole instrument of his technique*; the therapist, not the child, is conducting the psychotherapy. Some therapists cringe at the inequality of this concept, for they prefer democratic relationships. Still and all, the child, not the therapist, is seeking help. The power advantages and the "one-up" status belong to the therapist, not to the child. Prestige and authority belong to the therapist more than to the child. Every therapeutic transaction requires that greater power and greater domination lie with the therapist. This appears to be the case regardless of whether the therapist is humanistic and nondirective.

For present purposes, we can see *all* therapeutic processes as manipulative ones. The ones that show greater initiative on the part of the therapist are only more forthright than those which accomplish the same goal by a manipulation that remains more covert and even sneaky at times. All six of these processes are under the control of the therapist.

Transference and substitution. The child learns about his interpersonal relationships by learning the distortions to which he is prone; how he substitutes one person for another in his imagery and fantasy; and that his modal style of relating is derived from the way in which he formed relations early in life in his baby family.

Catharsis. The child learns what it is like to feel release from tension and conflict in the emotional sphere, to abreact, and to live with affects and feelings to such a degree that only his animal nature is sometimes at the fore.

Insight. The child learns that his problems have functional importance within the scheme of his interpersonal relations and that they are both bred and removed in the matrix of relatedness to others. The child learns insightfully − as the old joke goes, both by saying *Aha!* (paranoid position) and *Oi veh!* (depressive position) when he suddenly discerns what he is up to.

Ego-strengthening. The child learns aspects of his personality that theretofore lay outside of awareness. His self-picture is augmented, given an increased depth and acceptability. The child learns that, with help from a gifted outsider, he can make transformations that are far-reaching and deep.

Reality-testing. The child becomes more generally with-it. He learns more of the limits and real deficits within himself and within the world around him. He feels an intensified freedom, subjectively, and assumes a stance that enlarges his critical thinking faculties. He can cope better.

Sublimation. The child learns that his most imperious drives can be made a part of himself, and that he can control them. At times, he learns he must curb his raw appetites and rages in deference both to others and to his own inner self-image or conscience. Embracing his lusts as a part of himself, he becomes both tamer and more spontaneous through diversified expression of his cravings and longings.

Therapy Operations

Therapy operations return us to a focus more definitely on the behavior of the teacher, not the learner, in the teaching/learning dyad. I will try to discuss these operations as what the therapist leads and teaches. Psychotherapy is a trade. The eight therapy operations that follow can be used in a variety of therapy styles and processes.

Identification. This is helping the child to tell it "like it is"; it is a particularly valid teaching method when it helps the child to learn of feelings he has but does not countenance. It is an operation that the therapist shows to the child, making himself a model for truth-telling by the child as well as a model for seeking the real facts. Identification is candor. For example, "What you really felt, I guess, was *fear.*"

Clarification. This is the operation of dispelling fog and neurotic distortion from the perceptions and cognition of the child. It is teaching the child that behavior is not inexplicable, that it is determined and functional, and that it may always revolve around conflict or ambivalence. It is an operation to try to make sense out of what the child does and to see clearly and definitely what his deeper inclinations truly are.

Imparting information. Analysts such as Anna Freud condone giving a child information under the rubric of "educational measures," but some other analysts regard this as impure technique because it deviates from the analytic ideal of free verbalization by the analysand only. In truth, every child analyst, as well as any other child therapist, imparts information to children with whom he works. Some do little direct teaching but do teach a great deal by implication, by indirection, and by other, more roundabout interventions. Adults who work with children often find themselves being unabashedly teachers of the children. Psychotherapy is probably only an elegant approach to an individualized curriculum, using the personal touch, privacy, and confidentiality to facilitate the pedagogic process. Psychotherapy is tutelage, using the tutorial method [1].

Interpretation. This does not mean everything wise and bright uttered by a therapist in the presence of a child. Many child psychiatry residents speak of "interpretations" to mean any and all comments or utterances, I have discovered. I would go along instead with the more precise usage employed by Edith Buxbaum [16], who defined interpretation as "explaining irrational behavior in terms of fantasies and past experiences." Some interpretation is contained in such remarks as "I wonder if this is tied in with what you told me of the experience with your mother when you were little, maybe two years old"; or, "As you talked I got an image of a very small boy clinging to someone"; or, "Between the dream's ending and what you said about your clitoris you were very quiet for a few moments. I think the wheels were still turning, however, and I wonder if you will tell me what ran across your mind when you said nothing." Indeed, it is an operation whereby the therapist makes an explanatory comment, by which he attempts to tie up present behavior with either the child's fantasies or the child's early infantile experiences and recollections.

Advice-giving. Again, this is an ego-oriented form of pedagogy. It is done rather openly and directly by many therapists, although some therapists do not see it as quite cricket or kosher. Since I was trained to listen more than talk during therapy and to be unintrusive, I have a habit of giving advice in a very tentative way. For example, I say, "I am reluctant to say this because I do not understand enough to say much about it, but I do feel that you and your brother must put a stop to this 'vicious fighting,' as you describe it. How can I help you to understand and solve this problem?" Or I might say to a child, "I think you should understand that I would urge you to try out some newer ways, and that I do not think it has to take a hundred years for you to change." In other words, I try not to be too pushy, but I do try to declare my true colors whenever the child asks me for an opinion of his behavior.

Reassurance. This operation is easily understood. It is a teaching operation that says to the child that the teacher/therapist has confidence in the child's potential and capabilities. It uses praise, explicitly given, for good effort as well as for good results on the child's part. It reminds the child that the therapist has confidence he can grow and experience healing change.

Promoting regression. This operation is often used in role playing, in play therapy, and in psychodramatic exercises during the therapy hours. It is not always a bad idea, and often a good one, to influence a child to reexperience some of his more infantile behavior and to play the role of a baby. Water play, in particular, facilitates babyishness, as do feeding times and play times during the talking therapy session. In special circumstances, such as the situation of a hospital or school for residential treatment, the encouragement of regressive or more infantile behavior can be effective for reorienting the child into new ways of relating.

Confrontation. This is an operation initiated by the therapist that brings on rapid learning by the child. It juxtaposes an unfamiliar ideology or rationale beside the child's customary behavior and rationale. For example, if the child believes that a monster in his dream represents a younger sib, I am using confrontation when I offer the explanation, "What if we looked at the monster as being *a part of you,* which you put into the dream as a monster?" It is also confrontation when I ask a child about the message left by his mother with my secretary saying that he had stolen a hundred dollars. Confrontation is not always harsh, but it is good pedagogy and very elucidating for both child and grown-up.

Therapy Techniques

Therapy techniques are procedures that are usually instigated and offered by the therapist to the learning child. They include such procedures as:

Individual play therapy
Individual talking therapy
Peer group therapy
Family group therapy
Operant conditioning

Each technique has its special rationale, and parents and children may quiz us as to why we opted for one instead of some others.

In addition, there are certain *technical gimmicks* that ought to be mentioned, such as the use of pets, sandboxes, water sources, nude dolls with genitalia, role playing, relaxation, massage, or the use of squiggles.

General conduct, therapeutic style, generic approaches, processes, operations, techniques, and gimmicks are all the stuff of psychotherapy with children. Around them, many items of clinical lore, of sacred tradition, and of taboo have been built up, and occasionally some empirical research has been done in these areas.

In all modesty, however, we must concede that psychotherapy is an art (filled with conjecture, guesswork, and intuition more than with orderly, concrete behaviors) much more than it is a well-defined craft. We will have moved ahead considerably when, in referring to psychotherapy, we can speak of the state of the craft instead of the state of the art.

MAKING THE BEST USE OF COUNTERTRANSFERENCE AND SUPERVISION

Any young or beginning therapist who is worth his salt has the feelings of a real person while he is learning more and more of the professional skills of the art of psychotherapy with children. He responds with anger, greed, lust, envy, rebirth fantasies, rescue fantasies, competition, resentment, love, and dreaming about his child patients. He is in the process of learning not only how children distort the therapist's real role and function, but also how the therapist reacts to the child *as if the child were a real object out of his own past or among his real loved and hated persons* In children, of course, the countertransference is often stronger than the transference. At some point in nearly every psychotherapy transaction to which I have given my all, I have found myself fantasizing how *I* would do everything better if I were the father or mother of this particular child. Other therapists do not put this in print but will admit it privately. It is a risk, becoming involved and identified beyond the realm of professional necessity. All that going too far is positive countertransference. If not analyzed and corrected, it can be very sick. So can negative countertransference. I also spent a good bit of time early in my career as a psychotherapist learning (because people told me) of my negative feelings toward: (1) any child who voiced hatred for his or her father and (2) any child who was not in Operation Bootstrap — eager to work hard, shoulder responsibilities, and want to grow up. I revered fathers, I had contempt for children who were resigned to their weakness and dependency, and I found myself over and over imposing my own personal prejudices on my would-be therapeutic work with children.

Countertransference sees us taken in by our own values, the things we love as well as the things we disvalue. It is part of being lusty and human. When dragged out into the light of day, countertransference is an exceptionally nice reminder of our humanness and of our transferential proclivities as human beings. Again, our countertransference, when we are reminded of it in a productive way, is the occasion for some of our best learning, learning with ego involvement. The supervisor, if he is astute and wise, can be the personal tutor who leads us into greater self-knowledge and helps improve our talents as psychotherapists. Good supervision is very attentive to our own distortions.

Supervision is a precious commodity. It is rarely done well. Psychiatric social work is the mental health profession that has done most to study supervision in a systematic fashion; next comes clinical child psychology and then child psychiatry. Psychoanalysts have relied on personal "control" of the young analyst's cases since the beginning of the psychoanalytic movement. But what actually transpires in their supervision has not been publicized except by a few brave ones such as Stanislas Szurek [17], who wants to argue that there is little or no difference between supervision and therapy, or by an iconoclast such as Thomas Szasz [18], who wants to argue that in his view, supervision of analysts-in-training, like many other facets of psychiatric and analytic practice, is part of a big plot or conspiracy to deprive the learner (or the relatively disadvantaged) of rights and liberties.

Supervision should be taken very seriously by the beginner in therapy. It stands to reason that every supervisory session should be planned for. The best ones I have participated in are ones in which the child psychiatry trainee has let me have an agenda of what he wants help with during our next meeting. If he lets me have the agenda at least 24 hours ahead of our encounter, I usually do my homework and try to become a better teacher during the session. Both supervisor and supervisee should be prompt and businesslike about their interactions. The beginner should take care to bring up his blunders and failures as well as his triumphs and not to choose only the cases or case that will make a favorable impression because of the steady progress shown by the child. If one is open, honest, and risk-taking in using supervision of his psychotherapy, the supervision can become learning of a velocity that approximates the learning at first sight that Sylvia Ashton-Warner has described [19] with the Maori children whom she taught to read. Or, in accord with Szurek, learning from supervision can match the learning that occurs in individual psychotherapy by being both affective and cognitive.

Every three to six months during his training, the young therapist and his supervisor should set up a special session for evaluation, during which they appraise and rate the professional and personal assets and shortcomings of each other. Evaluation takes place informally, week in and week out, but a special session for a systematic and serious evaluation is an exceptionally fruitful scheme to adopt. Supervision is personal, "deep," and soul-searching. It is a democratic interchange in which both student and teacher try to help each other to improve their capabilities in their respective roles.

I have said it several times in this primer but will state it once more: The therapist who is serious, does not want to be lazy or greedy or a charlatan, and is not content to be second-rate in his work will seek out a competent colleague in his community from whom he will purchase supervisory time for the first several years after he leaves training and enters into practice. This is the most meaningful kind of help to our therapy, and it is an instance of peer review that protects the best interests of the children we serve.

HELP FOR THE HELPER: AN ADDED NOTE ON LIMITATIONS

The best young therapists are those who know the limitations of their realistic endowments and can gracefully work within them. One of the best ways that a young therapist can manifest his acceptance of limits is showing how well he makes use of supervision. If he can begin as a sponge, a passive but critical learner, and move from that inferior status to a position of full equality and mutuality with his helping teacher, he is on the right track.

Beginning therapists should also learn how to call in help when help is needed. Neurologists, speech and hearing experts, occupational therapists, pediatricians, and many other professionals, plus a growing list of paraprofessionals, stand ready as our colleagues in helping young children and their families. To be willing to depend upon these people, and to ask help from them, is a good sign of the humility that bespeaks honest-to-goodness competence in any of us.

Having touched upon some of the general treatment levels, processes, operations, modalities, techniques and gimmicks, I will now turn to some practical procedures for eliciting the fantasy productions of children.

REFERENCES

1. Rabkin, R. *Inner and Outer Space: Introduction to a Theory of Social Psychiatry.* New York: W. W. Norton, 1970.
2. Weiss, S. Parameters in child analysis. *J. Am. Psychoanal. Assoc.* 12:587, 1964.
3. Coppolillo, H. A technical consideration in child analysis and child therapy. *J. Am. Acad. Child Psychiatry* 8:411, 1969.
4. Klein, M. *Contributions to Psycho-Analysis, 1921–1945* (introduction by Ernest Jones). New York: McGraw-Hill, 1964. (Original paper, 1927)
5. Adams, P. Childhood ulcerative colitis: Outlines of psychotherapy. *Psychosomatics* 9:75, 1968.
6. Sperling, M. Psychoanalytic study of ulcerative colitis in children. *Psychoanal. Q.* 15:302, 1946.
7. Stein, A. Causes of Failure in Psychoanalytic Psychotherapy. In B. Woman (Ed.), *Success and Failure in Psychoanalysis and Psychotherapy.* New York: Macmillan, 1972.
8. Frankl, L., and Hellman, I. Symposium on child analysis: II. The ego's participation in the therapeutic alliance. *Int. J. Psychoanal.* 43:333, 1962.
9. Keith, C. The therapeutic alliance in child psychotherapy. *J. Am. Acad. Child Psychiatry* 7:31, 1968.
10. Mead, G. H. *Mind, Self and Society.* Chicago: University of Chicago Press, 1970. (Original, 1934)
11. Parad, L., and Parad, H. A study of crisis-oriented planned short-term treatment. *Soc. Casework* 49:418, 1968.
12. Levine, S., and Rosenthal, A. Brief psychotherapy with children: Process of therapy. *Am. J. Psychiatry* 128:141, 1971.
13. Rosenthal, A., and Levine, S. Brief psychotherapy with children: A preliminary report. *Am. J. Psychiatry* 127:646, 1970.
14. Hersen, M. The complementary use of behavior therapy and psychotherapy. *Psychol. Rec.* 20:395, 1970.
15. Slavson, S. *Child Psychotherapy.* New York: Columbia University Press, 1952.
*16. Buxbaum, E. Technique of child therapy: A critical evaluation. *Psychoanal. Study Child* 9:297, 1954.
*17. Szurek, S. Remarks on training for psychotherapy. *Am. J. Orthopsychiatry* 19:36, 1949.
18. Szasz, T. Some remarks on autonomous psychotherapy. *Psychiatr. Opinion* 5:4, 1968.
19. Ashton-Warner, S. *Teacher.* New York: Simon & Schuster, Inc., 1963.

FURTHER READING

Proskauer, S. Some technical issues in time-limited psychotherapy with children. *J. Am. Acad. Child Psychiatry* 8:154, 1969.
*Strupp, H., and Bergin, A. *Research in Individual Psychotherapy.* Chevy Chase, Md.: National Institute of Mental Health, 1969.

10

Learning the Child's Fantasies

In talking to children one has to be imaginative.
It is almost as though one had somehow to
try to get inside the child's skin, imaginatively
speaking, so as almost to feel oneself in the
situation in which the child is.
—David Maclay [1]

The ordinary child of school age is almost "super-square." With his unfreedom in relating to grown-ups he appears to be latent, conventional, and repressed. However, anyone who is the slightest bit perceptive can guess that the "latency" child is overdoing his mimicry of dormancy. Scratch a bit, and the world of early childhood, of pleasure principle, of primary process (use any set of metaphors you will) emerges. This chapter is devoted to how to scratch for and how to elicit some of the child's fantasies, thereby helping the child to see through his customary ways of perceiving as conditioned by the culture that engulfs all of us. The very releasing of fantasy is a release from some repression.

CONSCIOUS FANTASIES

A reticent child will catch on and share some of his inner life with a therapist if the therapist says, "Let's pretend . . ." or shares some of his own daydreams and fantasies with the child or narrates fantasies that may approach those the boy or girl will be having. Of all daydreams and conscious fantasies, the boy's or girl's masturbation fantasies are often the most difficult to elicit. Furthermore, on this score, therapists, too, have some reluctances that impede the production or elicitation of masturbation fantasies. Sexual association or fantasy of every description is supposedly readily available to most young men and women therapists in our "sexually free" era. But not masturbation fantasies. Masturbation guilt is a "hang-up," and the child will not be expected to want to share the fact of masturbation (or the fantasies either) until he has moved well along in the course of therapy. Indeed, as a matter of technique, only rather late in the game

147

should the child's report of his masturbation and incestuous fantasies be encouraged (see Chapter 9). The same goes for pregnancy fantasies of little girls, and boys, and of homosexual longings of both boys and girls. Hates and rages ought to be worked over first of all. Some of the basic reasons for this sequencing were presented in Chapter 9.

DRAWINGS

Drawings are a favorite way of "teasing out" both fantasy and clarity in a child's communications. When something is unclear, I say to the child, "I may not quite get you. Here, draw it, just a sketch, because the main thing is to explain it." Also, I rather typically ask children to draw houses, trees, and persons (the H-T-P test). I ask them to draw their own rooms, and then when my home visit occurs I have a chance to check the reality I observe against the drawing and the report that the child had given me. I ask children to "draw me a picture of your house (or apartment)." The bedwetters add gutters and downspouts. I ask them to draw a picture of the family, or more exactly, of "everyone at your house" (that is, the household). The household often contains more "significant others" than does the family. A drawing of the family doing something together, such as having a picnic or watching television or posing for a photograph, can be informative. Where the child places himself in the drawing is of greatest interest.

One little girl (who wanted to become a boy), whose family had just changed their geographic location and moved into a much higher income category, drew her family lifting a treasure chest. In her drawing she stood on her father's right and on the end. Nobody else, except her mother, was drawn in such close contact with the father, and her baby sister stood isolated at the other end.

The child is always encouraged to tell me a story about whatever he draws, and that story is the fantasy, the meaning, that I am so interested in. I see the drawing as a distillate and the story as the fuller fantasy.

Stan, a highly intelligent twelve-year-old boy, provided me with an unforgettable exception to the rule that drawing aids communication. He liked to draw, and, being rather perfectionistic, he drew with erasures and corrections, striving for a level of sure technique that would have been all right for a drawing class, but impeded the freer interchange that psychotherapy aimed to teach him. Ultimately, he did his drawings outside of the therapy sessions and brought them in (to describe to me the themes that he was attempting to portray in his drawings). In that way, technique with its attendant tedium was worked on outside the sessions, and his time with me was spent in more verbal activity. One of his drawings done at home was of a cicada emerging from its shell. It was elaborately drawn, carefully colored and shaded, and to me looked highly phallic in configuration. Stan, who had spent hours obsessed over the picture, said very simply, "It is the birth of a new personality. It means me coming out of a shell." That was a succinct wrap-up of long hours of work, in the consulting room *and* at home.

Sometimes, if I have an inkling that something of special importance is about to emerge into the child's awareness — for example, from a dream the child reports — I will call attention to the emerging insight by asking the child to try to make a drawing or a sketch of what it was that he "put into" the dream. This is a good way to get augmentation of the child's associations to specific parts of his dreams. It underlines what is coming forth. Drawings of children serve as reminders that a sketch (with elaborations supplied by a child) indeed becomes worth a thousand words.

IDENTIFICATIONS

Identifications are also useful to bring out, especially if we can elicit some of the child's own associations to them. I ask children about their likes and dislikes among animals, colors, persons, long or short pants or dresses, hairdos, beards, cars, and other objects. My assumption is that what we like, or hate, are somehow projections of our own wishes or aspirations. To the degree that this supposition is correct, I find it worthwhile and interesting to learn of these likes and dislikes.

I always try to elicit from the child an account of who his bêtes noires are; who it is that he feels he would least want to be like. For some white children this is blacks or poor whites, and for some black children it is whites. For some Irish it is Protestants or Jews, for some Cubans it is Anglos, and for some Jews it is *goyim.* Ethnic hatreds and contempt are acquired at a very early age in our racist society. Hence, at the same time that I am interested in the favorite hero of the child, I want to know who his anti-hero is. I try to have some sociologic sophistication in these matters, but I usually wind up thinking very simply that the negative as well as the positive reference groups constitute mere *projections* of the child's self-concept and intrafamily values. With children, as with adults, our hate objects (as well as our love objects) give away a lot about the internal state of our own souls.

Miguel, a six-year-old bilingual (Spanish and English) white boy, the son of Cuban refugee parents, was referred to a psychiatrist for "hallucinations." The child had nightmares of black things trying to kill him. He was ready to begin school, and his parents had elected to send him to a parochial school to avoid his studying with black children who, in the family's racial ideology, were stereotyped as wicked, unclean, primitive, and so on. Hence it was helpful to have the child articulate some of the parental ideas about their negative reference group. Unconsciously, Miguel was developing a conscience about some of his own lusts and rages, and from a slightly depressive perspective projected his inner attitudes of self-regard outward into *la cosa negra*. Hence the dual approach to overt family values and to the child's inner conscience paid off and helped Miguel to be more self-accepting and the parents to worry less about his fears of black people.

I also want to find out about some of the child's other identifications. I ask the child for his *favorite color* because I work with a rough rule of thumb that mother-centered children prefer blue, while father-centered ones prefer red. I do not care to defend that hypothesis and do not put much weight on it, but I do place a premium on the kind of talk that accompanies the child's telling me of his favorite color and what there is about it that makes it his favorite color.

Similarly, I ask a child to name his *favorite animal*, supposing that in general the cat and catlike creatures are feminine and the dog and horse are masculine objects in a child's fantasy life. Again, I would not put my hand on the Bible in defense of this opinion, but am happy enough with it to hold it as a tentative hypothesis. Moreover, I ask the child to name for me his *favorite famous person* and his *favorite parents*, "of all the people in the world whom you might choose to be your parents." When it comes to the child's *favorite jokes*, the evidence is mounting that a device of great utility is at hand. Atalay Yorukoglu [2] has found that the child's favorite joke furnishes the sensitive observer with a convenient index to the child's basic life setting, wrapping up his major conflicts in a neat package for us to open, helping the child. A ten-year-old girl (who was a lover of horses) had numerous dreams pointing to her oedipal attachment to her father. One day she reported her favorite joke:

A tailor had closed his shop to remain with his dying wife. On the night that the doctor had said would be her last, the tailor had become groggy sitting at the bedside when his wife tugged at his sleeve, asking him to have sexual intercourse with her. He could not believe that a dying woman would make this request and pinched himself to be sure he was not having a dream.

The wife insisted, and he granted her dying wish. He was half-dead from fatigue, so he fell asleep after coitus and awoke only the following morning when the doctor came to pay his respects. To his astonishment the wife was in the kitchen making potato pancakes and singing Jewish folk songs, miraculously alive. The doctor was overwhelmed by the wondrous revival, but the little tailor was sitting on the side of the bed sobbing profoundly. The doctor could not understand the tailor's weeping and asked him why he responded thus. The tailor answered, "I keep thinking of how I might — with no trouble at all — have saved Momma!"

Hence her favorite joke recapitulated some of her own central problems and cravings.

PLAY

As I have indicated in Chapter 7, it might not be necessary for the child who is highly verbal to play in the therapist's office, either for the child's progression in an abundant, competent life or for the therapist's need (through the play he observes) to get a handle on the child's fantasy in order to help him. Hence there is always a slight dynamic tension whenever play is used for understanding the child; that tension lies in the slight imbalance between play for the child's enjoyment and growth and, on the other hand, play for the therapist's greater understanding of the child. Both of these are noble enterprises, and although they need not conflict, they sometimes do.

A child's desire to play for enjoyment, for example, can sometimes take such precedence over his play for the goal of insight that a young therapist will become demoralized. When demoralized, young therapists often begin to impute evil to the child, evil at least in the form of resistance; or they will attribute an antitherapeutic narcissism and pleasure-seeking to the child. It seems to be their rationale that the pleasure principle makes therapy impossible. Young therapists begin to grumble that they are merely babysitters to the child and that all the work, if any, is being done by the person working with the parents of the child. Or, if the therapy becomes highly focused and diligent, the young therapist often regrets that the fun and spontaneity have gone out of the child's natural, free play. This latter is like the argument that a genius loses his genius whenever he loses his madness! Most therapy does have a regularizing influence. In all events, whether the play succumbs to the child's fun-seeking or the therapist's symbol-seeking, some conflict of interest has arisen between child and therapist, and a one-sidedness has developed in their mutuality.

Having mentioned the child's interest in fun and make-believe and the therapist's interest in insight or realistic understanding, let me take a brief look at a child's free play in several settings: at home, at school, and in the clinic or office of the professional psychotherapist. Free play, so called, is always context bound

and thus not entirely free: A child playing at home plays somewhat differently
from a child spontaneously playing in school or clinic. At home, the interruptions
by others are greater than at a therapist's workshop, and the regimentation is less
than it typically would be at a school. At school, the play is more likely to be
age-appropriate, more subject to group normative pressures, and more time-
limited than it would be at home, for example. Play therapy in the setting of a
university clinic is what I am used to.

Virginia Axline's writings about nondirective play therapy imply and rely on
the structure of a school or therapist's office, and the same is true of Moustakas.
In Melanie Klein's writings about play therapy, she takes it for granted that the
therapy occurs in a therapist's office (although the child's home was the setup
for most of the early child analysts); and the writings of Jessie Taft make it explicit that her views on child therapy refer to the context of a clinic only. Otto
Rank once persuaded her to see a child in Paris, as I recall. It was an abysmal
failure, Taft said, because it was undertaken in isolation from the clinic in which
psychotherapy must occur in order to be given the required outer limits and
boundaries so essential for its success. The relationship is always colored by the
setting in which the play occurs, even if therapist and child give little thought to
their milieu.

An eight-year-old girl, Fran, asked me in our fourth play-and-talk session if I saw
any other children than her. I said I wondered why she would ask me that, that
I was interested, and I soon would tell her the answer *if* she would please tell me,
first of all, what lay behind her asking. She replied, "Because I always see doctors
coming out of your office when I get here, or going in when I leave." I had been
guessing, not without some vainglory, that she was jealous of any other children
I might work with and wanted me exclusively for herself. Yet she claimed she
thought I might work mainly with grown-ups. When I said "I do see other children,
Fran. What about that?", she told me this surprised her, and maybe one day she
would meet one of them coming in or out of my consulting room. I followed
this up by asking her if she would have wished that I saw all grown-ups except her.
To this she said, "It would be all right with me. The things we do, the way we
work together in here — I thought you were used to having only grown-ups here,
except for me."

My pursuit of what it all meant persisted, and it ended up that she was, in her
child's way, thanking me for treating her with so much respect, giving her so
much time and attention, as if only adults deserved that form of attentive regard!
Hence for Fran, the setting, the structure, and the feature of her having so much
concern from a strange doctor were crucial, along with the play and talk secon-
darily, in giving her some relief from her daily routines and fears. Her mother
found Fran's restlessness greatly diminished, her wish to be a boy less insistent,

and her ability to form friendships greatly improved after only five sessions. It was evident that Fran needed "natural" play without interruption from her sibs and parents.

Some of the big differences between conflicting views about play therapy melt away if we take the trouble to specify the setting in which Axline or Moustakas, or Taft or Klein, carry out their therapeutic interactions with children. In the same way, we would try to account for the Kleinian view that *all* children could benefit from psychoanalytic work or the view of Moustakas that preventive play therapy can be an enriching experience for normal as well as disturbed children. Both Moustakas and Klein looked to prevention, not solely to the treatment of disturbances, and made good points in favor of the liberating end stage that the untrammeled release of fantasies, through play, could bring to a child. It is conceivable, although highly unlikely under our present economic and political dispensation, that the day will come when every child will have an opportunity to play, alone and in groups, at home and in school, with or without understanding grown-ups available to assist the play, to form relationships and to make interpretations.

A few more comments about free play and, by way of contrast, focused play.

Free play in any setting has a cathartic effect regardless of whether it is accompanied by insight. The play itself is therapeutic, in the sense of bringing pleasure and relief to the child. From the child's perspective, it is fun; from the therapist's perspective (as Erik Erikson stated it), play is our royal road to understanding how a young ego copes and (successfully) strives for synthesis. Because it is so therapeutic for them and enables them to attain a sense of mastery and fulfillment, children will not play for long periods of time before they experience a sense of satiation. Then they have "had it," and the therapist had better have something other than play that he can comfortably provide for the child. I am thinking of dialogue and clarifying, interpreting interchange, to be explicit.

It is small wonder that being in a playroom will facilitate a child's relatedness to the attendant grown-up, for it is a surrounding constructed for maximal tutelage. The playroom has some highly pleasurable gratifications associated with it, and it becomes an ideal learning and reinforcing environment. Both individual learning and learning in groups can be enhanced by play; but to many child therapists, play group therapy seems both more complicated and more superficial than individual play therapy. After all, not all teachers prefer classroom instruction; for many, only individual teaching and therapy are highly esteemed.

The therapist gets play therapy with one child started by saying:

This room is where we will do our work. Maybe you want to look around and get to know what the room has in it. Pick out something you want to explore and play with while you are here . . .

Yes, everything here is for you to play with. Only you and I will be here, and you can take liberties here, doing things you may not be allowed to do some other places where you are used to playing . . .

Since the therapist is permissive (to a high degree, yet not fully), the child tests, questions, and tries out some things that he longs to do outside. He rapidly catches on that play substitutes for some behavior that is tabooed or otherwise impossible. He can be babyish (regressive), energetic and lusty (aggressive), meditative (autistic or autocosmic), talkative, or whatever he wishes. He can be himself or can assume a role. He can pretend he is an airplane pilot, a copulating adult, a pregnant woman, Superman — anything his heart desires. Sometimes the child's free play upsets the therapist, odd as that seems.

Charlie, an eleven-year-old boy who was impulse-ridden, a borderline psychotic, and had an abnormal brain rhythm on EEG, demanded that we go to the separate playroom adjacent to the consultation room. He employed play there to test the therapist, playing baby and sucking on baby bottles in a way that made his therapist uncomfortable. The therapist considered himself to be unobtrusive and permissive in the interaction with Charlie. However, after several dozen hours of therapy that consisted largely of talking and "more age-appropriate" play, Charlie blurted out defiantly, "Adams, I want to suck on that baby bottle in the playroom and I don't give a goddam if you like it or not!" Free play carries some degree of license, and many children cling to that advantage. Hence, I realized that I needed to understand regression more than I had done in my work with Charlie.

Play therapy that is less free has considerable utility, provided it is chosen to be so and to illuminate a *sector* of the child's problems, or even to diminish a child's buildup of inner distress under special environmental circumstances; for example, when a new baby is born, when a surgical procedure has been recommended for a child, or when a child seems to be "thrown" by life crises like moving to a new city, divorce of the parents, a death in the family, sexual molestation by an adult, or a peaking of sexual unrest in the child himself. Under these circumstances, the playroom can be rigged to include materials guaranteed to elicit some focus on the child's current predicament. For the sexually stirred-up child, the realistic dolls that have genitalia might be furnished in the playroom. For the displaced penultimate sibling we can provide a doll family that matches his, with a new baby included. For the child who will undergo tonsillectomy or correction of hypospadias we can provide some materials for playing doctor, for drawing, and for rehearsing the impending surgery. In life's crises such as those mentioned, we can stack the cards so that the play materials will have attributes slanted toward the child's upset — the toy moving van for the family who have changed place of residence, for example. The main thing in such controlled or focused play is to help the child to abreact, to have a release of affect, and to undergo a corrective emotional experience.

I have seen children who responded (when I stacked the cards for purposes of focused and topical psychotherapeutic intervention) with suspiciousness toward me or their parents. Such children see a parental plot in everything they do with a therapist. They seemed to feel that what I called focusing was manipulation; and of course they were correct about my being manipulative, if not about my being an agent of their parents. Free play itself can be cut short by fears and taboos that weigh down on the playing child and by resistances and inhibitions that suddenly well up and lead to play disruption. No play equipment is immune from giving panic and paralysis to a certain child. The blocking is compounded when the play equipment is selected and structured for topical or release therapy. Still, focused or situational play therapy is usually successful (and not one bit problematic) for many children. The rigged playroom can lead to release, mastery, spontaneity, and a sense of fulfillment in the child.

Dottie was five years old, boarding in a fundamentalist Protestant farm home with her elderly foster parents and her three-year-old brother. The foster parents preferred the little brother, allowing him to occupy their double bed, lying between them, while Dottie felt banished to another room of the house. Dottie's mother was a chronic schizophrenic whose hospitalization had been required by the court, and Dottie and her little brother (under the care of the welfare agency) were given a long-term boarding placement while their mother was away.

The welfare agency and the foster parents concurred in requesting a psychiatric evaluation of Dottie because she seemed "wild, odd, and hyperactive." Her therapist, a young psychiatrist, proceeded to do play-observation interviews and to obtain psychologic testing and a physical examination. Simultaneously, the social worker studied and helped the foster parents in their relationship with Dottie and the little brother.

In the combined playroom and office, Dottie searched every inch of the desk, the toy cabinet, and every nook and cranny in the room. Only once, when she picked up a cigar from the ashtray and gave a loud and sexy guffaw, did her hyperactivity abate during the first hour. Hyperkinesis secondary to minimal brain damage was considered the most sensible descriptive term after the first play session. However, the young therapist cautiously added schizophrenia and extreme anxiety reaction as other possible diagnostic labels. The therapist's supervisor took a different tack, suggesting that Dottie was laden with sexual curiosity and confusion, advocating the use of dolls with genitals and the display of assorted phallic objects (pistols, spears, snakes, crayons) on the playroom table.

Dottie spent two of the following play sessions going repeatedly to the male dolls to examine the genitalia. She had no interest in the phallic objects, but would return repetitively from other "searching" behavior to look at the male genitals on the dolls. She did not seem to get the reassurance she sought through her restless, seeking manner or her constant exposure of the dolls' genitals. The social worker was called on for some help, to discuss this with the foster parents if their prudery would allow that discussion and to see if they could supply any notions other than Dottie's "original sinfulness" to account for her sexually related unrest.

The foster parents were greatly relieved to have this brought up, for they knew that they had been unsuccessfully trying to protect Dottie from some "bad" information. The thing they hid was that the little brother had a severe hypospadias, which necessitated his sitting down to urinate and gave his external genitalia the appearance of those of a girl with an enlarged clitoris. They had sensed Dottie's being worried by this.

When the foster mother explained the anatomic differences between boys and girls, and between the brother and most boys, Dottie began to play more freely, was less sexually alerted and less active, and lost the "bizarre" appearance that had brought her in for psychiatric evaluation. Obviously, the focused and rigged play therapy had been a vehicle for bringing on greater happiness and symptom reduction.

DREAMS

To be interested in the child's dreams it is only required that the adult enjoy learning the feelings, thought forms and concepts, and values of the given child. Many of our greatest mentors have had these interests in children and their dreams. Piaget [3] is a good mentor because of his keenness in direct observation, his seeing the dream as in the ludic mode, that is, in the mode of play, but with anxiety superimposed. When Piaget wrote about children's dreams, he diminished his reputedly strictly cognitive focus and bore down on the dream not solely as a way of thinking but as a way of experiencing, similar to play but under some anxiety. In other words, the dream tells us about our problems as well as being an example of our noninstrumental behavior. It makes some sense, but does not always show our best reasoning.

Sigmund Freud's [4] approach helps to enlarge and round out the Piagetan view of the dream. Freud, supporting libido theory by dream material, saw dreams as multidetermined, as wish-fulfilling, as protectors of sleep, and as originally unconscious substance of which only the manifest content was allowed by a censor to emerge to awareness. Freud also viewed the dream as primitive, childlike, and of the stuff of primary process. The dream, in brief, was a royal road to the unconscious of the dreamer. Freud regarded dream analysis as so fascinating that he justified it as a departure, within the transference relationship, from otherwise freer association. Jung, by contrast, tended to view the dream as an imaginative production, a "projective," which not only reveals our wildest and basest sentiments but also reveals our best problem-solving efforts, thereby serving as a kind of "signpost to the future." Freud, Jung, and Piaget have done the basic work on dreams, and every psychotherapist could benefit from reading them. Many other writers have provided an excellent rationale for probing the dreams of adults and children. Two good books on the subject, although they relate primarily to adults, are those of Erich Fromm [5] and Walter Bonime [6].

I ask children, often during the initial session, about their most recent dream, scariest dream, and recurrent dreams. I generally assume that what they dream and recall is of some import and may point to significant parts of the child's self-concept.

My statement typically is in interrogative form: "I wonder if you will tell me of the dream you had last night, or about the most recent dream you have had that you remember." And for the most frightening dream or nightmare I ask, "Of all the dreams you have had, what was the scariest of all?" For the recurrent dream, which, as a kind of rule of thumb, I consider to be indicative of a more abiding preoccupation of the child, I inquire, "Have you ever had the same dream, or practically the same dream, more than one time? Tell me what the dream was about."

It is difficult for some beginners in psychotherapy to realize how important dream inquiry is, or how easy it makes the interaction between child and therapist. Children respect their dream life more than adults do. They see dreaming as an indispensable part of living and take very readily to the postulate that we return in our dreams to problems that we tended to gloss over during the day before the dream. In other words, dream analysis is "made for" work with verbal children, and they do not approach it with the heavy and sometimes cynical outlook of some adult patients. I have conducted dream seminars in which we examined the first ten dreams of a child patient, using the characters placed in the dreams as portrayals of the most telling aspects of the child's picture of himself. It is a fruitful way to approach the child's self-picture, proceeding on the simple postulate that children dream about themselves in the guise of a numerous and varied cast of dream characters. The characters in the dream tell us a lot about the dreamer in all his roles, guises, and possibilities.

"Facilitating rap" is what more elegantly might be called "educational procedures" or even "explanations given to the child," but I consider "facilitating rap"
more descriptive and believe it helps a child to develop a little interest in the recall
of his own dreams. I know that when a child begins to recall dreams during the
course of therapy, a spirit of cooperativeness, and indeed a therapeutic alliance,
has developed. Anything that can help the process along is worthwhile, even if it
is as cognitive and directive as the rap I will describe here. The facilitating rap that
I put forth for the child is often something like the following.

I talk about the dream as a very personal product that is relatively uninfluenced
by the parents or siblings or doctor, and for that reason it shows some of the child's
real thinking, apart from whatever others may think. I say we all need to have our
innermost feelings that cannot be touched by others; a world all our own that is
hard to share is a very precious thing. (In this way I am introducing the idea of
individuation, of an unprogrammed area for ecstasy; and if this catches on even
a bit, it will be useful later on.) I say that in the dream *we* do it all, for the dream
is like a television program in which we serve as producer, director, writer, and
actors, and there is nobody but us. I lay before the child the humanity of dreaming, even if the dreams are scary. We need to dream, just as we need to sleep, to
eat, and to enjoy our bodies, getting pleasure out of the bodies of other people.
Even though we dream every night, sometimes children forget their dreams until
reminded of their importance by a therapist, I say, and chances are that a child,
if he tries, can recall what he dreamed. I might even go on to suggest that we need
to know what our dreams are, to make them a part of our *waking life of understanding.* A psychiatrist named Jung called dreams some of the best thinking we
do at times. There is an ancient Jewish saying that a dream not understood is like
a letter not opened. Even if children seldom receive mail, they know they would
be too curious to leave a letter sitting about unopened.

Sequence of Dream Analysis

I observe no rigid sequence in working with a dream the child reports to me,
but, ideally, it could go in this order:

1. The child tells of the dream fully, in his own words.
2. The child adds any extra details that occur to him.
3. He retells the story (on the therapist's request), with some designation of
its beginning, middle, and end.
4. The therapist repeats the dream, sequence by sequence, adhering closely to
the actual words employed by the child narrator.

5. Sequence by sequence, the child is asked to tell what he *felt* while dreaming that particular portion of the dream.

6. The child is told to pick out the main parts and to say whatever comes to mind about the different parts.

7. The therapist asks what this all means — "why are you having this dream at this time in your life?"

8. If time and inclination lead to it, the therapist might ask the child to "take a look at the dream as if each character in the dream is you in some way."

9. The therapist asks, "Now, what does your dream mean?"

What does the therapist gain from working with children's dreams? I believe he gains both fun and profit, the fun of Piaget and the professional benefit of Freud. The first accomplishment is that the therapist knows the dream reflects a trusting and working alliance. It shows a relationship with a healing promise. Second, he finds the dream to be a valuable road to the everyday reality of the child, for he learns things from dreams about the child's family life (also the child's cognitive constructs, emotional conflicts, and attitudes of co-culture or subculture) that he would never learn otherwise, because the material is so emotionally tinged and deeply private.

Working with one obsessive boy, I found the dream to be particularly useful for sorting out correctly seen reality from misjudged and distorted perceptions of reality. Only by working with his dreams did he reveal that he was preoccupied with guilt over his father's death. He could not talk of this except in the context of his "unreal dreams."

In the case of psychotic or borderline-psychotic children, the dream juxtaposed to wakeful reality makes a good avenue to initiate some very important cognitive repair. Such children do have problems sorting out what is going on around them, and by learning to categorize dreams as "only dreams" they are aided in demarcating a useful zone of irreality (the dream) from a reality in which others can share. The beginner should be warned that not every dream should be examined in every child. The severely disturbed child is working on more basic problems than the achievement of insight through work on dreams.

A third gain from dreams is that they serve as a "royal road to the unconscious" but to conscience and moral values as well as to antisocial id. A fourth gain is sharing knowledge with the child of an imaginative production that is very like play but more obviously bathed in basic anxieties. The dream shows how problems are approached and solved under some tension and conflict. The dream reveals

parts of the personality that are often kept covert; understanding dreams is therapeutic.

WISHES, MEMORIES, AND ASSOCIATIONS

Three Wishes. I like to ask children for the "three deepest wishes of your
heart." Then, if they are obviously conventional, I like to go on, asking "And
another? And another?" Some deprived children are rather mercenary. Some
obsessive children are rather cerebral, wishing for such things as world peace or
no more sickness and probably showing well enough how their reaction forma-
tions are structured. The three wishes can be elucidating.

Memories. The earliest memory, changing as therapy progresses, serves as a
useful index of the self concept. Alfred Adler and his followers gave us this rich
source of data. The earliest recollection of the child does not tell us much about
what actually transpired early in the child's life, but it does give us some often
nonveridical perceptions of how the child sees himself *here and now.*

Think back as far as you can remember, to some scene you recall when you were
very little. Please tell me a scene *you recall,* not what somebody else told you, of
something that went on when you were a very small baby. Go back as far as you
can remember.

Associations. When the child is talking rather freely, and I want to help him
go further in some self-discovery, I ask him to associate to "brown cow" or "a
child being beaten" or whatever he brought up. Children do this with some ease
after a time, and their associations during an interview give important information.
Some of the best therapeutic work is on-the-spot identification, clarification, and
interpretation of the verbal materials of the interview itself.

Word association tests are also fun, and I do not believe that the testing attitude
is contradictory to the therapeutic attitude, so I have no reluctance about giving
TAT cards, word association lists, sentence completion tests, and the like to a child.
In fact, several generations of child psychiatry residents have felt helped, if only
vaguely, by having some of these semistructured "results" available to them. The
sentence completion stems are favorites of mine. I cannot be certain from whom
they were plagiarized initially, and they have grown and changed over the years,
but the form in which I use them today is reproduced in Table 2. I keep prodding
the child to answer at once, with the first thing that enters his head when I read
out each stem phrase. I continue stressing that what he blurts out does not have

to make the slightest bit of sense. Children's pauses, blocks, refusals, and above all the substance of what they supply under the pressure of our rushing are of great interest to the psychotherapist who is willing to speculate about the child's inner life.

Table 2. Sentence Completion, Children

---

1. I would like to
2. Tomorrow I will
3. My mother
4. I wish that I
5. I cannot
6. If I only
7. I worry about
8. Girls
9. I am ashamed
10. I am afraid
11. I hope
12. My father
13. I like
14. I don't like
15. In school I
16. I love
17. Boys
18. It isn't nice to
19. Mother should
20. My teacher
21. There are times when
22. I hate
23. It makes me sad to
24. If I only knew
25. I would like most to
26. My home is
27. Father should
28. People think that I
29. I need
30. I dream about
31. Sometimes I think about
32. Nobody knows that I
33. The best thing that ever happened to me was
34. The worst thing that ever happened to me was
35. My biggest problem is

BODY LANGUAGE

Body language is an important kind of communication to be elicited. It is relatively easy to encourage its flowing freely and abundantly. The child gives an independent will to his bodily parts, saying, "My leg doesn't want to do that," and so on. I encourage this form of verbal characterization. Also, I like to use the principles of the associative anamnesis (Felix Deutsch) when talking with a child, particularly a child with a physical problem.

Roger was an encopretic ten-year-old boy. He soiled frequently, day and night. In all ways he was pleased with his soiling, except that he wanted it hidden from his schoolmates. He was reluctant to talk about the soiling for the first three sessions, and the therapist had allowed him to wait until he felt freer to talk. In the fourth session he described his fear of going to the toilet for a bowel movement. He said such things as "dangerous to let it go," and "I dread to think about it." The therapist encouraged him to describe what it felt like, from inside Roger's skin. Roger displayed directly his many-sided preoccupation with defecation and his anus; it made his feces his dominant mode of relating. He withheld his feelings, his trust, and his interest in others. He feared being dominated and downtrodden by others. He was angry, and his talk of his bowel movements was a parable about his way of life.

All aches and pains have a meaning apart from the objective pathology. Dynamic psychiatry helps other branches of medicine to illuminate the private meanings that accompany physical complaints. Body language gives us a good entry into the child's private world.

Polly was an eight-year-old asthmatic child, the fourth of six children and the only one who knew that her parents were planning to end their marriage because it seemed like an empty shell to them. Polly was afraid of what would happen to her should divorce occur. She appeared to be hyperalert and was forever monitoring with ear and eye everything that happened around her. Her facial musculature was tense. Her neck muscles (sternocleidomastoid and even the platysma) were taut and firmly developed because of the exercise from chronic tension and contraction.

Polly did very little abdominal breathing, even when she was free of asthma symptoms. A pediatric allergist found that she could precipitate an attack of asthma by acceding to the allergist's request to "show me what it is like when you get asthma." For what Polly did was to begin using her accessory respiratory muscles, turning off the abdominal muscles and breathing as if against great resistance — and presto — she had asthma! The pediatric allergist showed considerable wisdom in making a diagnosis of "asthma that has a large psychogenic basis."

Since the days of Wilhelm Reich's *Character Analysis,* it has been fairly well established that nonverbal postures and activities constitute a very telling clue to the personality of the actor. By the same token, as a child becomes happier and more natural during the course of psychotherapy, his physical gracefulness and naturalness will also improve. He will walk and move differently with a body that looks freer from tension and conflict. The change in bodily habitus and movement is especially seen in fearful, inhibited, obsessive children [7].

I have been arguing that we should "go for fantasies" in order to help the child to be freer emotionally, to claim his inner world as his very own, and to learn through a variety of media and approaches to share his internal world to some degree with his therapist. However, fantasies are not to be overrated or taken too seriously. One should certainly not try to elicit them in the manner of a prosecuting attorney — "Everything you say will be recorded and used in evidence." Fantasies are fun, so don't spoil them for the child.

Discovering children's fantasies has an interesting by-product in the therapist's own life. It stimulates the learning therapist to try the same thing on himself and enriches his own fantasy life. While I believe that a therapist gains empathy by this freeing-up, I also recall hearing a heated three-man debate involving a Meyerian psychiatrist and a Freudian and a Sullivanian analyst. They were taking up and defending their accustomed positions when they began talking about the encouragement of fantasies among psychiatric residents. The Meyerian, who thought the psychiatrist-in-training had the duty, fantasies be damned, to make a good diagnosis based on a kind of ritualistic recitation of the "mental status" questions, said "Discourage the resident's fantasies and let him learn to detect psychopathology." The Freudian said the resident should be pushed to elicit his patients' fantasies and to unleash *his* fantasies about his patients, to use his work with patients to help stir up his own empathy and inner processes. Thereupon, our hero, the Sullivanian, suggested that the resident should be encouraged to elicit fantasies from the patient, *primarily for the intention of helping the patient!* In my view, he won the argument.

REFERENCES

1. Maclay, D. *Treatment for Children in Child Guidance.* New York: Science House, 1970.
2. Yorukoglu, A. Children's favorite jokes and their relation to emotional conflicts (translated by the author from the Turkish). *Cocuk Noropsikiyatri. Rehberligi Dergisi* 3:105, 1970.
3. Piaget, J. *Play, Dreams and Imitation in Childhood* (translated by C. Gattegno and F. M. Hodgson). New York: W. W. Norton, 1962.
4. Freud, S. The Interpretation of Dreams (Vols. 4, 5). In *Standard Edition of the Complete Psychological Works of Sigmund Freud.* London: Hogarth Press, 1953. (2nd Edition, 1909)

5. Fromm, E. *The Forgotten Language: An Introduction to the Understanding of Dreams, Fairy Tales and Myths.* New York: Grove Press, 1951.
6. Bonime, W. *The Clinical Use of Dreams.* New York: Basic Books, 1962.
7. Adams, P. *Obsessive Children: A Sociopsychiatric Study.* New York: Brunner/Mazel, 1973.

FURTHER READING

Gardner, R. *Therapeutic Communication with Children: The Mutual Story-Telling Technique.* New York: Science House, 1971.
Robertson, M., and Barford, F. Story-making in psychotherapy with a chronically ill child. *Psychother. Theory Res. Pract.* 7:104, 1970.
Smolen, E. Nonverbal aspects of therapy with children. *Am. J. Psychother.* 13:872, 1959.
Tolor, A. Observations on joke-telling by children in therapy. *Ment. Hyg.* 50:295, 1966.

11

Winding Up Treatment

Termination of therapy is what the therapist had in mind all along. The child also sensed that a time limit hovered over the relationship with the therapist. This terminability made the working together more imperative and more goal-directed. Whenever the relationship was talked about or analyzed, the child caught on that this was not a "real-object" relationship but a professional one; not a usual relationship, but one that would be wound up when the therapeutic goals were achieved. Termination as a phase or process in the therapeutic relationship can be the high point. The discussion in this chapter will be centered first on the decision to stop and then on the matter of how to do it.

DECIDING TO STOP

Psychotherapy with a child is an episode to be ended. It is not an attachment for a lifetime, such as the child makes with a parent. It is not even like being adopted, although the child patient might have entertained such fantasies at times. As a helper, a professional one, a therapist seems different to a child. The therapist is not a person whom the child comes to love and hate in the way that he hates and loves the people in his everyday life circumstances. The therapist is a real person, of course, but he enters the child's life only as a helper when needed. The therapist is someone who is humane, who understands, who communicates, who respects, who listens, but he does not impose his own cravings on the child. He does not respond to child cravings with therapist cravings, but instead fosters a more businesslike, more professional, more helping relationship between an adult and a child.

A gifted therapist has made up his own mind that he will strive only to do his job and to be merely a therapist in the child's life, not a genuine love object. He is sure not to use his position to woo the child's affection or to direct the relationship into a long-standing attachment for his own benefit. The therapist's own treatment hopefully has aided him in the mastery of less-than-global relatedness to others. His own couch time has helped him to see, for example, his father as only his father and not as a god, and, even more urgent, his wife as only his wife and not as mother or sibling. This is not to detract from the importance of the therapist's being a real person or making "therapeutic use of the self"; but I might as well be explicit: I am disillusioned with therapists who are always looking for "bangs" and thrills for themselves under the guise of doing psychotherapy, for which they are often paid quite handsomely. They think their own great fun is bound to help others, but it simply does not always work out like that. Good humanistic ideas and intentions are not enough.

Aiming to end it is good agenda-making in psychotherapy. The end point is not totally precise, but there are some markers that inform us when termination has become appropriate. Termination is not a death sentence to be avoided or commuted, for it is an end point only in the way that a high school commencement marks both an end and a beginning. Indeed, we might not get so murkily sentimental about it if we called it "graduation" instead of "termination."

The young therapists with whom I have had contact do not move into the termination of psychotherapy in a considered, planned manner. They have grown accustomed to terminating exclusively when their patients get up the courage to stop keeping appointments. Under those circumstances the patient stops coming to the therapist, but he has not talked over and worked through the cessation of the therapy. As a consequence, the patient will be in for a lot of trouble if he ever takes up again with that, or any other, therapist.

Even more common for psychiatry residents is the tendency to keep going until they are transferred to another "rotation" and then to spring the news on the child, but as late as possible. The second therapist, who falls heir to a shoddy termination and transfer, is justifiably angry. It often takes weeks to "bury the dead," that is, the first therapist, and to get the child involved in a more meaningful relationship with the second team.

Therapists who do not know how to make parting into a productive, planned time of "sweet sorrow" often persevere until the child or the parents make the first move, the first bid for termination. If the parents suddenly must move away from town, the more-inept therapist is likely to breathe a deep sigh of relief. It is as if the therapist's prayers are answered, and the decision-making is not done in dialogue with the child but is left to an "act of God." This may be seen as a welcome gift to the lazy or unimaginative therapist, but it is seen as a deprivation of rights by the child. The child has a right to exercise some control over the termination, to make his voice count in the decision to wind up. Let other adults ride roughshod over children whenever we cannot prevent it, but let therapists give children a little consideration and respect.

A termination that is shared by child and therapist is to be sought. A termination that is planned for is better than one that comes about abruptly because of some unforeseen necessity, usually attributable to the domain of the parents or the therapist — that is, to grown-ups, not children. The decision to stop is not guided by the achievement of perfection, but on the other hand, it does have some direct correspondence to the achievement of therapeutic goals.

The decision to terminate does not await total changes within the child, with the child perceived as a culture-free person living only according to ethical-idealist standards. By "ethical-idealist" I mean that spirit I have already described in which the therapist will go on, almost interminably, urging the child to look within himself and to change whatever is wrong within him, until the child is free of anxiety, or until he has established "full genital organization," or perhaps even until the therapist has come to the old-time goal of rendering the analysand dream-free! These are superhuman aims, presupposing that our only function in life is to be privately and personally "a better person" and ignoring our necessity to strive for social change toward a "better world." The milieu as well as ego of the child merit the therapist's attention. It is not the child who changes the world, but the therapist who should aim to change it.

A more moderate ethical aspiration would seek to aid the child to develop into only a healthy *problem solver* — but, notice, not problem-free person — who has some utopical leanings, some *awareness of situations,* as well as having an ethical awareness of self and persons. Classic psychoanalysis has gone on too long preparing individuals for inner goodness at the expense of leaving unanalyzed their failing to understand contexts, institutions, and situations. A child who has become more spontaneous, more capable of tackling his problems, behaves more appropriately for his chronological developmental stage, and has figured out some of the patterns and games he gets involved in within his household assuredly can enter into planning to terminate his therapy. Termination is called for when the child gets on the right track, intrapsychically and situationally. He has what might be called the requisite insight into situations. As Anna Freud stated it, the child has caught up and is ready to progress; hence he is ready to terminate.

At the other extreme from lengthy analysis is a brand of the briefest therapy, sometimes offered to the public, which I would describe as hit-or-miss therapy. Such therapy entails an announcement to child and family at the onset that after ten sessions, come hell or high water, the treatment will cease. This seems to have been invented for expediency's sake, because of clinical manpower shortages. It does solve the termination problem through decisive calendar-watching and, in the process, perhaps stimulates a harder, more diligent working on problems. Even if someone does not get enough, there is a consolation that many have got a little. Without demanding the utter briefness of ten or twelve sessions that are mandated in some child guidance clinics, Jessie Taft [1] used time limits wisely and with utmost awareness of what was happening with respect to time. Her comments make highly recommended reading.

Time, then, as arbitrarily utilized to limit the therapeutic situation, is nothing more than the external symbol, the tangible carrier, of the inevitable limitation in all relationship, which becomes tolerable here for the first time, only because the patient is allowed to discover it one-sidedly, in himself, in terms of his own will and nature.

A related time-utilization technique that makes good sense in many clinics and centers calls for an evaluation and brief treatment period of perhaps six to ten sessions. Thereafter, all must wait for three or four months, testing out what they have reshuffled, or learned, before the family members return for a stocktaking and a consultation concerning their needs for the future. In this way, it is communicated by the structure of the therapy that dependency is not the desired goal. It is also made clear that changes are valued, changes that need not take a long time in coming. This technique also serves as a good reminder to convinced therapists, the author included, that personal change demands that family members give substantial help to one another. Therapy is a bootstrap operation. Therapists help, but children and their elders, their "real objects," *do it.* Termination is thus a growth phase in family life.

After having a breathing and growing phase, in which a certain amount of consolidation occurs, the family members might come back to ask for more therapy and to use it more directly than before. The child might have strengthened his motivation for therapy during the lull. In short, the rest period does not always serve to "cool out" or get rid of people; for some, it intensifies their longings for assistance. The wait has given the child some important clues, which his parents know just as fully as the child does: Therapy is not forever; therapy means work; therapy means change, uncertainty, and taking risks.

ENDING AT GOALS

Deciding to stop depends on the goals set and the goals reached. Looking at the opinions of some experts can help us here. Anna Freud, as has been mentioned, renounced hyperexacting idealism and, with a judgment grounded in a deep clinical wisdom, averred that the time to terminate is when the child gets caught up, having overcome the fixations and regressions that held him back. When the child is ready to progress with his own living, termination is called for, in the opinion of Anna Freud.

A Rankian, Jessie Taft [1], adhered to the practice of formal, structured end-setting in her psychotherapeutic work with children. Taft considered the child to be ready for termination when the child

... finally learns to use the allotted hour from beginning to end without undue fear, resistance, resentment or greediness. When he can take it and also leave it without denying its value, without trying to escape it completely or keep it forever because of this very value, [insofar as] he has learned to live, to accept this fragment of time in and for itself, and strange as it may seem, if he can live this hour he has in his grasp the secret of all hours, he has conquered life and time for the moment and in principle.

Here then in the simplest of terms is a real criterion for therapy ... It is a goal which is always relative, which will never be completely attained, yet is solved in every single hour to some degree ...

Another Rankian, Frederick H. Allen [2], stated the criteria for termination with perhaps no fuller definition:

... the therapist's major interest from the beginning must be in helping the patient eventually to finish with this particular episode in his life. Only in that way can this unique relationship have any value ... No therapeutic experience can provide a patient with a paid-up insurance policy against future difficulties although the anxiety centering about ending may activate the patient's need to have such assurance.

Carl Rogers, also impressed by Otto Rank, had a strong influence on the non-directive play therapy of Virginia Axline. And in a school of therapy that manifests some of the Rogersian verbal styles and word choices are writers such as Clark Moustakas, Eugene Gendlin, and others who make up the humanistic or existentialist school. Moustakas [3] expressed the changes that are characteristic of completed therapy in this way:

... the disturbed child experiences a process of emotional growth. He moves from the expression of diffused, generalized, negative attitudes which block him from fully developing his potentials as a human being to the expression of clarified positive and negative attitudes which enable him to feel worthy and to develop in terms of his real talents and abilities. With his self-capacity available and his self-regard restored, he ventures into new experiences and attains new meaning and value in his relations with others.

Virginia Axline [4] stated in a similar vein as an admonition to the therapist:

... change is a gradual process and ... some children move at a snail's pace. Let her [the therapist] remember that therapy does not always bring about the desired results. It is not a cure-all. Let her remember that the child is living in a dynamic world of human relationships. The conditions which have created the maladjustment may be still operating. The child may not be able to combat the other forces that stifle his psychological growth. The therapist should try to see things through the child's eyes, and should try to develop a feeling of empathy with the child. She should keep in mind the maxim that change cannot take place without the participation of the individual, and that worthwhile change comes from within. She should remember that growth is a gradual process.

From these injunctions it is difficult to fathom by what subjective or objective standards one can judge that "enough" treatment has gone on. In reading the Rankians and the experiential therapists one often finds these writers failing to suggest useful handles onto finite procedural reality. While one might be glad the experiential group insists that theories are no more real than what they describe, one laments that these experiential writers flirt with a real danger, as described by Eugene Gendlin [5]:

The danger is a therapy without theoretical perspectives and trainable principles. Existential psychotherapy can look like a mere rejection of theory and precise thought.

By contrast, the Freudians and their neo-Freudian relatives, although often less than "kissing kin" in their regard for one another, do work hard at a rational mechanical theory even though they flirt with the danger of sacrificing the unique quality of the experience in psychotherapy. Life instinct and death instinct are not very personal.

Clara Thompson [6] indicated her reluctance to demand perfection when she wrote that termination is due when the patient has obtained relief from neurotic suffering, has become able to relate to others with only minimal transference from his early life relationships, and has become capable of achieving as complete development of his powers *as will be allowed by his social position.* Thompson also recognized that the "clean bill of health" might have to be compromised by some neurotic concessions to a "sick society." The neo-Freudian Karen Horney [7], referring to adult analysands, wrote from a perspective that can help a child therapist a little:

When should an analysis be terminated? Again a warning is in place against seeking an easy solution by relying on outward signs or on isolated criteria, such as disappearance of gross symptoms, capacity for sexual enjoyment, change in the structure of dreams, or the like. At bottom, the question again touches upon a personal philosophy of life. Do we intend to put out a finished product with all problems solved for good and all? If we consider this possible, do we believe it to be desirable? Or do we think of life as a process of development which does not end until the very last day of existence? . . . I hold that the aim of analysis is not to render life devoid of risks and conflicts, but to enable an individual eventually to solve his problems himself.

But when is the patient able to take his development into his own hands? This question is identical with the question as to the ultimate goal of psychoanalytical therapy. In my judgment, freeing the patient from anxiety is only a means to an end. The end is to help him regain his spontaneity, to find his measurements of value in himself, in short, to give him the courage to be himself.

Finally, it was another neo-Freudian, Nathan Ackerman [8], who formulated the goals of psychotherapy and the features of a "cure" in a way that is general enough to include children as well as adults, but specific enough to give some sensible standards for appraising the movement toward health that real patients make.

The term "cure" implies, first of all, the therapeutic removal of symptoms, those specific signs of disordered functioning that characterize a particular illness. For some therapists this removal constitutes the sole meaning of cure; it is conceived as a significant result, sufficient unto itself. Perhaps for certain forms of mental illness, this outcome is good enough. For many therapists, however, and for a great variety of disturbances of mental health, this first meaning is the dissolution of vulnerability to illness. Treatment is expected to strengthen personality so that the patient will not fall ill again, to provide immunization against a further invasion of illness. Third is the idea that the personality of the patient must have undergone a basic change, signifying not only increased adaptive strength and capacity for resistance to illness but, in a positive sense, the ability to realize potential, to capitalize on personal resources so as to feel free and happy, satisfy personal needs, and be an efficient, productive person. Finally, cure may also mean that the individual, freed of crippling anxieties, can now unfold his capacity for loving others, can share with them both pleasure and responsibility, and can experience the full gamut of satisfaction in making a positive contribution to the welfare of family, friends, and community.

Stuart Finch, among others, emphasized the last Ackermanian goal of therapy with children when he affirmed the indispensability of the treated child's love for

From this look at some Freudians and anti- and neo-Freudians, we can see that there is true diversity when varied writers assess the signs of cure. We can see, moreover, that the goals range from very simple and commonsense ones, sometimes referred to by the snobbish term "simplistic," to goals that are murky, global, and mystical. In the finest formulations, from a strict perspective, the matter is left equivocal and inexact. The practice of psychotherapy assuredly requires some tolerance for ambiguity. However, let us try to remain tolerant but not reverent toward ambiguity.

ENDING IN FAILURE

At times, neither the optimal goals nor even the modified goals will be reached. Sometimes a therapist does not help a child. When this is the case, it is better to stop than to continue in a relationship that is completely unrewarding for the child. Sometimes it is good to acknowledge that the odds are insuperable. For example, if a child comes from an impoverished family who live in a remote farm area, and if the child is unable to come for therapy, treatment often ends before it is really started. Under such circumstances, the resourceful child psychiatrist gets busy and both works for social change broadly and also tries, in the case of this one child, to "beat the system" by finding a volunteer or a social welfare means to transport the child to the therapist. Then, too, the possibility exists for the therapist to reach out, to travel to the child's home.

Every time therapy does not get going, it is good for the therapist to recall that the onus is on the therapist, not the child. None of the insuperable odds, whether in the form of child and parent resistances or reality factors such as poverty, mental retardation, unforeseen physical illness, or countertransferences that are, alas, unmanageable is a serious reflection on the child who cannot be reached. The therapist is the one who has the greater responsibility, the greater accountability, and hopefully the greater freedom for negotiating the changes that make therapy go along better. Therefore, the therapist must not wash his hands of the case as soon as he has effected the termination because of failure; for there is, after all, no special novelty in the fact that both parties can agree nothing worthwhile has transpired. The complete task is finished only when the therapist has arranged a transfer to other and more promising resources than himself.

Psychotherapists, both young and old, can easily fall into laying a burden of grandiose expectations on themselves, overvaluing their competence, and devaluing the importance of the child's participation in the psychotherapy. The therapist has never lived who can be successful with everyone. Wisdom urges and prudence affirms that we must not expect always to be all-purpose helpers. There will be some children — notably, psychotic children — who make no progress in our "best show" of psychotherapy. There are many other treatment failures, too. How lucky we would be if the only children who were not helped by us were the psychotic ones!

After all is done and said, psychotherapy is a technique that works best in unburdening a child of "hang-ups" and thereby restoring him to normal developmental progression. If he slips back into "regressions" or becomes stuck at "fixations" in the course of that development, then therapy helps to free him of the hurdles and restore him to the normal developmental line for his age and sex. But if a child has never been socialized or habilitated, then *rehabilitation* or restoration is a meaningless goal. The child described needs to *get started* on humanization.

The psychotic child, through no fault of his own, cannot be reached by the usual psychotherapeutic skills and know-how. Psychotic children are so weakly responsive that work with them taxes not only psychotherapists but also the psychotic children's parents, occupational therapists, speech therapists, child care workers, social workers, teachers, and others. The gratifications are minimal and satisfactions scarce. The gratifications that Rankians get from "the living relationship" would never have been deduced had they worked mainly with psychotic children. (Here I refer to Otto, not Beata, Rank.) Talk of living relationships and unfolding of full potential makes a little sense, probably, with severely disturbed children too. But with disturbed children who have been unable to relate from birth onward, we are "in a different ball park" than when we are waxing poetic about what can be done with inhibited, neurotic children. For autistic and other psychotic children, unrelated all their lives, very specialized and intensive therapy, rather different from the major approaches that are discussed in this primer, is required. Certainly, with the approaches I have been suggesting, the rate of "termination, no improvement" would be very high with psychotic children.

A change of therapists does not seem to have the deleterious effects on psychotic children that some writers have contended it has. Therefore, if one therapist cannot accomplish any gains after as long as two years, the decision to transfer to a different therapy or therapist is a step in the right direction. All of us can stand to live with some degree of therapeutic failure.

PARENTS AND THE DECISION TO TERMINATE

We cannot terminate therapy expecting that a child will forever after be the independent, heroic, and Promethean creature epitomized in idealized statements of what the "cured product" of psychotherapy must be. We deal in child psychiatry with dependent children, that is, young people who depend on their parents for both physical and mental security. We do not restore the "product" to his job at the bank, but to his family, peer group, and school. The parents "own" their child, both legally and through an extralegal loving identification as conveyed by "my own," and the parents must be reckoned with if the child is to survive after termination. In 1926 Anna Freud [9] contended that

... the child's education suffers no interruption even at the termination of analysis, but passes back, wholly and directly, from the hands of the analyst into those of the now more understanding parents.

The matter is not merely academic. It is practical and compelling. Parents have rights. Parents must be involved fully in the decision to terminate treatment.

As an illustration of this rather pontifical assertion, let me use the example of a child who has school phobia; I could easily illustrate the same point with a stammerer, bedwetter, or thief. In this situation, as soon as the major complaint (of the parents, but about the child) goes away, the parents want to get off the hook straightaway. Children with school phobia are not experiencing a mild and unimportant malady, for even if we dislike compulsory education, the child is still legally required to attend school. The child with school phobia is not a rebel against school attendance anyway, nor is he a truant. He does dread to leave his mother, and his fear of separation from her is one more expression of his adverse response to the hostile symbiosis that endures between him and the mother. The mother, and the father also, keep feeding the symbiotic ties. These interpersonal relations, by definition, require participation of more than a child.

If the parents do not recognize, at least, that the trouble is more than skin deep, involving more than a short-lived refusal to attend school, they will beat a hasty retreat as soon as the child is back in school. If the parents are simultaneously involved, however, they know from their own side that something is brewing that is not to be solved by a simple return to school attendance. If the parents are only tenuously involved, it becomes difficult to reason with them when they have already come to a decision to stop therapy. That is to say, because nobody had their confidence earlier and nobody was trying to help them directly, nobody can stop them now from calling for an abrupt termination. Parents sometimes want to assert their rights to terminate psychotherapy for their child.

In the next section I will come back to ways to coordinate termination with the parents. For now, however, I want to make one concrete, mundane suggestion concerning abrupt and unilateral termination by the parents. It is a simple injunction: *Do not allow the parents to stop without adequate notice.* Hold out for at least two more sessions with the child. Be angry and bully them if they do not allow you to have at least one more good-bye session with the child. Even though it smacks faintly of moral blackmail, tell the parents that, regardless of whether or not they have caught onto it, a relationship has grown between the child and the therapist. This relationship deserves to be respected, and abrupt withdrawal does a disservice to child and therapist. One may go on to remonstrate, "I would never break the contract so abruptly." Sometimes the parents can be persuaded to grant the child and therapist an additional couple of hours if the therapist offers to set no charges for the sessions. That kind of offer shows that the therapist's demands have a certain indisputable earnestness. Obviously, a therapist who offers free sessions is not in that classic tradition that avows the necessity to pay through the nose for all services rendered. The affluent may show their devotion only by paying well for their therapy; to them, free sessions may seem to be an affront. But, as I have observed many times [10, 11], such peevish misunderstanding is not the case with poor people. The poor are little impressed by getting only what they pay for; they are much more impressed with the therapist's making some special monetary commitment or outlay. They like free sessions very well, as I have seen, and they profit without paying.

HOW TO STOP PSYCHOTHERAPY

Let us look at the "how-to" of termination under the topics of setting an end point, coordinating termination with the child's parents, rehearsing the ending, the termination rap, and the child's behavior on ending therapy. A good overall rule in planning the termination of psychotherapy with a child is to be as decisive in the "elective" termination as you would be in an abrupt and unforeseen kind of ending. In other words, be definite and try to stick to the time limits. With a mutually understood anticipation of ending, the termination can become the best part of the treatment process.

Setting an End Point

Setting an end point is basic. Despite the fact that it is chosen and imposed arbitrarily to some extent, it is made easy and natural if it has evolved from one of the review sessions with parents and child such as were discussed in Chapter 9. In those review sessions the stocktaking has occurred, and a new phase of therapy has been mapped out, including the termination phase. The parents, child, and therapist(s) have all worked over some of the fundamental issues. And a consensus has emerged from the joint work, which bodes well for the termination process.

"Let's aim to wind up on May first," exemplifies a sensible statement from either child or therapist when the stocktaking shows that the end may be in sight. In the decision-making the child's voice is second in influence only to the therapist's. The parents' voice ranks third even though they give orders to their child, are often paying for the expensive therapy, and may keep trying to usurp the therapist's place at the top of the power pyramid. This is something we must recognize: Work with families is not devoid of power strivings and power allocations; hence it is a political phenomenon. Fortunately, everyone has enough power allocated to him so that, usually, nobody employs violence! Identifying the power moves and power plays is good practice in psychotherapy with children. I especially like to help the child to see clearly and forcefully that his parents do not control the therapist!

If, in a conference back in March or April, May first was selected as the date to stop, the therapist sticks to it and uses the agreed-upon end point as a control that facilitates the child's growth toward health. If the child begs for clemency and says, as I have often heard, "Please let's not quit when May comes. I want to keep coming here until school is out," then what? The therapist resolutely maintains, "Let us see if we cannot be ready by May. What is there that we have to work out before then?" If both are lucky, the child tells the therapist of something he regards as a problem that depends on therapy for resolution.

Coordinating the Ending with the Parents

Since it is important to coordinate the ending with the parents as well as with the child, let me suggest some ways that this can be done. If the parents are being seen by a social worker or other colleague, a meeting of child, both therapists, and the parents might be the easiest way to do it. It can be a session to evaluate how things have been progressing, which doubles as a leap into the world of the home-and-hearth reality of the child. Not only the child but also the therapist must face up to that reality. I used to think that it was unseemly for the child and his therapist to join in such a meeting, but I learned better from my collaborators, primarily psychiatric social workers. However, I sometimes think that I might have been exceptionally blessed by having social worker colleagues who did not flex the muscles of territoriality by opposing the psychiatrist's getting together with a child's parents. Some social workers do not want any psychiatric resident "messing with the parents" of disturbed children; their claims are foolishly inappropriate in a setting that purports to teach child psychiatry to psychiatric residents. If your supervisor cannot read the riot act to them, you need to be learning child psychiatry elsewhere.

Assuming that the team members are thinking first and foremost of the welfare of the patient and not of their own professional prerogatives, teamwork can be the educational approach of choice and can help all of the family seeking help. When attitudes are cooperative and fairly pleasant, the two therapists can hold a parents-child session, ask where things stand, and set up an end point along with an informal agenda of work remaining to be done. Some of the generalities that follow will make some sense both for collaborative work and for therapy with a solo therapist; by solo I mean that a child is seen for the most part alone, eventually bringing the parents into the session toward its end, either routinely or intermittently. I like this modality, especially with adolescents (see Chapter 12).

One question must be raised in this parent and child conference, and answered in the affirmative: *By the time we stop, are the parents going to be in shape to resume parenting unaided?* Further estimates should be forthcoming in response to such issues as these: Do the parents need to continue in treatment longer than the child because of their personal or conjugal problems or their problems in being parents of other children in their family group? (If the parents will need more time, let them know that it is available to them.) Should the parents do further work with someone else? In other words, should a transfer of therapists be arranged, perhaps in another setting? Or should a different modality be sought, such as a switch to family group therapy?

Rehearsing the Ending

Rehearsing the ending is also an important item in termination technology. There are several opportunities for it: (1) If the practice has been to do an evaluation and brief treatment and then to rest a while, some rehearsal of the ending has occurred already. (2) The child's vacations offer a convenient rehearsal. Trips to summer camp or holidays away with the family — more abundantly available to children from middle-class families than from working-class or lower-class ones — provide the stimulus for a lot of identification of affects concerning parting and losing and for working maturely with issues of separation, autonomy, and death. (3) The therapist's vacations also provide ample opportunity for such work. When the therapist goes away at a time that is not convenient for child and parents, in that his vacation does not coincide with theirs, the fuller is the yield for working through termination. (4) Temporal spacing, or tapering off, is also a favorite way to prepare for the complete parting that is due to follow the "weaning." If a child has been coming to therapy sessions four times weekly, reduce the frequency to three or two visits per week, eventually to one a week, and perhaps allow a full week's lapse between the penultimate and final sessions.

It is fun to watch young therapists start an elaborate tapering-off ritual only to discover that the child gets the message and effects a wholesome termination more quickly than the therapist had anticipated. On such a discovery the therapist is wise not to beat a dead horse and to acknowledge that therapy, in truth, has already stopped. Still wiser is the one who is honestly glad that the child set his own timetable.

Termination Rap

A termination rap can help to clarify what treatment has accomplished and what the ending signifies. Without falling into the fallacy of those intellectuals who believe in verbal magic, we must concede that there is something very potent about the talk between child and therapist concerning termination of psychotherapy. A sampling of useful remarks might include: "What will you do without me, when you stop coming to see me? What is it that we have been up to? Why did you come to see me in the first place? What big problems have we worked on? What big problems remain? What kind of things do we need to get settled for you to be happy enough that you can do without me? How might I have been of more help, better help, quicker help to you? Do you recall a time that I did something that was awful from your way of looking at it? Do you remember a time when I did something that was just right, just what you needed me to do? Who will be able to help you with some of the problems that come up after you and I stop therapy?" And so on. This verbal rap is not to be minimized, no matter how cathartic and releasing the nonverbal aspects of therapy might have been. Of course, it is not a time for the therapist to pound away, hell-bent on implanting an ideology or carrying out brainwashing; but it can be a useful time for eliciting the kind of ideology the child has been in the process of forming for himself. The child does have a head for thinking, after all, and the gift of speech is valuable — speech carries messages.

The Child's Termination Behavior

I will present five classes of termination behavior in the hoped-for sequence of their appearance, although they may coexist or appear in reverse order: (1) fear, anger, and aggression; (2) recrudescence of old madness; (3) open bid for interminability; (4) recapitulation of the therapy; (5) the rap of accepting termination.

Fear, Anger, and Aggression. Fear, anger, and aggression can be surprising. Such expressions are crude, childish ways to try to ease the pain of parting. A placid and ingratiating child who has spent much time in treatment putting his best foot forward will suddenly become almost vicious, overtly destructive, and abusive. He will voice his murderous wishes, engage in direct assault and assaultive play, and verbalize an ideation that is starkly delusional, with a paranoid flavor. The time is at hand not only to *confront* the child with the fact that his acting-up response to ending therapy is a "no-no," but also to *identify* several components of his response: his frustrated longings to be accepted; his fear of not being worthy; his outright solicitation of a rejection that he controls and which goes the therapist's "rejection" one better; and his wildness in the face of an impending loss. *Interpretation* would be very much in order if one has evidence that the child was abandoned — as, for example, with an adopted child — or neglected in infancy.

In milder form, the child might become pointedly and strategically "lost" when the parents try to find him and bring him to the next appointment after a termination has been plotted out. Again, such behavior means that he is trying to take charge, to reject before being rejected. In still milder form, but just as irritating to parents and unwary therapists, are such activities as passive-aggressive lateness, yawns and proclamations of boredom, becoming inattentive and selectively "hard of hearing," reading books during the therapy hour, and so on — a lovely juvenile repertoire.

Recrudescence of Old Madness. These reactions bespeak nostalgia and reluctance to terminate but must not be adjudged to mean that the child requires more prolonged, extended psychotherapy. The long-dry mattress will become wet again; the renovated school phobic will vomit on school days; the spontaneous ex-obsessive will resume a frantic touching of door knobs; the reformed thief will steal from the church collection plate. The dead horse gets a thorough beating, and the therapist had better be on his toes to account for this as a form of protest against ending the therapeutic relationship. If the therapist is set to expect some of these responses, some rerunning of the crazy old flicks, he will not overreact to them. I find them funny, sometimes, and I do not mean to ridicule the child in stating it this way.

Bid for Interminability. The child can make a bid for interminability precisely when termination is proposed. It is another manifestation of reluctance to grow through separation and individuation. Occasionally this bid will come shockingly late, even as late as the final session, when, at the very instant of departure, the child comes barrelling back into the treatment room to embrace the therapist and exclaim, "Doctor, I don't wanta quit seeing you." Therapist, try being Doctor Cool under those circumstances!

Sometimes the child will bid for an "unending" by bargaining with the therapist for a gift, asking to pick out his favorite toy and "keep it always." The child might want only a firm promise from the therapist that he will write letters to the child, ranging from one a day to a letter on each birthday anniversary. An obliging therapist can certainly do the latter for a little child. Or, along this same line, the child may try to schedule some future appointment with the therapist; "a year from now" might be all that is asked. My own inclination is to end it, clean and simple, but I always try to get the message across to the child that I would value a friendly contact now that the professional one has ended.

That attitude has had two noticeable results: First, many years later, the child may suffer from similar or totally new problems, and even if he cannot recall my name, he will ask his parents to contact the doctor who "wanted children to be happy" whom he saw at age six years. Second, unless they should have a recurrence of serious difficulties, most of the children whom I have seen do not show any penchant for hobnobbing in later years with that doctor who tried to help them, once upon a time, to be happier and freer. That in and of itself speaks well for the expatients, I must say.

Recapitulation of the Therapy. This is indicative of the child's determination to claim the treatment, to clutch it to himself. This is a good omen during the termination phase. One way in which the child reenacts the more moving facets of the treatment is to repeat, sometimes uncannily, the varied activities of the initial session or of the first two or three sessions. This is not a deadly ritualized repetition, however, for there are modifications that proclaim to the observing therapist, "Watch how I grew. See how I made changes!" Whereas in the first session he picked up a gun, tentatively and asking for permission, the child now answers his own questions in an authoritative tone that shouts out his mastery of his former murderous longings. He has made big changes. He is now back on the track.

Another way the child enacts his progress before the therapist's eyes is by staging a rerun of all the play activities in which he has engaged throughout the therapy. Or, alternatively, he may squeeze into the final hour a review and résumé of all the things that he and the therapist talked about during a year or more of treatment. It is a private showing of a most meaningful psychodrama, and I think therapists should feel privileged to be a witness to this kind of heartfelt presentation.

Rap of Acceptance

The rap of accepting the terminating relationship is still another important index of the child's ability to grapple with the ending of a relationship that has helped him. Frederick Allen [2] wrote:

The child needed a period of time in the beginning to find what he could be in this new relationship. And, in the ending phase, he will need to have a planned period in order to learn the meaning of this anxiety that is aroused by the prospect of assuming fuller responsibility for the changes he has effected through the help of the therapist.

The child needs to conceptualize the relationship and put it into words (hence, the rap), to render it as he perceives it. Although his version is ordinarily not like a psychodynamic "pearl," it is a needed, curative operation. All of this — the mama bears I have heard of, in this phase of child therapy, taking their cubs out to graduate them and allow them to fend for themselves henceforth, the imagery about weaning, the talk of growth, the "I will miss you," and the earnest consideration of how life soon will be with "only" the parents to turn to — is the stuff of poetry, if it is not already poetry as the children themselves express it. The intelligent therapist will encourage a child to talk about the ending, to give some rap that shows he accepts the ending.

Indeed, it bears repeating — termination is what psychotherapy aimed for from its very inception.

REFERENCES

1. Taft, J. *The Dynamics of Therapy in a Controlled Relationship.* New York: Macmillan, 1933.
2. Allen, F. H. *Psychotherapy with Children.* New York: W. W. Norton, 1942.
3. Moustakas, C. *Psychotherapy with Children: The Living Relationship.* New York: Harper & Row, 1959.

4. Axline, V. *Play Therapy* (rev. ed.). New York: Ballantine Books, 1969. (Orig. ed., Boston: Houghton Mifflin, 1947.)

5. Gendlin, E. Existentialism and Existential Psychotherapy. In C. Moustakas (Ed.), *Existential Child Therapy.* New York: Basic Books, 1966.

6. Thompson, C. *Psychoanalysis: Evolution and Development.* Camden, N.J.: Thomas Nelson, 1950.

7. Horney, K. *New Ways in Psychoanalysis.* New York: W. W. Norton, 1939.

8. Ackerman, N. *Psychodynamics of Family Life: Diagnosis and Treatment of Family Relationships.* New York: Basic Books, 1958.

9. Freud, A. *The Psychoanalytical Treatment of Children.* New York: Schocken Books, 1964. (Original, 1926)

10. McDonald, N., and Adams, P. The Psychotherapeutic Workability of the Poor. *J. Am. Acad. Child Psychiatry* 6:663, 1967.

11. Adams, P., and McDonald, N. Clinical cooling out of poor people. *Am. J. Orthopsychiatry* 38:457, 1966.

12
Therapy with the Adolescent

The adolescent is a special type of patient and a special type of person. Throughout this primer I have mentioned the special needs and the distinctive aims, methods, and techniques appropriate to children of different ages. Occasionally I have pontificated about what must or must not be done and then added as an afterthought: *This does not apply at all to adolescents.* In this final chapter I will try to pull together some of my general ideas about young people in this age group and to summarize what is special about working with adolescents in psychotherapy.

Except for some of his politically conservative overtones, Erik Erikson [1, 2] has put his finger on what the required developmental challenges and tasks are for the adolescent. Certainly anyone working with an adolescent should be "checking him out" for his moves toward emancipation from the parental nest; for his working and achieving in the realm of sexual freedom, all within a basically if not exclusively heterosexual orientation; for his accomplishment of some unalienated work and movement toward a vocation, and for his sense of selfhood or ego identity. All four of these tasks can be explored with an adolescent and can even be laid out as goals of his life stage for which therapy could have some relevance.

I tell parents of adolescents that they need to allow freedom for their son or daughter, unless they can find it in their hearts to go further and promote it. Parents can be most helpful if they change gears, stop bossing the sexually mature young man or woman, and start dispensing added choices, duties, and privileges. For middle-class adolescents the best thing parents can do is to stop insisting that the parents "know it all." Then again, following Erikson, I suggest to parents that they try to have some empathy for a young person who lives in the Kingdom of the Body (many parents do also, by the way), where body image is all-important and where acne seems to be a devastating disorder. Parents need also to acknowledge that sexual ignorance, so-called innocence, is a rarity, and that the point of adolescence is to make progress toward ultimate parenthood. Sexually mature people can beget babies unless they are apprised of the best contraceptive technology. Further, when parents complain that the adolescent does nothing useful, I launch into a work history-taking from the parents themselves. Many parents then realize that they, too, have not known much of nonalienated work. Further, whenever parents speak for their adolescent offspring, I always try to get the adolescent's views out into the open, pointing up the separate identity of the adolescent. By operating with the Erikson "checklist" [3], I have been helpful to both adolescents and their parents.

VALUES AS WELL AS PHYSIOLOGY

Adolescents live immersed in values as much as adults. They are often very alive ethically, unless they have become dropouts, delinquents, or zealots. Even some dropouts — potheads, acid heads, hippies — are sensitive to ethical issues, and if we extend some outreach they can be reachable. Ethical sensitivity, I would insist, is what makes anyone become a friend and supporter of psychotherapy. It is fashionable for some psychotherapists I know to play it cool and to dwell only on mechanics, ignoring values. They talk about "screwing" (when talking with their adolescent patients); they condone sexuality and encourage it, but refrain from finding out the framework of real values in which the patient lives. Fortunately, one does not have to be a puritan to recognize the folly of this. Sexual intercourse has no intrinsic magical influence on the teen-ager's problems, except when it occurs within a context of livable and acceptable values and when it is congruent with the person's self-concept; when those conditions are met, wonderful! *Blushing* is as important as lust when we are working to help adolescents, trying to help them solve problems in living. Young therapists who do not understand this make very poor sex counselors.

HOW TO INCLUDE AND EXCLUDE PARENTS

The parents of adolescents are eager to involve themselves in the adolescent's psychotherapy. They will artfully lay traps to get the therapist to talk with them behind the child's back. For adolescents more than for any other age group of young people, it is essential that confidentiality be totally protected. One move to spill the beans to parents, and the adolescent, with considerable justification, will denounce you with gusto and zeal and may even try to crucify you. If this should ever happen, it is unfortunate, and as the therapist you should apologize for your unethical behavior. But stop at two or three expressions of regret and apology. Do not submit to crucifixion by the teen-ager. He, too, can learn to be right and "get the goods on us" once in a while without feeling entitled to gloat and to annihilate us. Anyone doing therapy is allowed a few mistakes, and the victim of our misdeeds is allowed to score a moral victory occasionally without making a federal case of the whole matter.

Parents should be excluded totally except when the adolescent is present. That still allows the parents to join in family group sessions or to see a therapist or caseworker separately and concomitantly. Another possibility, which I have found more and more congenial as I have accrued more experience in working with adolescents, is to see the patient for a portion of the hour in individual, one-to-one therapy, and then to ask him to go and fetch his parents during the latter part of the hour. This works so smoothly that I have come to suspect family group therapists of endorsing this particular therapy mode with enthusiasm because they tend to work mostly with families in which adolescents or young adults are the primary or "identified" patients. They certainly have a point when they commend this way of working with an adolescent and his parents.

Excluding the parents sometimes gets us into situations in which we are made to look unduly rigid in our relations with them. A father will call to ask, very gently and with concern, about something the therapist thinks safe enough to comment on. Besides, the therapist feels like a stickler if he refuses to answer the father's question, so he gives a benign and general statement to the father. Thereupon, something infernal breaks loose, and the father misuses what the therapist has said. The adolescent instantly has a profound grievance — he knows that he had a right to expect the therapist to say *nothing* to his father.

It should be pointed out that my preferred modus operandi — namely, seeing the youth individually and then concluding with a family (parents and offspring) group session — does increase the risk of having the parents try to get to the therapist outside of the sessions. If they are seeing a separate therapist, they can be more readily shut out by the son's or daughter's therapist. After all, I can say in good conscience that I will not discuss anything behind the adolescent's back and simply remind the parents that they have someone they can talk to about their concerns. It is almost as risky that confidentiality will be compromised by irregular communications between parents and therapist when family group therapy is the adopted approach. Family group therapists, however, as a group are rather scrupulous about urging the parents to bring their question up in the adolescent's presence; and since the parents do participate in the entire session with the adolescent, they seem to feel that the therapist's proscription is a just one.

To finish summing up how the parents can be brought in or kept out, it must be added that while we must preserve confidentiality, we have no right to be abusive toward parents, and we should honor their insistence to be involved in the therapy with their son or daughter. After all, parents own their children, for children are like chattel until they are eighteen years old, and that means that all the folkways and stateways that protect the sacred institution of private property protect parents in their concern for ruling their children. If we do not like the idea that parents own their offspring, perhaps we should work to change the law and bestow some human rights on children [4].

SELECTING GOALS AND TECHNIQUES APPROPRIATE FOR THE ADOLESCENT

The adolescent is so readily stereotyped by both his friends and foes and has had so much written about him from a psychodynamic viewpoint that I find much of the literature on adolescents downright boring. At the same time, much of it is sound. In some ways, the more theoretical the literature is, the less sound it is; and the more practical and empirical the literature, the more sense it makes. The books by John Meeks [5] and Donald Holmes [6] are interesting and helpful, I believe, but those of Blos [7, 8], for example, seem at best to fit the old world and maybe another era too. Try them for yourself. Maxwell Gitelson [9] too was a psychoanalyst, but he was enough of a freethinker to advocate rather early on that what adolescents need is character synthesis, not character analysis. The Gitelson article is a classic and is required reading. The most exciting literature nowadays about adolescent life-styles and strivings is that of the sociologists and social scientists, for the psychiatrists and analysts have grown a little stale and jaded.

Character synthesis makes sense as the basic objective in working with adolescents, for many adolescents suffer from "identity neurosis." They do not know who they are, what they stand for, and what they will become; but they are at least seeking some identity, at least are on the move, and that in itself gives a more favorable prognosis. They often know how absurd their lives have been and, if they do not manage to take control, will forever be.

Adolescents make careers out of spotting the fakeries of all of us, above all, of therapists who are trying to get people to fit our institutions in lieu of trying to get our institutions made over so that they fit people. The smug and alienated therapist should be made to work with adolescents for the good of his therapeutic soul. Adolescents laugh at such cop-out therapists.

A therapist needs a capability for gluing (people, not cracked objects). Some of the truly positive parental attitude described in Chapter 6 is a good model, if not carried too far. The therapist needs to be able to watch without intruding too much, but always be ready to proclaim some of his own real values (if he has any!) and to show by his very presence as an integrated person that adolescence can be survived. The therapist has to remind the adolescent that he has a growing integrity. For example, with an eight- or ten-year-old child I might say, "Let's imagine that every person who appeared in that dream represents some part of *you.*" With the adolescent I would add a prefix or suffix such as, "You are just one person, I know, but sometimes we might put several characters into our dreams to represent different wishes, different values, different problems, and even different aspects of our personality." The therapist is intent on hearing out and tolerating the most dire psychopathology, for that is ego-supportive too; but he sees to it, at the very same time, that the adolescent is regarded as an autonomous, rather well put together person. The therapist must somehow get across his confidence to the adolescent: You can make choices; you can be self-governing; your intuition and judgment can be excellent; you are a "good egg." The therapist must take the young person seriously. He is sexually mature and he deserves our respect for having grown up to that extent.

Respect is shown on the surface by usage of courtesy titles. Therefore I advocate that any adolescent more than fifteen or sixteen years old be addressed as Mister or Miss, or Mrs., or the more Southern-style respectful appellation, Ms., which some of the women's movement have adopted as a generic title for adult females. I have harangued residents with this idea of courtesy titles, which I find so productive in my own clinical work, but I have observed that they consider it embarrassing and improper to address people in their late teens by courtesy titles and so call them by their first names. I practice what I preach on this score but hardly expect that I will make big waves in convincing others. I should add that if I have known the adolescent on a first-name basis previously, *both he and I* will use first names during therapy. If he won't call me Paul, I insist on calling him Mister. If the adolescent objects, saying she wants to be called Karen while she calls me Doctor Adams, I refuse, for therapists do have some rights. My acquiescence and my refusal are not important ingredients in our power struggle, I feel. However, as grist for talking about the longings of the patient for a subservient role, wanting to stay a humble, docile child, my yielding or sticking by my guns is important.

If the adolescent lives nearby or has good access to transportation, I prefer to see him twice as frequently as I would a child — and for only half-hour sessions.

Some younger children do well with one hour once a week. Adolescents move rapidly in therapy with sessions that last only a half-hour but are held three times weekly, for example. Obviously, this cannot be extremely analytically oriented treatment, but it helps. The model of flexibility — to help in any way possible — on the part of the psychiatrist is not to be undervalued. Incidentally, more adolescents than children, knowing that I am not an analyst, refer to me as their "analyst," I have discovered. Their defense for using this misnomer is that I try to psych them out and show great interest in their dreams and fantasies and that they want something simple to tell their friends!

I do not play with adolescents. Play therapy is for younger people. I encourage adolescents to talk. I do go for their fantasies, and their dreams are particularly useful vehicles for getting to know the intimate twists and turnings of their inner lives. As with patients of other ages, adolescents have shown me that dreams are not just a royal road to the unconscious but are also a royal road to the everyday reality of their private ecosphere. Dreams and their associations give revealing glimpses into the value systems and the deeply felt reality patterns of that particular adolescent and his family.

I have said that I advocate flexibility in dealing with the adolescent patient. I do not mean that I refrain from holding the work as serious and that I have no expectations for personal change. None of that accurately depicts what I do and expect of the adolescent's work. I say flexibility to show that I am not intent on doing rigid, analytically oriented work with adolescents. I will lend them books — money occasionally — and though we discuss all these transactions, there is no hidebound tradition to cramp the relation between us. Again, it seems to be a virtue to be somewhat flexible.

What about the number of evaluation or diagnostic sessions? I need more than one or two sessions to evaluate an adolescent, more than is usually needed to evaluate a younger child. An adolescent can present three or four different faces, or masks — say, one for each of the first four sessions. Therefore it is best to see and hear a bit more of his repertoire before trying to conclude anything of great merit and seriousness. It takes four or five interviews to obtain a broad sampling of the adolescent's repertoire. Conclusions based on fewer interviews than this are premature and all too often stand in need of thoroughgoing revision by the end of four or five sessions. I would prefer to wait and have a better basis for knowing what I deal with in my diagnostic formulation.

Adolescent therapy differs in procedural approach from younger children's therapy. With the adolescent it is more imperative than with the child that the therapist help to uncover feelings before he uncovers the defensive patterns, and that the therapist encourage a full expression of anger before discussing lust in any detailed way. The here-and-now is where we work with the adolescent. The therapist encourages frequent consideration of any unprofessional, "extracurricular" feelings that the adolescent experiences for the therapist. To encourage a strong, passionate, quasihallucinatory transference is out of the question in therapy with the adolescent. Transferences are to be examined and held up in contrast to reality at every step along the way.

Furthermore, the therapist with an adolescent clientele should give serious thought to the aptness of more therapy for himself before, during, and after his training period. Therapeutic work is vital and serious, and we need to bring it the best preparation and self-knowledge that we can muster and foster for ourselves. If we do not engage ourselves in psychotherapy, what right have we to dispense our services as psychotherapists to others? If we are not willing to be among the friends and supporters of psychotherapy (for ourselves), what right do we have to dispense these wares for others to buy? I think personal therapy is always good medicine for a therapist to take, but in the instance of the therapist who works with adolescents it is especially to be pushed and recommended. Adolescents are not easy to treat unless their therapists have the best kind of training.

PARADOX AND ABSURDITY AS COGNITIVE STYLE FOR THE THERAPIST

There are certain features of thought, of *Weltanschauung,* of general frame of mind that make it easier to work with adolescents in therapy. Some of the more doctrinaire old maids (of both genders) whom I have known will just never be able to acquire the necessary frame of mind. They realize it, usually putting the onus on the adolescent, but, fortunately, refusing to attempt to engage themselves in psychotherapy with adolescents, confining their professional work to younger children. Then, when they really become old, they skip the adolescent and work with adults exclusively. Without some of the components of the frame of mind that I will now present, the therapist of any age or sex would be well advised to work with age groups (or generational groups) other than those between twelve and twenty years old.

The adolescent requires a therapist who is not convention-bound and literal. He needs a therapist who has some *affinity for paradoxes* and who can see through the humdrum of everyday existence in a mass culture that is bureaucratized and pretends to make sense simply because it is overly structured. Somebody who has never questioned the faith of his fathers, who has never had a vibrant adolescence of his own, is in no shape to help most adolescents of the 1970s. A contentment with paradox, such as a willingness to do only "dynamic" work with no "genetic" focus, and yet to agree when the patient says, "What do you mean, that we have not talked about my infantile experiences and my Oedipus complex? We haven't talked about *anything but that.*"

This affinity for paradoxical thought is seen in therapists who have an openness and tolerant acceptance for irrationality and for defensiveness. I remember one time when I congratulated an adolescent for having the feelings attendant on resistance, wanting not to change, wanting to stay neurotic, missing the obsessive symptoms he had almost forsaken while becoming more spontaneous; and as soon as I had shown my respect for the humanness of his wanting to tune me out, the adolescent seemed to turn a corner, and the therapy became increasingly and steadily helpful to him. Respect for ambiguity is another way to say what I am getting at.

The adolescent vacillates from dependency to omnipotence, from altruism to greed, from wanting freedom to wanting masochistic bondage, and so on. He knows that he is somewhat inconsistent but that he is gradually finding himself. If the therapist can accept this ambivalence and contradictoriness, the adolescent is relieved and helped immensely. Some therapists, we must admit, have to have everything compulsively honest and consistent. They turn off adolescents before any possibility of a relationship can emerge. Attunement to ambivalence is a necessary ingredient of one's life-style and cognitive style if one is to be a therapist with adolescents.

Another feature of the therapist who can work well with adolescents is an eagerness to listen with respect even if nothing is said. Just as it was in the middle ages when Christian legend held that Mary was impregnated by the Holy Spirit through her ear, for some therapists the ear seems to be sexualized. Whether the ear's *listening* functions are sexualized for these therapists I am not prepared to say; however, I do notice that there are some therapists who cannot shut up and listen. Only the sound of his own voice gives a feeling of security to such a therapist. Or a therapist may be arrogant and feel he cannot waste time hearing from "an untrained teen-ager" how some sacred wheel is being reinvented. The therapist then talks, and even if he ritualistically observes some times of silence, he does not really attend. In the end, he neither sends nor receives. He does not really communicate. He is preparing his next pronunciamento. The adolescent senses his lack of empathy and knows that, except for occasional diversion and joking, such a therapist is no good for him.

If we are to speak to the condition of the adolescent, we must learn to listen attentively and respectfully. Naturally, we all know that promiscuity was not *invented* by the current crop of adolescents, but we also ought to have enough sense to let them live their own lives, relish their own enjoyments, and make their own personal experimentation.

Cultural traditions can help out, but the adolescent must discover this for himself. I would say that a good therapist for adolescents is one who assumes that it is only what the adolescent learns by direct, unbuffered experimentation, by direct engagement, by total participation, that has real merit for his growth as an unalienated human person. Even Erikson [10] has come to the point — not that his delay held back the adolescents one bit in making their own discoveries — where he can write that a certain amount of "playing with ego boundaries" is not gravely pathologic, as seen when adolescents lose control (perhaps even with the assistance of some drugs for recreational use) and subject themselves purposely to a blurring of boundaries. A self that has genuine worth can afford an occasional dissolution, perhaps. Norman O. Brown [11] wrote that a self that is really healthy can imagine its own dying and nonexistence without going into panic. Brown is one of the rare orthodox Freudians who has a style that shows real affinity for "where the adolescent lives."

Not everything the adolescent says during a therapy session makes a lot of sense, but that is not a serious indictment, for the same is true of the therapist and certainly of the child and the adult. The adolescent will surprise anyone from time to time with the sagacity and freshness of his utterances. Agreeing with Paul Hahn [12], I have found poor people to be highly articulate; poor adolescents have a verbal and cognitive style that makes for true enjoyment and gratifying sharing of the human condition, even across race, class, and age barriers.

Therapists working with adolescents (and with parents of adolescents) should know that their good advice, freely given, may often go unheeded. The adolescent gets corroboration and confirmation of what he is from his age-mates, people in his own generational group. He does not depend on middle-aged people, aged 25 to 50 years, to supply him with the standards by which he judges himself in the large or small scale. His worth and his shortcomings are validated mainly by his peers. The older generation has done almost everything it is capable of doing by force. From here on out, the middle-aged must be content to run the country, bribe the cops, condone law and order, control the wealth, and leave adolescents alone to a great degree. My own age group can do "consultation" whenever requested, but there is little that we can do to force our values and standards, however respectably superior they may seem to us, on adolescents.

It is indispensable that the therapist stand for his own values and not hold back on asserting them whenever asked by the adolescent where he (the therapist) stands on a given issue. Adolescents can accommodate very well to people who are not nihilistic, doubting all values and claiming that all values are merely "defenses" waiting to be unmasked by the Grand Inquiring Psychodynamicist. An adolescent can accept our having values that we assert, if we do not nag. Yet the adolescent wants to have his or her values, too, and to cherish them, as they are, after all, the things that matter most.

I know that I am on shaky ground in the next attribute I will mention, but what I am attempting to get at is valuable, so I will try. The competent therapist of the adolescent is a person *who possesses a nose for nature.* This is a person who is serene in witnessing the generative cycle close, with the sons and daughters becoming transformed into fathers and mothers. The kind of therapist whom I have in mind is able to see things in a broad perspective, is willing to go easily at some things that may look alarming at first blush. This kind of therapist is filled with trust in spite of some of the hair-raising qualities of the adolescent's behavior.

The therapist himself is no stranger to such paradoxical and unsettling views as those of psychoanalysis, Zen Buddhism, and the theater of the absurd. Perhaps in a more old-fashioned vein I could simply say, with Altenberg [13], that the therapist who works best with adolescents is a therapist with a sense of humor

STYLES IN DIAGNOSIS AND THERAPY

A friend once told me that I have some of the mannerisms of traditional psychiatrists whenever I undertake to help a teen-ager to figure out, identify, and not deny his problems; but that when I undertake therapeutic work I become an energetic optimist, trying to set goals that seem rather more than can be achieved. Or, he would say, I am a diagnostic pessimist and a therapeutic optimist. I know there is some criticism contained in these remarks. However, I would rather accept my friend's estimate than a suggestion that I am a therapeutic pessimist. Hope is crucial in therapy.

Clinical psychologists have been extremely helpful in identifying adolescents' and children's intellectual and personality problems (see Chapter 8). However, I have found that psychologic testing reports often seem both to overdiagnose (pessimism) and to cast grave doubt about what treatment can do (pessimism, again). I mention this, not to start up a battle, but to give a clue to the beginning therapist; that is, to take psychologic testing as only one more ingredient in your diagnostic assessment and to give priority to your clinical intuitions about the seriousness of the diagnosis. If not done by someone as astute and clinically sound as you are, testing will tend to overrate the seriousness of the adolescent's pathology.

All of us need to consider repeatedly with our colleagues from other mental health disciplines what our orienting philosophies (as seen in the fruits of our daily work) really are. That kind of feedback can be helpful to anyone. Even after analysis, we need a peer to tell us we repeat certain mistakes. People who work in solo or unidisciplinary settings always run the risk that their blind spots are being encouraged and perpetuated. This is where colleague review of our work can be helpful as long as we are engaged in the practice of psychotherapy. This is why a new therapist who leaves his training to do private practice had better line up a "supervisor" who will consult with the young therapist for the first few years of his actual practice. This always merits its costliness. Only by some such mechanism will skills improve and our patients benefit from our steadily increasing helpfulness. With adolescents particularly, we can only stay open, alive, inquiring, and empathic if we keep in touch with our own intrapsychic worlds and keep current with what is new and productive in our larger field of psychotherapy and society.

ADOLESCENT, GENERATION GAP, THERAPY, AND SOCIAL CHANGE

Most of the adolescents whom I have worked with are very much like their parents. The astonishing thing is that there is so little rebellion and rejection of their parents' values, mannerisms, and deeper-lying attitudes. In itself, this makes for an easier communication between parents and adolescents almost as soon as it is pointed out in a family group session. Now, the big exception is that if the father and mother are dishonest about what they really are, the adolescent might identify with some part of their value system that reigns in the parental lives despite denial. The adolescent, under those conditions, is asserting what the parents really are but disclaim that they are. In any event, the clarification of their value hierarchy is all to the good. Often, the adolescent can do it with only minimal support from the therapist.

The real dilemma for adolescents is that they are making the transition from being consumers of security into being providers of security. They are in between, caught in an existential conflict, looking both ways. They are recasting their whole outlook on the world of relationship styles, for they are in the process of giving up the sucking in of security for the dispensing or providing of security to others. When they have become providers much more than consumers, they will have mastered the challenges of adolescence and hence will no longer experience the agonies, and joys, of adolescence. They will, as I date it and define it, be middle-aged. Some of what happens in our psychotherapy is that the identity of a young middle-aged person emerges, squeezing out the identity of child/adolescent. The reorientation from taker to giver of security, achieved by nature but aided by a slight push from nurture, is what therapy is set up to illuminate whenever we work with adolescents.

The only generation gap that counts is that between givers and takers of security, those who suck in nurturance and those who give it. Consequently, the gap between a therapist and an adolescent is smaller than that between a child and a therapist. Only a teen-aged demagogue or a rather dim-witted therapist tries to make a sharp and total distinction between adolescent and adult. An aging business executive is reputed to have said, "I personally will not feel safe until all adolescents are behind bars." That outlook, however, is not proper for a therapist. Our outlook as therapists is one that shows what fun it is to look after our young, and if we in mental health work cannot measure up to what decent parents are, it stands to reason that we deserve to lose the respect of young people.

Some therapists, as they approach old age (over 50), find themselves despairing of or getting bored by young people. They find that they have lost a former empathy for children and youth. As they do this, they begin restricting their clientele to adults. That is a fortunate career change for everyone concerned. Certainly the young people will benefit from the absence of therapists with strong negative countertransferences for youths. Other therapists, however, seem to mature and mellow with age, keeping open to paradox, remaining empathic toward people who are learning to be both adult and child simultaneously, and growing old gracefully while enjoying their continued practice of therapy with adolescents.

Adolescents are provocative people, as a rule. They bring out the most hidden features of the best of therapists, and the worst.

REFERENCES

*1. Erikson, E. Growth and crises of the healthy personality. *Psychol. Issues* 1:50, 1959.
  2. Erikson, E. Youth: Fidelity and Diversity. In E. Erikson (Ed.), *Youth: Change and Challenge.* New York: Basic Books, 1963.

3. Adams, P. A pediatrician's checklist for adolescents. *Clin. Pediatr.* (Phila.) 5:54, 1966.
4. Adams, P., et al. *Children's Rights.* New York: Praeger Publishers, 1971.
5. Meeks, J. *Fragile Alliance: An Orientation to the Outpatient Psychotherapy of the Adolescent.* Baltimore: Williams & Wilkins, 1970.
6. Holmes, D. *Psychotherapy: Experience, Behavior, Mentation, Communication, Culture, Sexuality, and Clinical Practice.* Boston: Little, Brown, 1972.
7. Blos, P. *The Young Adolescent.* New York: Free Press, 1970.
8. Blos, P. *On Adolescence: A Psychoanalytic Interpretation.* New York: Free Press, 1962.
*9. Gitelson, M. Character synthesis: The therapeutic problem of adolescence. *Am. J. Orthopsychiatry* 18:422, 1948.
10. Erikson, E. Reflections on the dissent of contemporary youth. *Int. J. Psychoanal.* 51:11, 1970.
11. Brown, N. O. *Life Against Death: The Psychoanalytical Meaning of History.* Middletown, Conn.: Wesleyan University Press, 1959.
12. Hahn, P. Jiving Among the Gentry. In P. Adams. (Ed.), *Humane Social Psychiatry: A Book of Readings in Honor of Robert Ollendorff in Celebration of His Sixtieth Birthday.* Gainesville, Fla.: Tree of Life Press, 1972.
13. Altenberg, H. Changing priorities in child psychiatry. *Voices* 4:36, 1968.

Index